The Man Who Read the East Wind

By the same author:
The Inn With The Wooden Door

The Man Who Read The East Wind

A Biography of
RICHARD HUGHES

Norman Macswan

Kangaroo Press

Acknowledgements

I acknowledge gratefully the assistance of the Literature Board of the Australia Council.

I am also indebted to André Deutsch Limited, publishers of 105 Great Russell Street, London, for permission to quote from Richard Hughes' books *Foreign Devil* and *Hong Kong: Borrowed Place, Borrowed Time*.

My thanks are due also to innumerable friends — Denis Warner, Dick Hughes, Cyril Pearl, Walter Simmons, Hazel Sproule, Roma Pemberton among them — and finally to the Merlin of them all, Richard Hughes himself.

The back of the jacket shows Hughes and author Ian Fleming in Kyoto during Fleming's tour of Japan to research one of his James Bond novels You Only Live Twice. *Hughes said of the picture: 'Fleming and myself in spiritual converse after early morning mass.'*

First published in 1982 by Kangaroo Press
3 Whitehall Road Kenthurst 2154
Typeset by BudgetSet Pty. Ltd.
Printed in Hong Kong by Bookbuilders Ltd.

ISBN 0 949924 20 2

Contents

For David and Andrew

Listen to the East wind and keep your arse to the sunset
— Advice from an old China-hand

Two of the five silent men at the white-clothed table stood up when the Australian foreign correspondent came into the room.

The taller of the two, in a well-cut English pin-stripe suit and a dark red-spotted tie, held out his hand, his smile tentative. 'I am Donald Maclean', he said. The shorter man, plumpish and wearing a similar suit and an old Etonian tie, grinned widely. 'And I am Guy Burgess.'

Richard Hughes was instantly cold sober. For a moment he was speechless. The pain from his abscessed teeth thudded. His voice when it came was high. 'Gentlemen', he said, 'this is the end of a long trail.'

And it was the end of a five-year hunt for two of the most extraordinary spies of modern times, the British diplomats whose defection after a lifetime of deceit rocked the western world.

For Richard Hughes their dramatic appearance in the cold of a Moscow night in February 1956 was the highlight in a life that began in distant Melbourne fifty years earlier. And now he had the prize — the scoop of a lifetime — within his grasp.

1 Early Days in Melbourne

The 'long trail' for Richard Hughes began in Melbourne's Prahran in 1906, the Chinese year of the horse. His birth came just five years after 'the birthday of a whole people' as Prime Minister Alfred Deakin referred to the proclamation of the Commonwealth of Australia.

Queen Victoria was dead, Edward VII was on the throne and the iron grip the British royal family had on the affections of the people of the newly-formed nation was beginning to loosen. Sectarianism, the blight that was to shadow Hughes for much of his life, was stirring more openly in the young nation.

Hughes' father — Richard senior — was of Welsh descent and Protestant, and his mother, Catherine McGlade, was fiercely Roman Catholic. She was a direct descendant of the Irish people whose persecution still had a long way to go. They were both children of Victoria's goldfields country. He was the son of a miner who worked the Bendigo fields and died when the boy was five. When he was thirteen the family went to Melbourne and by then he had left school and was working to help support the family.

In Melbourne Richard senior took on two jobs. One was pasting labels on bottles in a chemical factory and the other involved reading judgements to court shorthand writers needing practice. His total wages came to the equivalent of about a dollar a week. At the same time he read widely, took lessons in elocution and boxing and tried his hand at writing. One of his early pieces was called simply 'Working in a Chemical Factory, by a Factory Boy'. He was thrown out of the first editor's office to whom he tried to submit the piece.

Australia was then passing through a decade of gloom and despair. A land boom in the 1880s collapsed but this was merely a precursor to the total collapse of 1892, when banks and other financial institutions failed. There was nothing gay about the nineties for the small boy, wearing his obligatory hat, as he battled to help his family and lift himself out of the rut. He was to say later in his long life that his story was that 'of a little man plodding along, looking for wealth, fame and power and finding only limited fortune, obscurity and insignificance'.

But he rose far above this denogratory view of himself and his life. Improbably, ventriloquism was the key. He was convinced that ventriloquism was not a gift, but was something that, with application, could be learned as one learned to talk and write. Confidence and perseverance were the keys and he practised day and night.

At fifteen he joined a small group playing suburban halls, eventually being able to stay on the grubby little stages for fifteen minutes. His confidence high, he arranged a complete postal system of self-tuition in ventriloquism. In the process he earned the ire of other practitioners by claiming that the art was merely a clever illusion, and could be acquired by anyone possessing sound vocal organs.

By now he was a good mimic and elocutionist, so he grasped the nettle and took his one-man-show to Queensland. He was nineteen. Drovers, shearers, bullock drivers, railway workers and even the lonely kanakas — the islanders who had been dragged from their Pacific paradise to work the Queensland cane fields — were his audiences. At the little town of Razorback one kanaka crept out from among the trees to the small hall where the show was being held. A blue cattle dog slunk at his heels. He had no money and offered the snarling dog as the price of admission. Hughes refused the offer and told the black man to go in free. After the show he asked the islander how he liked it. 'Glad I kept me dog', the kanaka replied.

Financially the tour was a failure. Dejected, he headed back towards Melbourne but was broke by the time he arrived in Brisbane. He took on a job there as a sparring partner for a boxer before returning to the lonely road south to Melbourne.

But his first book *Secrets of Ventriloquism,* was selling reasonably well and he followed with *Ventriloquism, Ancient and Modern* and then his popular *How to Become a Ventriloquist.* In this latter book he guaranteed that ventriloquism was something that any man or boy of average intelligence could learn after a few weeks of painstaking study. He said the claim that ventriloquists 'threw' their voices was bunkum. They merely deceived by modulating their voices. A voice would be imitated, not as it was heard at its source but as it fell on the ear of the listener after travelling from some distant spot. The illusion was aided by means of appropriate gestures or facial expressions. The audience's imagination would be aroused, by which time they were waiting and willing to be deceived.

By now he was something of a minor celebrity and he had added to his gifts the ability to play the piano, which he taught himself. He toured Victoria and was widely acclaimed.

10

One of his unpaid jobs at this time was on a suburban chain of newspapers to which he contributed articles and theatre reviews. In return he got tickets to see some of the great entertainers touring the country — Carrie Moore, Dante the magician and Houdini among them. He wrote about them all and as his confidence rose he went beyond the suburban chain and became a successful contributor to the *Age* and the *Sporting Globe*. He wrote about his experiences, show business people, successful businessmen. The flowery prose fashionable at the time came easily to him, and he loved the feeling of power that writing gave him. But he was the breadwinner and full-time journalism had to remain a dream.

Catherine McGlade was born in Ballarat. Her father was a sergeant of police and at one time was involved in the chase after Ned Kelly and his gang. One of her earliest memories was of household talk about the wild Ned. Ballarat offered nothing for a young woman so she went to Melbourne to live with a sister. She was a big handsome girl, a devout Roman Catholic and for a time she thought seriously about following another sister into the convent. But she became a seamstress and worked at Rockes, a big furniture store in Melbourne. It was there she met the young Hughes, who had put aside his dream to become a furniture salesman.

He was shy and gentle, with a great love for books and learning. Catherine was more of an extrovert and inclined to be dominant. On the surface it was an improbable match. Each of them knew and respected their families' views about mixed marriages. Catherine's was the stronger view; his was more a stubborn refusal to concede than the love of faith that she had.

They became engaged, but each family forbade the marriage, Hughes' mother, dominating and Calvinistic, demanded he should break off the relationship. Catherine's family, equally bigotted and with memories of the Irish persecution they had brought to their new land, were just as adamant. If Hughes became a Catholic, they said, they would consider giving their consent. He refused, and Catherine, despondent, joined her sister Rose in the convent.

The shock move jolted Hughes. He agonized for weeks about his loss and gradually began to rationalize the stupidity of his stubbornness. No faith, he reasoned, could compensate for a life without Catherine. So he agreed to take instruction in the Roman Catholic faith and promised he would raise any children as Catholics. The nuns released a happy Catherine and they were married in St. Francis Roman Catholic church.

Richard Hughes was born on March 5, 1906 and was baptised in the Catholic faith as his father had promised.

His first memory is of being circumcised at the family home in Prahran. His second memory is that he once told a visitor that when he grew up he would marry his mother. A third, and vivid, memory is of getting drunk at the age of four. It happened at a wedding reception being held at his parents' home at 2 Arkle Street, Prahran. The guests left some sweet wine in glasses and Hughes and his cousin swigged away happily at the dregs.

Years later he recalled the improbable scene. 'Apparently I was resplendent in a silk shirt and some type of silken bloomers but that didn't stop me from wrestling silently with my cousin Greg for possession of disputed glasses. I've been told since that eventually I fell on my back under a table and went into a dreamless sleep. My cousin however didn't share my cunning and he lurched into public view, clearly and grotesquely drunken. He staggered into the family group and fell heavily. There was stunned silence as he crawled towards the bride and threw up over her white shoes.'

His drunken cousin was carried off and Hughes' mother was smugly pleased until she discovered him sleeping it off under the table. He was forgiven because he had not brought his shame into the open.

His mother dominated the early years but as he grew older he turned more and more to his father for talk. At home he was inclined to shyness but when schooldays began he burgeoned.

He was aware of his father's increasing interest in spiritualism and aware too of the unspoken schism in the family about attendance at church. His mother was rigid in her adherence and accepted doctrine without question, but his father often spoke to the boy about any aspects of belief that didn't equate with the conformist views his mother did not want him to question.

Richard senior encouraged his son to read early, and by the time he was enrolled in Christian Brothers College at nearby St. Kilda he was showing signs of the articulate, intelligent and driving man he was to become. He was a large boy, towering above his school fellows, and he objected strongly when his mother made him wear his school trousers buttoned differently from the older boys — above the knees. His father had taught him to box, however, and there was no teasing and no fights because of his size and known prowess. And there was only one beating.

The punishment was for a childish misdemeanour. The sense of injustice was as great as the pain as the cane swished down and the big, tough boy cried. He went home that night, humiliated, and, when pressed, told his father. His father agreed that the punishment was too severe for the misdeed and immediately took him away from the school and enrolled him in a nearby government school.

Within days of his leaving Christian Brothers College the teacher who beat him arrived at their home, bearing a book for Hughes' father, and offering apologies for the too-severe punishment. Within a week, he was back at CBC, eating his lunch at the college of soup, cold meat and vegetables or stew and pudding. He remembers the pudding as dried bread with custard on it.

Lunches were presided over by a lay teacher, Paddy Logue. He would have his lunch with the boys and they would watch fascinated as he appeared to strain the soup through his luxurious moustache. Logue taught the small boys and he loved them. At the end of the closing period for the day they would line up and shake hands with Logue and sometimes, such was his love for them, he would bend down and kiss them on the cheek.

On the long walk back home, Hughes would make up stories for the other boys and tell them of the latest adventures of Sherlock Holmes. His father had started him on Conan Doyle's hero and his love for the sardonic Holmes was to grow stronger over the years. (To this day he can identify virtually every character in every Holmes book and will not concede that Holmes died but that he lives on his bee farm in Sussex. 'If he died *The Times* would have announced it', he still claims indignantly.)

He would also regale the other boys with bawdy songs, based on knowledge far beyond his years and on one occasion he produced from some unknown source a set of 'wicked' pictures. A school friend remembers them as the type once fashionable at seaside resorts — 'all bloomers and tits' — and complete with unsubtle innuendo.

They exchanged insults with boys from other schools — particularly Protestant ones. The 'proddies' would sing: 'Catholic dogs, jump like frogs, eat no meat on Fridays' and Hughes and his mates had equally vulgar replies. 'Public bummers' — a reference to the state school boys being educated at public expense — was one of the more polite insults Hughes and his friends shouted at the Protestant boys. Stones flew too at times, and occasionally there would be fights under a convenient tree after school.

The childish shouting and fighting was merely a prelude however to a greater schism that began to divide the whole country when Australians went to war in 1914. On the surface there was public acceptance of the 'last man and last shilling' rallying cry, but the latent bigotry epitomized by the childish insults soon came to the surface. An Irish prelate was the improbable key.

He helped let loose a flood of intolerance, based understandably on memories of the dreadful persecution of the old world, onto a country struggling to find its own identity. His effect on all the people he touched, including children, was to last for decades. His influence extended from the children to whom he preached to the easy-going, 'she'll be right' adults almost prepared to live together in tolerance. Yet strangely, he touched a chord of nationalism in a land bereft of it.

He was Dr Daniel Mannix.

Mannix arrived in 1912 as coadjutor archbishop of Melbourne.

Bigotry was in many instances just beneath the surface yet Mannix, fresh from the memories of persecution in Ireland, stirred it to the surface. He talked about the inequality Catholics received at Australian public schools, called some state schools 'sinks of iniquity' and claimed that Australian Catholics had been persecuted.

Many Australians opposed Catholicism but on the surface there was reasonable tolerance along class lines at least. But Mannix thought the voice of those who openly opposed his faith was representative of the whole country . . . and he prickled. At first his speeches — and they were numerous — stirred antagonism towards himself, but later, in a growing swell, towards his church.

Mannix, too, had been educated by the Christian brothers, but at Rathclurc, in Ireland. As he progressed in his brilliant career Ireland was going through one of its darkest periods. The tall, handsome cleric became a professor of theology at the Royal Catholic College of Maynooth. It was there, where he was ranked among the brightest minds in Ireland, that he was tapped for the Melbourne post. He often spoke to the boys at St. Kilda's Christian Brothers College and Hughes remembers him as a spell-binder.

As the war in Europe dragged on and more and more bodies piled up, Britain asked Australia for more men. Fewer and fewer volunteers were coming forward and conscription was being openly touted. William Morris (Billy) Hughes was Prime Minister when it was announced in 1916 that there would be a referendum on conscription for overseas military service. Prime Minister Hughes, small, ill-tempered and a bit of a larrikin but a brilliant orator, threw all his Welsh fervour into the 'Yes' campaign. Mannix became the virtual leader of the 'No' campaign.

The boys at Christian Brothers College took their cue from their beloved Dr Mannix, and Richard Hughes followed fervently, wearing his 'No' badge with pride. The campaigns divided Australia neatly, with nearly all the non-Catholic churches in favour of the 'Yes' campaign.

The Labor movement backed Mannix, distancing itself from Billy Hughes, the Labor Prime Minister who was becoming more and more identified with the war party. The campaign was vicious. When the dust settled the 'No' cause won by 1 160 000 to 1 087 000.

According to Niall Brennan in his excellent biography of Mannix, the vote had a marked effect on the outspoken prelate. From that moment, Brennan wrote, Mannix became the 'most notorious political prelate' Australia ever had: 'He was the leader of a whole faction which was trying to give a new dimension of a concept of a new Australian patriotism'.

Mannix, unceasing in his opposition to conscription, resumed the leadership of the 'No' forces when Prime Minister Hughes announced

14

yet another vote on the issue. This time the Australian people rejected conscription more firmly. They were helped by Mannix, who claimed that the war in Europe was an ordinary trade war. He also related Britain's concern for small European countries to her lack of care about the plight of Ireland.

Again the boys at CBC went into the campaign with enthusiasm, Richard Hughes among them. But the young Hughes was beginning to think and the chord of nationalism that Mannix had stirred began to take form, even in his young mind as also in the minds of countless others.

At school, Hughes would listen fascinated but unconvinced as the principal, Brother Tevlin, deplored vulgarity, and preached nationalism. With the memory of his recent caning fresh he listened closely, too, when Tevlin expressed his dislike of corporal punishment. He called it a method 'rightly considered out of date in modern educational establishments' and asked the boys to remember the virtues of discipline, hard work and good manners.

At home, Hughes was inclined to moodiness and was often alone. He read avidly, played little sport, but would occasionally play cricket with his younger brother, Walter on the back lawn. His growing flamboyance and extrovert nature were for outsiders and within the family he was considered merely stubborn.

Mass on Sundays was obligatory. His mother and the children would tramp off, greeting the neighbours along the way, but Hughes' father would not be part of this ritual. His absence hurt Hughes' mother but not once did she refer to it to outsiders. The father explained it later in his life: 'I didn't really believe all that. I would not go along with it. I'm a religious man but I'm not sectarian. I believe in God and after-life but I dislike sects of any kind.'

Despite this once-weekly hurt, Hughes' mother would not listen to any disparagement of her husband. He could do no wrong in her eyes. She was strong and rigid in her acceptance of what she saw as her duty. There were blacks and whites and few, if any, greys in her outlook. She ruled the house, fierce in her loyalty to her family and her faith. Yet her rigidity sent the children to their father for comfort and he would quietly take over the discipline, making up his own mind about the rights and wrongs of the particular issue. But having made it up he would not change, and his stubbornness sometimes negated the peace he tried to instill in the children

The home was large and comfortable, school was fascinating and love and security cocooned him, yet the younger Richard was beginning to show a rebellious streak. It surfaced when his mother, observing to the letter the law of her church, forbade him to read H. G. Wells. She told him Wells was an evil man and that his works were on 'the index' (*Index Librorum Prohibitorum*). A great number of well-known books were placed in this category by the Roman Catholic Church and Roman Catholics were forbidden, under pain of mortal sin, from reading them. If a book propagated anti-Catholic views, or what were considered to be immoral attitudes, that particular book, together with all other books by the same author, were banned to Catholics. And Wells, in his excellent and scholarly *Outline of History*, for instance, raised the ire of the Roman Catholic hierarchy when he dealt with the Czech, John Huss.

In his *Outline* Wells tells how Huss delivered a series of lectures at the University of Prague based on the teachings of the English scholar Wycliffe who, among other things, translated the bible into English 'in order to set up a counter authority to that of the Pope', and denounced the doctrines of the Roman Catholic church about mass. Huss' teachings aroused the Catholic church to excommunicate him. Tried for heresy, he would not recant and was burned alive at the stake in 1415. There were many other instances of Wells' criticism of the role of the Roman Catholic Church in history.

So Wells, for these statements and others, was on the infamous list. Innocuously, Hughes was reading *War of the Worlds* when his mother announced the ban. He rebelled and, over-reacting, declared that if he could not read what he chose and had to be ruled by the dictates of the church, he would have nothing further to do with it. Hughes was fourteen at the time. One thing led to another. Hughes' father, perversely, came into the argument and decided on one of his stubborn moves. He removed Richard from Christian Brothers College, cutting short what promised to be a brilliant scholastic career, and told him to get a job and to honour and obey his mother.

The young Hughes over-reacted again. That night, from his comfortable attic room which he shared with his younger brother, he ranted —in what the family said at the time was a nightmare — that he had sold his soul to the devil. At the time, some members of his family put his outburst down to what they said was his flamboyance.

Yet sixty years later, Hughes still maintained his intellectual opposition to the Roman Catholic church. But in those years, filled with adventure and contact with the famous and infamous, spies and writers, intellectuals and world leaders, he has been known to seek a blessing from a Russian orthodox priest, Laotian monk and a gentle, brave priest in the island of Quemoy, and to have asked forgiveness for his sins from a priest in the Vatican. ('What were they', asked the confessor. 'I don't remember', Hughes said. 'If you don't remember them — but I think you do — they can't have been very important', said the priest.)

In 1920, he went to his first job as a poster artist with a Melbourne firm, W. W. Reid. As well as stencilling the posters he had to stick them up in the streets. He would return home after work despondent,

16

his hands and clothes covered in ink and grease, and go to his room and escape into his beloved world of Sherlock Holmes.

Then an opening occurred in the Victorian Railways and he started work as a boy shunter. From that moment, trains rivalled Sherlock Holmes among his great loves. He progressed to being a time-table clerk and at this time, encouraged by his father, he began to write. He bombarded the *Railways Magazine* with articles on every conceivable subject. His greatest success was the publication of a short piece in the *Bulletin*, the most prestigious target then for any budding writer. He called it 'Clerk'. He also had a drawing published in the *Bulletin*.

Some of the pieces he had published in the Victorian *Railways Magazine* were noticed by the then Commissioner, Harold (later Sir Harold) Clapp, a brilliant administrator who transformed the state railways into the most efficient system in Australia. Clapp, who had worked for some years in the United States and retained a slight American accent, was ruthless. If he wanted something, he got it. If he wanted a particular person, he tapped them. And he tapped the young Hughes for his public relations staff.

So Hughes was finally set on the road of journalism. He wrote thousands of articles for the *Railways Magazine*, under a profusion of by-lines ranging from his own name to 'Nowurk' to 'Hugh Richards'. Whenever he used his own name he attached 'Jnr' to it because his father was a well known contributor to various newspapers at the time.

He did his compulsory military service in the signals corps, and became a member of the railways debating team. Subsequently, as a debater, he won the title of debating champion of Victoria against all comers for four consecutive years. Harold Holt, who was to become Prime Minister of Australia and who died so tragically at the height of his power, was among the young debaters Hughes encountered. (On Sunday 17 December 1967, Holt went for a swim off Portsea in Victoria. He disappeared in the boiling surf 'like a leaf being taken out' an eyewitness said later. A huge search failed to find his body.)

Hughes found debating hard but stimulating work. He also found that the successful debater's most crushing counter argument, sparkling repartee, and the swiftly forged white hot arguments had to be laboriously hammered and shaped beforehand. The first task was to draw up all the arguments for his side and the other side.

In the army, he fought as an amateur light heavyweight. A tough semi-pro, Paddy McQuirk, broke his nose in one forgettable encounter and Hughes eased away from the sport.

He published a piece at this time, by-lined 'Ex-Sarge', which dealt with an imaginary invasion of Australia by Zulus. He called it 'How I Saved Australia' and deliberately miss-spelt the words. 'Suddinly the dor opened and in rushed my old frend major general roarer, waring his medals and a terrefied expresshun. He flunged himself on his nees beside me and clutcht my hands, grate tears rolling down his cheeks. "sargint" he bellered, "Australier needs yu. The zulus have arrived intending to invade the commonwealth".'

So Sergeant Hughes took over the defences and organized his signallers to mount their heliograph mirrors in a straight line and he directed them to flash the sun at the zulu battle cruisers, then off suburban St. Kilda. "My simpel but clever roos was immeedyatlee suckcessfull. The bright lite dazzled the zulu gunners, conserkwently making it impossible for them to take proper ame.

'From the beach we could see the enraged admirals running about the decks cutting the throtes of the unfortunit gunners and putting noo ones in their places. But it was all in vane. One of the beems of lite hit the cheef engineer of the zulu flagship in the eyes, blinding him so that he pulled the tiller the rong way and rammed a mine layer beside him which bloo up and then sank down taking half the flagship with it and leaving the other half behind. That was the last strore.' The Prime Minister hurried down from Canberra, made Sergeant Hughes 'a guverner, gave me six racehorses and two tin hares and a dozen greyhounds, theater passes to all the best shows and a fashunable house to live in and so Australyer was saved'.

Life was good. He was writing furiously, debating, and learning typing and shorthand. He neither drank nor smoked. His nickname in the railways was 'Snow' because of his blond hair. Like all men in those days he wore a hat. He was a strangely shy man at times and never seemed to know how to hold his hands, and yet, despite his 'loner' reputation, was popular among his mates. He was articulate, witty and good company, though reserved and unsure of himself with women.

A quiet little prostitute in Melbourne's bohemian Little Lonsdale Street helped the transition to adulthood and greater sureness with women. Late one night she took his money and sent him smiling home to the suburbs, his elation mixed with guilt. He was ninteen.

At work there was a heady mixture of achievement, pride in his increasing sureness as a writer, the stimulation that Commissioner Clapp generated to all around him, and the wit that filled his days.

One particular foreman who was a fawning, pompous type, and who had achieved the stature of one who could wear the obligatory hat at all times — even in the office — was the butt of one joke. Hughes and a friend packed a paper bag full of horse manure, sneaked it into the office and tipped it into the upturned brim of the foreman's hat. Chief Commissioner Clapp came into the office and the foreman stood and nodded his head graciously to the boss. The horseshit scattered down all over the foreman's shiny desk and onto the floor in front of the surprised Clapp.

Hughes often travelled with Clapp throughout the railways network.

He was an inspiration to Hughes as he shook the system into shape. He electrified Melbourne's suburban railway system, literally, and the entire state railways figuratively.

Clapp was something of a dandy. His initial imported weakness was for green Stetson hats though he overcame this. But he never overcame another weakness for gleaming shoes and even if he did not leave his office he would move away from his desk three or four times a day to polish his already spotless footwear. He was a tough disciplinarian yet Hughes saw many instances where he would ignore transgressions by his employees provided always that his beloved railways did not suffer. In their travels Clapp and Hughes found that there was an astounding sequence of seduction of girls in parcels offices at railway stations. Hanging bicycles, stacks of unclaimed luggage and lost umbrellas were hardly the aphrodisiac trappings that encouraged seduction, but apparently once a girl was in there, Hughes recalled later, 'she was on the counter'.

A cow manure cake coated with icing sugar and decorated with strawberries that was sent to a church bazaar as a goodwill offering from the Victorian Railways was one instance where Clapp's readiness to forgive small transgressions was tested. The deception was not discovered until the camouflaged cake was cut. The responsible party was found guilty of 'grossly obscene and disgusting behaviour', fined £5 and reduced to the position of porter.

Clapp's influence on Hughes was to last throughout his life and in a tribute many years later Hughes said Clapp had helped him most when he was young, striving and uncertain. He recognised Clapp's genius at the time and subsequently saw him as one of the truly great Australians he had known.

Hughes met May Lillian Bennett at one of the rare parties he attended. He was attracted immediately to the tall, strikingly beautiful model and shortly afterwards they were married. She was a Protestant but Hughes did not care. Others did. His mother and some members of his family objected, despite Hughes' dedicated non-attendance at church and his professed agnostic views. His father, remembering the trauma that preceded his own marriage and grateful for the peace and love he had found in it, offered solace to his troubled son. Richard was troubled because his mother tried hard to discourage the marriage and he did not want to hurt her, but Richard senior told him, 'It's all right if you love, Richard'. So they were married in a registry office and for a time the uneasy dream of travelling overseas and becoming a great writer was stilled as he settled down to domesticity in suburban Brighton.

Hughes found his stimulation at work and threw himself into it. Sometimes he would contribute four or five lengthy articles to each issue of the *Railways Magazine*, each under a different by-line.

Gradually, and particularly after the birth of their son, also named Richard, there was a lessening of the ill-feeling from some members of the family. His father was supportive, but he would walk away from an argument and retire to his room to read and write.

The first muted blow came in 1932 when May was found to be suffering from chronic bronchitis. Further specialist examination diagnosed what the specialist called the presence of tubercle bacilli — the then dreaded tuberculosis. She began tuberculin treatment and for more than a year she attended the central tuberculos bureau for treatment. Her physical progress was satisfactory, she gained weight, and within a year there were no signs left of the disease.

Her specialist said subsequently that at no time during the treatment did she appear mentally depressed or worried. Yet Hughes and his mother were concerned. His mother noticed the depression and recalled that May was afraid she would give the complaint to her son. 'One of these days I will go far out in the sea and not come back', she told her mother-in-law on one visit.

On 6 July 1933 Hughes arrived home at his usual time of around 5.30. After supper May retired to a sleepout as usual, to have an hour's rest. Afterwards, she bathed the baby and put him to bed. At 9 pm Hughes saw his wife coming from the kitchen. She was on the point of collapse and the only word he heard her say was 'finished'. Hughes tore through the cold Melbourne night to her doctor in a nearby street. When they returned, within minutes, she was dead. In the kitchen they found a glass with some wine in it together with a small bottle containing a white substance. At the subsequent inquest the coroner found that she had taken her own life by drinking cyanide. She was twenty-five.

Hughes was shattered. Although he knew she feared the tuberculosis and that she had threatened to take her life because she felt she was not getting better, he had no inkling that she would take that final desperate step.

He took his young son to his parents and another chapter in his life was beginning.

2 First Assignments

'So you're becoming bored, Richard'.

Chief Commissioner Clapp, as elegant as ever, rarely gave the impression there was ever anything more important than the matter he was dealing with at the moment. His flat, American-accented voice went on: 'Well, I will approve your departure on one condition. You must promise me that, when the time comes, you will concentrate on Asia. None of this tearing off to Europe, as most stupid Australian newspapermen do. Australia belongs to Asia you know and the future of this country will be as part of Asia.'

The year was 1934. Hughes had agonized for weeks about his decision to leave the railways, but the restlessness that had been dormant had come to the surface after his wife died and he knew he needed more experience. He had sold his house in Brighton, talked for hours with his patient father and had seen the love his mother and father were lavishing on his young son, before he finally came to a decision. He would get a job on a newspaper and eventually go overseas.

But the decisions to leave the 'family of railwaymen' as he was to call them later, and to break with his mentor Clapp, were both hard to make. Each night, at home, he would read again some of the stories he had published in the glossy, beautifully-produced *Railways Magazine* and the nostalgia that came when he read his version of the drama and the pathos and the wit he had encountered over more than ten years made his decision to leave even more difficult.

One of the stories dealt with the adventure of a parcel on the rail system: 'The doubts and fears that agitate the breast of one making its first journey, the other parcels it meets, the friendships it makes and rejects, the stories it hears . . . give it a tongue and what a story it could tell . . . .' He also recalled writing about his first journey on the footplate as the roaring steam-powered giant thumped its way from

Melbourne to Albury; the 'Right away' cry from the guard before the wheels gathered power and the train rushed through the quiet, moonlit countryside.

One story he recalled with particular pleasure.

It was about an old man of ninety-three who had come from England to help wind up the affairs of the Hobson Bay United Railway Company before the Victorian Government took it over. 'Meet John Wakefield', he wrote, 'a distinguished looking old gentleman, thin white hair and beard, arched nose under a high forehead, dark suit, neat bow tie, immaculate linen. He is writing at a table, pale sunlight filtering into the quiet room and touching his frail hand as it moves slowly over the white paper . . .'.

The old man told Hughes about his arrival in what he called 'the colony' in 1855. The Crimean War was on. There was no water supply, so they drew their water from the sweet Yarra, meandering unpolluted then through the fledgling city.

Hughes always wrote his pieces at home in longhand first. Then he would type them. He used a wide arm of an armchair for the first draft. (Many years later, his father told Richard that he had heard the scene described to him in minute detail by a medium. The old man was at one of his spiritualist meetings and the medium described the room and his son's appearance and predicted that Richard would be married within a few weeks. At that time Richard had not told his family he planned to marry May).

His time with the railways had been stimulating and fun but he felt he had drained it. The life had been too protective and he was beginning to feel stifled both at work and with his family. His shorthand and typing were now excellent, his memory had sharpened because of a course in Pelmanism — an Edwardian method of memory training — and he had read through his father's extensive library. Nor could he maintain any great interest in his father's love of spiritualism although he relished the chance to see and meet his boyhood hero, Arthur Conan Doyle, who was also on a spiritualism kick.

Conan Doyle came to Australia earlier to lecture on spiritualism and Hughes' father was involved in the arrangements for the visit. To his intense delight, Hughes was entrusted to pick up Conan Doyle from his hotel and take him in the family Oakland to the theatre where the great man was to lecture. Young Hughes told the author how he used to tell his school mates some of the Sherlock Holmes stories. Conan Doyle merely smiled. 'He wasn't very forthcoming', Hughes would recall forlornly in later years. Doyle's primary interest at the time appeared to have moved away from Holmes.

The great Depression that was to blight so many Australians' lives was on and, although there were signs of recovery, Hughes was advised time and time again not to give away the security of the railways. Clapp's understanding helped him make his choice and he joined the *Star*, a rumbustious, sturdy evening newspaper that had gone to battle with the mighty *Melbourne Herald*, which was to become one of the great evening newspapers of the world.

The *Star* first hit the streets in 1933 and for a short time the people took to it with gusto. Some of the great names of Australian and international journalism had been enticed to join the paper — Jack Waters, King Watson, Roland Pullen, Cyril Pearl, Cecil Edwards, Reg Leonard, Roy Macartney, Lachie McDonald, Allan Dawes among them. Hughes, studious and diffident at first in this comparably exalted company, began to hit his straps after a few months. For a start, he had his first drink — whisky and lemonade.

He was assigned as western roundsman and his beat, happily, included the railways. Clapp, of course, was among his best contacts. He often wrote under the by-line 'Greenlight'. The free-wheeling, intemperate world of the *Star*, with its larger-than-life characters, struck a reciprocal chord and the extrovert nature of his personality, so long subdued, emerged.

Cyril Pearl, fresh from the academic world and regarded as somewhat of a dandy because of his by-line — C. Alston Pearl — became one of Hughes' first and dearest friends on the paper. The no-nonsense approach of the other tough, hard-drinking and cynical reporters who had been raised in daily newspaper journalism wore down both Hughes' and Pearl's reserve. Cyril, later to become one of the great Australian editors and a distinguished author, dropped the 'Alston' and Hughes too emerged into the light from his relatively cloistered past.

Hughes' salary was half what he received from the railways but he relished the life — the tough reporters, hats tilted the same way, humming their dirty songs and drinking far into the night. They had a lust for everything they did, whether it was writing the story of an underground railway or the change of name of a railway station from 'Bumbang' to 'Robinvale'. There was one daring cut-and-run tradition that appealed to them all: the nightly march up Flinders Street to the basement of the *Herald* to join the long queue of *Herald* staffers to pick up, illicitly, a free staff copy of the rival paper.

Newspapermen sense the end quickly and when the signs appeared more openly that the *Star's* days were numbered, Hughes joined Cyril Pearl and others in the exodus. He went to Sydney to join the *Daily Telegraph*. Before he left Melbourne, Hughes, Pearl and King Watson went on a madcap jaunt by car to Victoria's Lorne-Apollo Bay region. There were a lot of refreshment stops along the way. Finally they came to a narrow, fast-running brook emptying into the sea under a humble wooden bridge. They found some loose rocks near the then 'mouth' of the river and diligently carried them across to the eastern slope which was wider than the real mouth. They placed the rocks with drunken cunning, the water began to rise immediately, and within a couple of hours the little river had a new mouth, some hundreds of metres from the original.

He made a last nostalgic trip with his young son to Sandringham, by train to Victoria Docks to see the ships and goods train. And he talked for hours with his father about the old man's increasing interest in spiritualism before climbing on board an aeroplane for the first time in his life for the flight to Sydney.

Frank (later Sir Frank) Packer, also born in the Chinese year of the horse, acquired the *Telegraph* in 1936 when its circulation was some 90 000 daily. Packer, tough and dynamic, cast his net wide when he assembled staff for the revitalized paper. They were regarded at the time and afterwards as one of the most brilliant groups of journalists ever assembled to work on one newspaper.

Packer swept aside with one huge hand a half empty tomato sauce bottle and some biscuits when Hughes arrived in his office for the first interview with his new boss.

'So you're Hughes?'

'Yes, sir, I am.'

They sized each other up for a moment. Each was tall, powerfully built. Packer looked tougher than Hughes had imagined and his slightly belligerent air was accentuated by one eye that remained fixed. He had lost partial sight in it earlier as a result of an accident.

'What makes you think you're a good journalist?'

Hughes was sweating. His coat was too tight across his massive shoulders and he was aware suddenly that his hands were in the way again. His voice seemed lighter than usual, contrasting with Packer's growl.

'I don't think I'm a good journalist; I know I am.'

He hadn't rehearsed that. It was spontaneous. It seemed the right touch, however, and Packer grinned.

'Confident big bastard, at least. Well, we've got the best here. So good luck.'

Sid Deamer, small and dapper, met him outside Packer's office. He noticed Hughes' sweat. 'Don't take too much notice of Frank. He looks tough, but he's all right. Stand up to him and you'll have no trouble.'

Deamer was the first editor. He had enormous enthusiasm and was a scintillating, bohemian type and he attracted the brightest talent. He was a cult figure even then, and his contribution to journalism was enormous.

Packer was in partnership at that time with E. G. ('Red Ted') Theodore, a former deputy Prime Minister and Treasurer. The

24

partnership, on the surface, was a strange one, yet fruitful. Theodore's background in the labour movement and his undoubted financial wizardry and drive, coupled with Packer's experience in the newspaper world, were to prove a formidable combination that eventually silenced the critics and harbingers of doom who tried to strangle the lusty infant that was to grow to become such a giant.

The new paper became the *Daily Telegraph* and was first published on 23 March 1936. It was a broadsheet modelled on the style of the London *Daily Express,* and within eighteen months circulation had nearly doubled.

Under Deamer, and inspired by the talent surrounding him, Hughes blossomed. He began as a sub-editor and at times was acting chief of staff and all the time he was writing, writing.

One of his chores was to review mystery stories and he assumed the by-line 'Dr Watson, Jnr'. When there was a dearth of mystery stories he would make them up and review imaginary books, much to the bewilderment of Sydney booksellers. He used the pseudonym 'Pakenham' for these reviews.

Whenever he could, Hughes would travel to Melbourne to see his young son and his mother and father. Somehow the boy would know when his father was coming and for a few days there would be another visit to Victoria Docks and the zoo and the railways. The little boy lived in a fantasy world peopled by characters his grandfather invented and his happiness was complete when the big man wearing a hat would appear magically at the front gate and make up other stories to complement the gentle ones his grandfather would tell.

Back in Sydney, life was becoming more Rabelaisian. The pub next door to the *Daily Telegraph* was the rendezvous for the wild, scintillating group of journalists Packer had gathered around him. Stories were re-hashed, dreamed up and fought over. At 6 pm, when the pub officially closed, they would troop upstairs for their nightly battle to bring out another paper for Packer who, seemingly omnipotent, shouted and cajoled to help shape another daily miracle of order out of chaos.

Packer fought with his staff and they fought back but there was enormous pride on both sides. Reports of Packer's 'bastardry' was one topic that has never palled, and many of his staff, Hughes among them, disagreed violently with the newspaper's political views. Yet they poured out their talent, often grumbling and rebellious, but with great professionalism.

Hughes was known as 'the railways boy' when he first started on the *Telegraph*. Despite his stint on the *Star*, he was a relative newcomer to the tough professional world of Sydney journalism, with its cut-throat competition. By comparison, his Melbourne days were sedate.

He soon lost the 'railway boy' tag as he rose from a sub-editor to become acting chief of staff. Cyril Pearl, sure and erudite, was still his mentor and dear friend. Hughes' bulk and his increasing habit of using biblical quotes, together with the name his friends had coined for his apartment in Double Bay — 'the monastery' — were building a legend about him. His nickname became 'monk' — though not because of celibate habits.

He had 'taken on' Packer, too, and on one occasion the two huge men, enraged over a comparative trifle, stood and glared at each other when Hughes invited Packer to stand up. 'Stand up so I can knock you down', he glared at his boss. Packer, a former amateur heavyweight boxing champion, smoothed down the incident, as he was to many other times. He had great pride in the array of talent around him and he recognized that passion was one of the most important ingredients in the make-up of a top newspaperman.

Hughes clashed with Packer often. Once, without thought, he referred to Packer's bad eye. 'You know, Frank', he said when Packer took a stand on a political issue that Hughes thought was too narrow, 'in the country of the blind the one eyed man is king.'

Packer flared. 'Never mind your smart arse cracks about my bad eye.'

Hughes apologized. He was aware that his wit and erudition often hurt others. Sometimes he didn't care when this happened, though on other occasions he was filled with remorse when his quick wit stung the less articulate. Often however, his remorse was too late and private.

Drinking, under the absurd 6 pm closing law was always a problem, but cunning and strategy overcame it. One strategic move was to gain access to a club. Hughes' non-membership of a nearby Masonic club, together with one of his close friends, solved the problem at one stage. He was invited to visit the club by a high Masonic brother and he enjoyed the rich surroundings and the availability of good cigars. He went in once or twice alone to await his member host, was mistaken for a brother and given immediate service. By this time the portly doorman knew him as 'Brother Hughes' and would salute him respectfully as he entered.

Occasionally he would take in visitors — also non-members — and was welcomed by the bar staff, to whom he occasionally slipped a surreptitious tip . . . not a widespread practice among the actual members.

Hughes, and one particular newspaperman friend he would usher in, lordly drank as much as they could of the rare stock of Bass Ale and smoked their way through the precious Corona coronas which were reserved for them. Eventually, ashamed of his deception and feeling guilty about the acceptance by the 'brother' drinkers, Hughes withdrew from the comforts of the club. He was also aware of the risk of being uncovered as an imposter.

The 'monastery' was a great gathering place too for the articulate and bohemian friends, mostly from the *Daily Telegraph,* who were making his life so full.

Hughes began to live up to the legend of the 'monastery' and the biblical quotes and one day he and another close friend purchased a biretta, the square cap with three projections and a tassel on top worn by Roman Catholic clergy. Hughes' friend explained that another close friend, 'Father Murphy', had risen in the clerical world and was entitled to wear the headgear. Such was the eloquence, laced with appropriate biblical quotes, that the assistant sold them the biretta, which Hughes promptly adopted. Occasionally he shared it with his friend, and they took to blessing each other.

A journalists' fancy dress ball saw the emergence of the biretta into the world outside the 'monastery' cloister. Hughes went dressed as a monk, complete with cowled robe and crucifix. With him was another friend dressed as an English gentlemen, bowler-hatted and with pristine spats setting off his immaculate appearance. On their way home from the ball, the two revellers stopped opposite the old Stadium at Rushcutters Bay to buy cigarettes from an all night hawker's stall. Some youths heckled them because of their dress and words were exchanged. There was a police car parked nearby in a prohibited area. Hughes' friend strode across, thrust his head through the window of the police vehicle and berated the two policemen inside for breaking the law and for not controlling the loutish youths. He was promptly dragged inside the car which headed for the nearest police station. Hughes tried to intercede but it was too late. He scrabbled his monk's gown to his knees and ran after the policemen and his outraged friend. He finally caught a taxi and shadowed the police car to nearby Darlinghurst police station. When he got upstairs, his friend was being searched and measured up against a wall after being charged with drunken and offensive behaviour.

Hughes, dignified by now, approached the seated desk sergeant who was checking his friend's money and other belongings. 'Take care, father', his friend cried, 'they are taking me to the triangle.'

Obsequious, Hughes asked the desk sergeant if his friend could be released. 'He meant no harm', he said earnestly. 'I know him well at my monastery. He is a good, law-abiding believer but has perhaps been drinking a little too much tonight. I promise to take good care of him'.

The sergeant rose respectfully. 'I am sorry, father', he said in a rich Irish brogue, 'but the charge has now been entered against him. But I promise we'll take good care of him and release him on minor bail tomorrow morning.' He lowered his voice and bent his head closer.

'Your friend needn't appear in court. We won't press the case but must keep the bail of course. I wish you had come earlier. Please excuse us. I, too, am of the faith. Please bless me father.' Hughes blessed him and they reverently shook hands. As Hughes left, his friend, unblinking, bowed to him. The next morning Hughes' friend told him that he had been treated with great care, given a late supper, comfortable bedding and early breakfast before being released on ridiculously low bail. The case received no publicity.

Shortly afterwards, Chief Commissioner Clapp was in Sydney and called on Frank Packer at the *Daily Telegraph*. He inquired after his one time protege and Packer dialled Hughes' home number. Hughes answered: 'The monastery here'.

'I don't want any monastery', Packer growled, 'I want Richard Hughes.'

Hughes recognized his boss' rusty voice and apologized and Packer, grinning, handed over the phone to Clapp who chatted for awhile then repeated his earlier advice about Asia.

Packer, going from strength to strength, launched the *Sunday Telegraph* in 1939. It was an instant success, and Hughes was appointed chief-of-staff. Cyril Pearl was editor. Australia was by then out of the Depression years but was becoming more and more aware of the clouds boiling up over Europe and uneasily looking again towards the north, aware of the growing emergence of Japan as a belligerent world power. But in Australia the great daily appetite for the bright, sensational and sordid continued to be met. Occasional feuds with Packer erupted and died away again, and Hughes' uproarious, exhilarating life went on.

One night, just before he went to the *Sunday Telegraph*, Hughes was having dinner with Sid Deamer — often referred to as 'the last of the great editors' — and Pearl. They were discussing a fascinating crime in New Zealand involving Gordon Robert McKay, a Sydney skin dealer who had disappeared there after his arrival together with a companion, James Arthur Talbot. Talbot told police that McKay had been burnt to death at the beach resort of Piha after the shack he was living in caught fire from a cigarette McKay was smoking in bed. Some charred bones were recovered. Soon afterwards it was discovered that McKay had been insured earlier for £50 000.

Deamer, in a frivolous mood, said to Hughes: 'Dr Watson, Junior, you're a great authority on crime. Why don't you go over to New Zealand and solve this mystery for us?'

Hughes replied: 'Certainly. I'd be delighted.'

Several of his friends saw Hughes off when the ship to New Zealand pulled out of Sydney Harbour. Several toasts to the success of the mission had been hoisted and there was some hilarity as the ship eased away from its berth. The term 'mug' was the 'in' honorific among some of his friends at the time. 'Good bye, mug', they called, and 'have a successful mission, mug' as Hughes blessed them from the deck high above.

Within hours of the ship dipping into the Pacific swell a fellow passenger approached a pale Hughes as he stood on the deck watching Sydney blur into the distance. 'I believe you're the reverend Mug', he said respectfully. Hughes, deadpan, acknowledged the greeting.

In New Zealand, Hughes pitched into the McKay mystery with enthusiasm. He interviewed everybody he could find who had seen or spoken to McKay. He also inspected the site of the fire and saw the handful of charred bones the police had collected.

Then, in true Sherlock Holmes style, he wrote his story: 'I have been courteously made privy to the scientific evidence which the police are collecting on the case. I must now regretfully testify that I cannot accept the statement that Mr McKay perished in the Piha fire.'

He went on portentously: 'Consider the facts. The Piha shack was destroyed by a blaze which burned irregularly and fluctuatingly for from thirty-five to sixty minutes. In that time, it is declared, all of Mr McKay, from teeth to sacrum, was burned to dust, except a small section of skull and vertebrae, two or three knuckles of bone, and a couple of pounds of scarred flesh.'

Relishing a change to write in the style of the master, he continued: 'At the outset, therefore, we are asked to accept the monstrous supposition that Mr McKay could leave some of his flesh behind him in the fire even while all the bones charred away.'

He recalled in his story, which was published at a time when police still believed that McKay had been burned to death, that the skull in the fire had no teeth. Meanwhile the human debris from the ashes were solemnly buried and notice of McKay's death was quickly served on several insurance companies in Australia. As McKay was heavily insured, the insurance companies were suspicious. Police told Hughes that the two men had arrived recently from Australia and had taken rooms in an Auckland boarding house. They told the landlady that McKay had trouble with his teeth and all had to be extracted.

They intended they said, to go to Piha so he could recuperate. They hired a car and parked it in a suburban garage until the day before the fire at Piha, leaving a shovel which did not belong to the garage's owner. A pea-sized piece of clay was found on the handle of the shovel. The garage owner also recalled seeing the two men who had rented it with a round, long bundle, wrapped in sacking.

Police, spurred on by the suspicions of the insurance companies, finally traced the tiny piece of clay to a nearby cemetery. There a Government analyst pointed dramatically to a grave site. 'If you dig up that grave there will be no body in it', he said. He was right and the search was on in a big way.

The grave was that of a Mr Stone, whose son recalled that two men had come to his home the day after his father died and asked if Mr Stone had served in the World War. One of the men said he thought he was a mate of Mr Stone's but he would know for sure if the late Mr Stone had false teeth. He had, the son agreed.

Talbot was soon arrested but there was no sign of McKay when the remains buried as his were exhumed and the skull found to be Stone's. Police finally tracked down a man who said his name was Tom Bowling. Fingerprint tests proved that Bowling was McKay. But he denied it and feigned lunacy and neither he nor Talbot showed the slightest recognition of each other when brought together. But the strain of acting as a lunatic was too much and McKay, alias Bowling, finally admitted his real identity. McKay and Talbot were brought to trial, found guilty of desecrating a grave and sentenced to gaol terms. Their ingenious scheme had been meticulously planned, even to the painful extent of McKay having all his teeth extracted so that the skull found in the fire would not be in doubt.

Hughes' careful investigation was a triumph. He had not believed the provisional police theory. 'I am convinced', he wrote for his paper before the case was solved, 'that the late Mr McKay will be recovered alive and unburned.'

Hughes' report was published in the *Daily Telegraph* in Sydney on March 21, the day before McKay was arrested.

It was Hughes' best story and he returned to Sydney in triumph. He came back on the trans-Tasman ship *Awatea*, dining at the captain's table and instilling some awe among the other passengers when he ordered Bombay duck from a supercilious steward. 'I'll have the Bombay duck', he said grandly.

'You mean, sir, you'll have the dish which includes Bombay duck', the steward said loftily.

'Nothing of the sort. I want the Bombay duck and nothing but the Bombay duck.'

Confronted eventually with a stinking mess of dried, putrid fishy substance and conscious of all eyes on him he had no recourse but to reach for a fork and force down a dish he had never seen previously, and had ordered only because he heard that King George liked it.

Later in 1939 Australia went to war, with thousands queuing for the privilege of being among the first. Hughes, who had trouble with his knees, was unfit. So he threw himself into his new and exciting job as chief of staff of the *Sunday Telegraph*. But as he watched the first troopship leave Sydney Harbour late that year the old dream of overseas travel recurred and Clapp's 'go to Asia first' advice became an obsession. He began to plan, saving some money and reading everything he could about the China-Japan conflict. He said goodbye to several friends who headed for Europe as correspondents. Among them was Ronald Monson, destined to become a household name and who later was to perform a feat of bravery in Syria that would have won a Victoria Cross for a soldier.

A final visit to Melbourne to see his son and other members of his family preceded his plunge into the outside world. He took long leave, borrowed £400 from his newspaper to add to the money he had saved, and boarded a Japanese boat for Japan. Three weeks later, wiser and slightly more tolerant towards Japanese than when he left Australia in a haze of farewell parties, he landed in Japan, a virgin foreign devil.

On the long voyage he taught some members of the ship's crew Australian slang and they in turn told him some of the more gentle customs of their country. Hughes called his sessions with the Japanese captain and crew 'an earnest study group in pornographic semantics'.

The war news came over the ship's radio but the Japanese crew would insist to Hughes that Japan would never go to war against Australia despite the broadcast threats by Japanese statesmen against the West.

When he landed he was the only Australian journalist in Japan and he went into his unofficial assignment with gusto. He installed himself in Tokyo's old Imperial Hotel, nestling with spies and other foreigners. And it was there he met one of the greatest spies of them all — Richard Sorge — who was in Japan posing very successfully as a German newspaperman and rabid member of the Nazi party.

Sorge was the epitome of the German tough — ruthless, arrogant, coldly intelligent and with great fascination for women. Hughes disliked him intensely — the cruel, scarred face repelled him. Nothing that Sorge did or said gave anyone the slightest clue that he was head of the Soviet spy ring in the Far East. He never allowed women or liquor or friendship distract him from his role and never once did he give a clue that he spoke Russian.

Sorge headed a Russian spy ring of sixteen men and women. Some were Western and some Japanese and for seven years they operated with ruthless efficiency, pouring in their invaluable reports to the Soviet Union. Sorge himself had access to the German embassy and through one of his aides he had access to the Japanese government. German and Japanese military moves and policy shifts were fed back to Moscow diligently. One of Sorge's greatest spy coups was his alert to Moscow that Germany would strike at the Soviet — a week before Hitler struck. He told the Kremlin that Japan would not attack Russia and he told them also that Japan would strike south into the Pacific.

Richard Sorge was forty-five when Hughes knew him, over 180 centimetres in height and heavily built. He was born in Russia of a German father and a Russian mother. He went to Germany as a child and served in the First World War. After the war he joined the

Communist Party, secured a doctorate in political science at university, then worked as a school teacher and coal miner in the Ruhr. In 1924 he went to Russia, had special training and became an agent, eventually with the highly efficient Fourth Bureau of the Red Army General Staff. He served in Scandinavia and Britain, using his cover as a journalist.

How then did Sorge become a trusted German agent? Hughes, in his excellent *Foreign Devil*, an hilarious and intelligent account of his thirty years reporting from the Far East, comes to the conclusion that the master spy was in fact a triple agent. The Germans had a complete dossier on him and they obviously trusted him. Hughes felt that Sorge had manipulated the German backing for the greater advantage of his only real interest — the Soviet Union.

Hughes' amiable disposition made it easy for him to mix with Sorge and others in the heady days of the old Imperial Hotel. He drank with them at the Imperial and mixed at other times at restaurants. It was at one restaurant, Ketel's Rheingold on Tokyo's Ginza, that Sorge intervened when a giant student-prince type German aimed a punch at Hughes when the Australian ebulliently asked the assembled Germans how they felt about losing the war. Sorge grabbed the furious German giant and spoke to him savagely. He then asked Hughes to be polite. Hughes said he was merely returning a compliment as some other Germans in a bar across the street had told him Britain had lost the war.

Sorge was arrested long after Hughes left Japan. The Japanese secret police, Kempei-tai, dragged him from his bed and among his possessions they found the draft, in English, of his uncabled message to Moscow urging that he should be recalled immediately. He was hanged in 1944.

Just before Hughes' arrival in Japan in 1940 another story involving allegations of espionage shocked the Western world. The ramifications of the arrest and subsequent death of Melville James Cox, a Reuter correspondent, were still echoing when Hughes arrived. Again he took copious notes and spoke to everybody he could find who knew something about the mysterious death of Cox who, together with thirteen other Britons, was arrested on a charge of espionage. He was taken to the Kempei-tai headquarters not far from the Imperial palace and held in a stone cell in the basement, his bed a plank.

The secret police, for whom Hughes formed a savage hatred, claimed that Cox leapt to his death through an open window while under interrogation. They explained puncture marks on his broken body as being from the injections they had administered in an effort to save the fluttering life that was still there when they picked him up. The Kempei-tai produced a letter, unsigned, which they claimed Cox had left for his wife. It was found on his body they said. In it, according to the police copy read to foreign correspondents, Jimmy Cox said, among other things, 'I know what is best .. always my only love . . . '.

Hughes arrived a week after Cox's death and in the tense atmosphere of the time he remembered, with some anxiety, his own detailed diary of his arrival and impressions of the explosive country. Few of Cox's friends to whom Hughes spoke doubted that he had been brutally killed after being drugged and beaten, but Hughes had his doubts. He spoke to Japanese newspaper friends who assured him that the Kempei-tai methods did not involve a prisoner dying on their hands; the secret police method was to question inexorably day after day. They had plenty of time.

So Hughes formed the opinion that Cox, dispirited for months before his arrest and worried about Britain's fate, had jumped to his death. With his news files and notes, however harmless, he knew he had no hope under the espionage laws. But Hughes was equally sure that Cox, in jumping to his death, was a brave man as surely murdered by the Kempei-tai as if they had thrown him from the window.

This theory was reinforced in 1960 when an eyewitness of Cox's death, Yaroku Shimazu, told the Japanese Ministry of Justice he had seen Cox jump from a ledge outside an open window on the third storey of the Kempei-tai building. Shimazu, who was dying at the time, said he heard a shout and looked up to see Cox climbing out on the ledge. 'He looked calmly round him, raised his hands to his face and deliberately jumped', he told ministry officials.

Hughes knew Shimazu during the occupation and Shimazu also told Hughes his story. He was a highly respected reporter on the newspaper *Asahi Shimbun* and was covering Kempei-tai activities when Cox died. He told Hughes he did not report what he had seen at the time because he detested the secret police and had no wish to help them out of their embarrassment or help to acquit them of their suspected responsibility. He too believed that the police had broken Cox so badly that he was forced to throw himself to his death.

Interest in Cox came about not because he knew the man but because Hughes felt that 'a brave Englishman and good newspaper man should not have a question mark over his grave'.

Hughes wrote only innocuous pieces during his 1940 foray into Japan. He was technically on leave for the first two months though he took copious notes and collected news clippings about crop failures and shortages and every conceivable aspect of pre-war Japanese life. He knew also that his room at the Imperial was searched diligently, regular as clockwork at a certain hour on a certain day, so he had left the material — as incriminating as that Jimmy Cox had collected — with a friend at an embassy.

At the time he was getting thundering cables from his office in Sydney demanding his return. He turned the growing wrath to one side with disarming lies about the unavailability of berths on ships destined for Australia. He was completely fascinated by Japan, and Tokyo itself touched a chord, even in those tense days, that was never to be broken.

Before he returned to Sydney, he had a brief foray into nearby China, convulsed then by the Sino-Japanese conflict. He went to Shanghai, but it was a fast trip and he was depressed by Japan's growing dominance over the fragmented Chinese and by the attitude of so many of the old China hands, still steeped in the worst aspects of colonialism.

Back in Japan briefly before his ship left for Australia, and beginning to feel guilty about over-staying his leave, Hughes swung straight back into the life that exhilerated him so much. The drinking sessions and nights on the town were interspersed with contact in the diplomatic world and with high Japanese officials. He formed a sneaking regard for the then Japanese Foreign Minister, Yosuke Matsuoka. A hard-drinking, dwarfish, bandy-legged caricature of the prewar Japanese diplomat, Matsuoka revelled in indiscretions at mass press conferences and Hughes found great delight observing the impact he made.

He spoke English with an American accent picked up when he worked as a hotel employee and attended a U.S. university. Sometimes, even when sober, he delighted in embarrassing his career advisers by ostentatiously throwing away prepared statements at press conferences with the remark: 'That's what they wanted me to say. Now I'll tell you what I want to say . . .'

But he was a clever politician and a political driving force who had 'sold' Japan both the non-aggression pact with the Soviet Union and, subsequently, the tripartite pact with Germany and Italy. He had taken his country out of the League of Nations when Japan was condemned for her rape of Manchuria. It was reported at the time that Matsuoka, uninhibited as always and perhaps with a shot or two of sake bubbling in his veins, shouted as the Japanese marched out of the doomed League building that Japan was 'another Jesus of Nazareth, crucified by the West'.

Hughes' muted liking for the unconventional Matsuoka deepened when the little man provided a curiously Japanese alibi for his drinking. Sometimes, he said, he was troubled by inner doubts because of his contact with the mysterious West and the possible evil and infectious influence of that contact upon his immaculate Japanese conception and continuing chauvinistic integrity. So he devised his alcoholic apologia: 'When speaking and sober I always think in English. This has led me to wonder at times whether I'm more western than Japanese, but I have found out by studying my reflexes while under the influence of alcohol that I must be a Japanese at heart because I can't think clearly in any language but Japanese when I have taken a little sake.'

Matsuoka, who was reported to be the only civilian who knew all the details of the Pearl Harbour attack of 1941, died of natural causes before the war crimes trials began, perhaps with a sake bottle beside his bed.

Packer's recall cables by this time were taking on a threatening note. 'You are ordered to return', one of them said ominously. Hughes was reluctant to leave, yet he was in a fever to return and publish his forecast of doom. He believed that war with Japan was only months away. He collected his bits and pieces and his detailed diary, his memory of Jimmy Cox's brave death still fresh, and left Tokyo in December to board his ship from Kobe.

The farewells in Tokyo were continued in Kobe. His guide there, a Dutch shipping company representative who shared Hughes' Rabelaisian outlook and non-celibate habits, took him on a hilarious tour of the seaport. The highlight was a visit to a sex shop, a modest building crouching, as Hughes said, 'with a discreet leer' on a side street corner. Hughes intended to buy some of the shop's merchandise as gifts to the Australian Journalists' Association and the pair finally selected appropriate souvenirs, including two posters remarkable for their lurid colour and exquisite detail. They packed them into a trunk and headed to a bar near the wharf for another final drink.

Hughes climbed the gangplank and turned for a farewell blessing to his friend. Happily, he started towards his cabin. Two squat figures barred the way. One was a security man in civilian clothes and the other an officer of the dreaded Kempei-tai, complete with red armband and two holstered revolvers. They escorted a suddenly sober Hughes to his cabin and instructed him to open his trunk. Inside the trunk, packed into pockets of his clothes, were notebooks full of his observations about Japan and news clippings from Japanese and Chinese newspapers. The December night became colder and the thought of Jimmy Cox and his lonely 'always my only love' note to his wife slipped into Hughes' mind. A return to shore and the inevitable interrogation seemed certain. He would be arrested, miss his ship and lose his job. And what about the Axis flags he had exuberantly pinched from a German embassy car the night he left Tokyo?

The trunk was in the corridor just outside his cabin. Hughes opened it. The two officials bent over it and out came the German and Italian and Japanese flags. The Kempei-tai man shook them out, stared for a moment then handed them to Hughes. He suggested Hughes should put the flags in his pocket on his arrival in Australia. The Australian government might not like them, he suggested.

'Why do you have them?' he asked.

'They're happy mementoes of my stay in your country', Hughes said. He tried to assume what he thought was an innocent look. Perhaps we can make an issue of the flags, he thought, and waste a bit more time over them. He shook them out again and spread them on the deck. The Kempei-tai man gathered them, ostentatiously placing the Japanese flag on top of the others, and thrust them at Hughes again. 'You keep', he said, and turned back to the trunk.

Then came the posters. The civilian unrolled one which depicted a strange, simply-drawn apparatus which, the text explained in English and Japanese, was for 'body building exercises by a man with markled fleelings of sexual infleriority'. It was sedately called 'the happiest invlention of the century'.

The two officials, grinning now, examined the poster minutely. A passing ship's officer halted, bowed to Hughes and the security men, and joined in the animated discussion. The second poster followed. Comparably it was mild. The box of sex shop souvenirs then spilled onto the deck and the four men scrabbled to collect them. The security men were hissing with laughter and one of them perched one of the objects on his head. Sweating, Hughes grinned with relief.

The final touch came when a fellow passenger, an elderly female Western missionary, paused as she passed and peered short-sightedly at the array of pornography. The first poster caught her eye. She drew herself up fiercly and stamped down the deck, followed by the delighted shouts of the now relaxed security men. They restored Hughes' treasures, packing them on top of the incriminating material underneath, closed the trunk and shook hands with the still trembling Hughes. The female missionary avoided him religiously on the three weeks voyage back to Australia.

Back in Sydney, he reported to his office, put off for a few days the inevitable shouting match he knew he faced with Packer, and headed for Melbourne to regale his small son with some of his experiences.

3 Japan to Egypt

Hughes' stories on Japan hit Australia early in 1941. He wrote most of them on the voyage home and when Packer saw the first of them he relented. 'All right, you bastard', he said. 'You win. You were on assignment after all — not leave. I'll pay all your expenses.'

So the *Daily Telegraph* blazoned across the first of the stories 'We sent our man to Japan' and devoted huge space to them. Hughes, the newspaper trumpeted, was the first Australian journalist representing a newspaper to visit Japan since 1934. They called him 'one of our ace reporters'.

He forecast that Japan would be embroiled in the war within six months and that the Japanese people had been trained to accept and even welcome the most bitter personal sacrifice in the name of their national family. Yet, he wrote, really the Japanese people wanted war as little as the American people wanted it and the government actually dreaded the idea of war with the U.S. But a strong section of the Japanese Army felt that the European conflict provided Japan with a heaven-sent opportunity to snatch the Dutch East Indies, the Philippines as well as China and that their view would prevail.

The stories had a mixed reception. Many politicians derided Hughes as a scaremonger, despite the subdued tone of his writing. There was little of the flamboyance often associated with his newspaper and his name. The stories were sober yet entertaining. Australians at that time were looking at Europe, and were being regaled daily with the agony of the British people. The top talent from many newspapers had been sent to Europe, some with the Australian divisions, others to London itself. The motherland was again in danger and all other threats, irrespective how close to home, were uneasily dismissed.

Underneath the apparent indifference, however, there was a growing sense of fear of the danger from the north and Hughes' articles, perhaps because of the passion he put into them and because they had been so carefully researched, helped the slowly growing awareness of Japan's belligerence.

Hughes reported that, if ordered to do so, and the signs were growing that this would happen, the solid, disciplined phalanx of Japan's 100 000 000 people would fight the U.S.A., the Soviet Union or the whole world. Without a doubt, he wrote, Japan could stand up to a major war. He warned about complacency, about the average Australian's penchant to dismiss the Japanese as little, short-sighted and funny men who could never stand against the big, bronzed Aussies.

In one piece on the hard drinking Matsuoka — 'the ruthless and garrulous little man with the thick spectacles and bristling, boot brush scalp' — and on the sinister war minister, Tojo, he said they had respectfully bullied the Emperor into acceptance of Japan's alliance with Germany and Italy. The Emperor, he said, was opposed to the alliance with the Axis powers. Hirohito, he wrote, was pro-British royal family but not pro-British.

In a personal aside, he told how, at one of a series of 'spontaneous celebrations' of the signing of the Axis pact, he had been mistaken for a German. 'Processions of youngsters, students and soldiers carrying flags usually ended up outside the Emperor's palace. They had all the elan of a Jehovah's Witness rally on a wet Sunday afternoon at La Perouse [a Sydney coastal suburb]. I was watching one of the processions when some students, thinking that any big, blonde, heavy moving, slightly stupid looking foreigner must be German, gave me the Nazi salute.'

Summing up Japan's strength in the event of war in the Pacific, Hughes said the country's navy was powerful and dangerous. The army was tough but weak in mechanical forces. He was not impressed with Japan's air force and said the country's air raid defences were weak. Contrary to the widely held view in Australia, he said Japanese soldiers were brave, first-class infantrymen who obeyed orders without question. They were a queer blend of the stoic and the fanatic.

Dealing with the tri-partite pact, Hughes wrote that some influential Japanese he had spoken to claimed the signatories should have been Japan, the U.S.A. and Great Britain. These insiders, he said, also claimed that Japan had made overtures to Britain and the U.S.A. and that Britain, at least, was prepared to encourage this mood. Britain, he said, even began to work out a new face-saving formula for Japan in China and a new deal on trade, markets and natural resources in the Pacific. But all this would have required American co-operation that was not forthcoming.

The Emperor, he wrote, had fought a courageous, losing battle against the desperate extremists who had forced Japan into the alliance with Germany and Italy. He called the Emperor an intelligent, highly-respected and popular man, but he had no friends and was the loneliest man in the country.

Of the average Japanese man, whom he called 'suzuki-san', Hughes wrote: 'This type, since he began to talk, has learned to do what he has been told — at home by his father, at school by his teacher, at work by his employer, in the street by the police — always, everywhere, awake and asleep, by the divine and infallible emperor.

'His mental attitude is one of complete, inspired resignation. He seeks to avoid all personal responsibility, all expressions of individuality. He belongs to a great family of which the emperor is the supreme father. His duty to that family, his loyalty to Japan, his reverence for the emperor shape and colour all his mental processes. He believes sincerely that Japan is liberating China.'

He poured in thousands of words, day after day, drawing a picture for Australians of an enigmatic race with values quite alien to those taken for granted at home. He tried to destroy the myth that all Japanese ships overturned, that Japanese planes were toys made of paper, and that their bombs often did not explode. The majority of Australians at that time were still imbued with a belief that British ships, planes and vehicles were second to none and that most others, including American but specifically Japanese, were pale imitations. The shock of Pearl Harbour, the taking of Singapore, the death of two of Britain's greatest warships before the year was out need not perhaps have been such gut blows had Hughes' articles been taken more seriously.

Packer and the brilliant men around him were convinced, however, and planning began for Hughes to visit the United States to report on her attitude towards the war. But Australia's eyes were on the war in Europe and specifically on the campaign in the desert. Tobruk fell in January 1941, with Australians playing a big part in the capture. Some of the great names of Australian journalism were covering the action and Hughes began to feel restless again as the weeks passed and prospects of the American visit seemed to fade.

He made another visit to New Zealand, this time to cover the dedication of a monument to Michael Joseph (Mick) Savage, a former Prime Minister who had died a year earlier. The homely, white-haired Savage was an Australian miner who became New Zealand's first labour prime minister. Hughes said all Auckland seemed to turn out on a bleak, drizzling Sunday to attend the service: 'From all the folklore about Savage there emerged certain constant qualities of simplicity, honesty and gentleness which clarified but did not fully explain the New Zealand people's abiding idolatry of him', Hughes wrote in his touching tribute. 'He was not a great politician, statesman, great speaker but he was steadfast, sincere. He kept his word. He was never intolerant or bitter although he had a Celtic fire which flared up in moments of crisis.'

More and more stories were coming out of the United States about the country's covert preparations for the war that Hughes was convinced would also engulf the Pacific. President Roosevelt, in his third inauguration speech in January 1941, warned against the peril of inaction. He said democracy could not and would not die because it was built on the unhampered initiative of individual men and women joined in a common enterprise. The speech was regarded as one of the President's greatest and one newspaper said of it: 'The people of England, listening to Roosevelt's dramatic tone, could see the flame of liberty burning'.

So the scene was set for Hughes, particularly in the light of his Japanese visit, to bring home to Australians how a deeply divided America viewed the conflict. A poll at the time showed that 60 per cent of Americans wanted to aid Britain, even at the risk of war, but only 12 per cent wanted to go to war deliberately.

Hughes had flair and imagination and one great attribute that set him apart from many others in his craft: the ability to give the impression that he was not eager to obtain information. He knew that men who were engaged in important affairs would refuse to talk to him if they suspected his motive was to collect information. He also knew that if he gave the impression that he had more information than his prospective informant, the informant would give with a smile. And with his knowledge of Japan and his conviction that she would lash southward when the time was ripe, he was confident he had enough information to give him an edge.

His arrival in the United States got off to a strange start. One particular news service reported from the West coast that Hughes had arrived to cover the American scene for his newspapers, but some curious gremlin got at the simple message and when it was re-transmitted from New York on the network he was referred to as 'Premier Hughes of Australia'.

He ranged over the vast country, not confining himself to the big cities but taking in the mid-west, the prairies, and the grassroots generally, looking for the elusive average American. He came to the conclusion that most Americans were convinced the U.S. already was in the war and were reconciled to complete belligerent participation very soon. But he felt they were sliding towards war rather sullenly and resentfully. As a people they had no particular warm or friendly feelings towards Britain. She was doing a 'swell' job, they agreed, but they were prepared to sit back until there was no alternative. Primarily their attitude was selfish, thought Hughes, though he also called the American war effort 'the greatest industrial revolution in the history of the world' and said it would perform in two years what Hitler's Germany took seven years to achieve.

He found that West coast people at least were aware of the Japanese menace, but the remainder of America thought it a nebulous threat. 'I'm still surprised at the bitterness of anti-Japanese sentiment along the Pacific coast', he wrote. 'It is no phase; it is abiding and angry and positive. They believe that war in the Pacific is inevitable.'

He interviewed everybody he could. Roosevelt, Hoover, head of the Federal Bureau of Investigation, senators, congressmen, union leaders, dock workers, farmers, miners, negroes and whites fell into his wide-cast net. The interview with Roosevelt was off the record and Hughes had to confine his remarks to the President's looks and attitudes and to the fact that Roosevelt was pressing on confidently with his aid programme to Britain.

Everywhere he found enormous interest in Australia and New Zealand. Their exploits in the desert war, their breezy scorn of convention and their alleged singing of 'The Wizard of Oz' as they went into battle struck a chord with all Americans and appealed to their sense of adventure.

In Washington he was invited to attend a Negro revivalist meeting and to speak to the congregation. A Negro he met in a bar invited him. He was sitting in a corner, playing quietly on a mouth organ as Hughes ordered a drink. Hughes had to repeat his order when the barman apparently did not understand his accent, still pure Prahran. The Negro tapped the mouth organ on his hand to remove any spittle. 'Where you from, man?' he asked.

'Australia.'

'Where's that?'

Hughes turned over a coaster and sketched his country's outline. They started talking and when the Negro told him about a revivalist meeting nearby, and that he played the mouth organ in the choir, Hughes happily went along.

'So I stumbled up the aisle, crawled up three steps to the stage on which the choir orchestra of silver trumpetist, violinist and two mouth organists and a beaming, be-spectacled elder were assembled.'

'I told them in a halting rumble that I was very happy to attend the service, that white people in Australia didn't enjoy their church service as much as black people in America, that we thought Joe Louis was the world's greatest boxer and that I wanted to hear the choir singing again. They kept interrupting me with "yeahs" and "hallelujahs".'

He felt his statement didn't exactly measure up to a public testimony of faith, but he was convinced that one-third of his audience didn't understand his accent, one-third thought him a dull pleasant enough fellow who didn't understand the English language, and the remainder thought he was from Austria. At one stage, he said, his arm jerked up of its own accord to give them a blessing reminiscent of the far-off days at the 'monastery' in Sydney, but he dragged it back guiltily.

He had several love affairs, some one night stands in the most improbable of places, and was entertained with typical American hospitality wherever he went. He made lifelong friendships, many with American women, whom he admired, yet treated warily. He said he didn't believe that American men always did everything their womenfolk told them to do but he had no doubt they felt they should. 'I want to pay humble, slightly scared tribute to feminine authority on the American scene', he wrote at the time. He was convinced that men's ties were so bright because they were made to please women, who chose them. On beer, of which he was fond, he claimed that the light, frothy, sweetish beverage had been largely influenced by women's palates. 'But I must sadly report that American women's intellectual development has not matched her material development', he wrote. American women, he said, had the leisure, the opportunity and the money to establish a feminine authority unknown in any other country in the world. Yet it would be a grave mistake — and the Japanese were likely to make it — to think of America as degenerate. It was immensely strong and once it became united over spilt blood it would roll over anything in its way.

On the West coast, Hughes met and talked with one of the most controversial Australians anywhere in the world at that time — Harry Bridges. Bridges was the union boss of the West coast waterfront workers and at the time was about the most hated man in the United States. Communism was only one of the 'crimes' alleged about him as Bridges led strike after strike in his effort to improve conditions. All efforts to deport him failed. 'Hanging is too good for him' was one of the least abusive expressions that normally cultivated, pleasant Americans used about him.

Hughes found Bridges brisk, incisive, slightly suspicious but supremely confident. The dapper, thin-faced Bridges, with a disconcerting habit of closing his left eye when emphasizing a point, told Hughes he was not a member of the Communist Party and did not have an attitude towards communism: 'I'm a trade unionist and nothing else. I stand and fight for trade unionism'. He fought so successfully and against such tremendous odds that he secured the world's best working conditions at the time for Pacific coast waterfront men.

Hughes stayed six months in the United States. One of his last pieces, strangely, dealt with Pearl Harbour, so soon to be decimated by one of history's greatest acts of treachery. He wrote that plans to make Hawaii self-supporting in the event of war in the Pacific were complete. Foolproof anti-sabotage measures for all vulnerable points had been taken. The harbour itself, he said, was equipped with all facilities to enable the U.S. Pacific fleet to operate indefinitely on a war basis. There was nothing to indicate then that Japan's military leaders and the half-drunken Matsuoka were preparing feverishly for the holocaust that was to hit the base within weeks.

Back in Australia, Hughes found that former journalist John Curtin had succeeded Robert Menzies as Prime Minister and Australia began to rise to his nobility. People turned to Curtin with enthusiasm and trust as he took on a stature that surprised his critics. Under Curtin, Australia's advisory war council spent more and more time assessing the Japanese threat. Many of its members felt now that Japan's entry into the war was inevitable.

Again Hughes went to Melbourne to see his son and family. His young son, by some prescience possessed by children and dogs, knew his father was coming and raced to the gate of his grandfather's home to meet the hero he so rarely saw.

Life was more serious in Sydney now and there was little left of the wild and exciting days of the 'monastery'. Hughes' obsession with the Japanese threat was reinforced when many military observers claimed that Japan was preparing to strike South from Indo-China, where she was already established, to obtain oil and other resources preparatory to an attack on Siberia and thence into Russia itself. Russia was fighting a step-by-step backward action against the Germans and the scenario seemed highly probable. Singapore began to get jittery. Troops were everywhere and two of Britain's greatest battleships were berthed at the naval base there.

Despite the presence of British and Australian troops — Curtin had sent Australia's Eighth Division — the old colonial attitude still prevailed in the Far Eastern bastion, so soon to prove so fragile. The clap-your-hands-for-a-boy mentality, the cricket, tennis, swimming and parties still held sway, albeit somewhat uneasily as the rumours spread.

Australians were anxious for the coming fight, particularly after the news broke about the sinking of *HMAS Sydney*, and the loss of all on board, after a duel with the German raider *Kormoran* off the West Australian coast. The war was near home now and Australians knew in their bones that the Japanese were about to hit though, together with their British counterparts, they remained supremely confident.

Hughes shared all Australians' anger when the blow fell on Pearl Harbour on 7 December 1941. But he did not share the initial disbelief that the 'little nips' had the resources and the guts to flay giant America so close to home. Admittedly Hughes had not admired the Japanese Air Force eighteen months earlier, but he had praised the navy and it was from Navy carriers that the Japanese planes had swooped down on the unsuspecting base on a lazy Sunday morning.

He wanted desperately to go overseas again but with Labor in power under Curtin, the local political scene had taken on a different flavour and Hughes soon found himself involved. The *Daily Telegraph* and the *Sunday Telegraph* were fiercely opposed to the Labor government. Packer and Menzies — who Hughes once called 'the poor man's Churchill' — were friends. But Hughes and many of his colleagues maintained the trait of most journalists — that curious, admirable ability to stand apart from political bias yet continue to do the job.

Curtin, quiet and unassuming, had quickly taken on the stature of a war leader to whom most Australians looked with faith. He was later to be called the greatest leader the Australian Labor Party ever produced and even enemies said of him that he was the biggest figure in Australian life. He was credited with having started to change the course of Australian history with his decision to bring home Australian troops from the Middle East to help stem the Japanese tide sweeping down from the north. He had defied the mighty Churchill. Then he cut the umbilical cord that had held Australia so firmly to Britain when he made his 'Australia looks to America' announcement; 'Without any inhibitions of any kind, I make it quite clear that Australia looks to America, free of any pangs as to our traditional links or kinship with the United Kingdom.' He added that the Australian Government regarded the Pacific struggle as primarily one in which the United States and Australia must have the fullest say in the direction of the democracies' fighting plan.

Early in 1942 Australia was locked into an all-out war effort under Curtin, who had warned that the position Australia faced internally exceeded in 'potential and sweeping danger' anything that confronted the country in its history. From such a seemingly colourless man, his ringing demand that Australians everywhere must realize that their country was now inside the fighting lines was not taken seriously. Not until Darwin. There, on 19 February 1942, nearly 200 Japanese aircraft swept in from the North in Australia's own version of Pearl Harbour. The northern port city, 'defended' by a comparative handful of sailors, soldiers and airmen, was hammered. More than 250 people were killed, and 400 wounded. Buildings were razed, ships sunk, storage tanks destroyed. The ensuing and understandable panic was kept from the Australian people by censorship and only the barest details of the raid itself became known.

The tiny garrison thought the huge raid was the prelude to all-out invasion. Many took to the bush on every conceivable form of transport. One airman, according to a later royal commission, got to Melbourne, 4000 kilometres away in about two weeks. Others managed only a piffling 640 kilometres. One stubborn defender who kept his .303 rifle pointed out into the sun-glazed Arafura Sea admitted ruefully later 'the nips could have taken us then with a bagfull of fuckin' oranges'.

Curtin's austere measures were tightened even more in the wake of the raid and Canberra, for a frustrated war correspondent, was the scene of the nearest action. So Hughes went to the capital early in 1942 as a columnist for his newspaper. His ebullience and wit were never far below the surface and in the comparatively cloistered seat of government he began to blossom again. The clerical and biblical references and episcopal blessings, now trade marks, became part of the Canberra scene.

But Hughes went too far when he wrote a facetious, tongue-in-cheek story about the Senate throwing out a regulation to give the Commonwealth power to override the states and secure the release of beef for the Army. Hughes was serious in his intention to show the action as being against the interests of the country's fighting men, but his presentation of the men who made the decision shook the hallowed precincts of Parliament House.

His story read in part: 'Cackling an old man's fool laugh, the Senate jabbed a long darning needle into the war-weary rump of the Government this week. The old boys of the Upper House pulled down their woollen stomachers with weak, arthritic wrists and in their wheezing voices threw out a bill from the House of Representatives that would have released urgently needed supplies of beef. Don't ask me why they did it. Most of those who voted against the measure wouldn't know.'

He went on to tell of one member 'choking down his reasons in his thick throat with clotted accent' and referred to the chamber as 'a comfortable home for old men'. He called one Senator 'red faced and bespectacled, looking like a stern Mr Pickwick'. Another, he said, had 'the itchiest nose in the Senate'.

'But the real ruler of the Senate is a thin, querulous fellow with a beaky nose, light angry eyebrows and with a small wig. He hisses acid instructions to the timid senators like a bad-tempered stage prompter.' (This last reference was to the Clerk of the Senate, Robert Arthur Borinowski.)

The story was published in the *Sunday Telegraph* and Perth's *Sunday Times* and was headed 'Those Meddlesome Old Men of the Senate'. In the uproar that followed, the war was temporarily forgotten.

The Senate acted with amazing speed. Their decision, announced by the President, Senator Cunningham, excluded all representatives of the *Daily Telegraph* and the *Sunday Telegraph* from the Senate precincts, with immediate effect. The President said the article could only be construed as 'a deliberate attempt by the newspaper concerned to discredit the Senate in the regard of the people and to bring it into contempt'. The Senators demanded publication of an apology, also setting out the form the apology should take.

Packer reacted furiously. He refused to comply and asked that before any action was taken his organization should be given a hearing. The President duly granted the requested interview but neither side budged and the standoff began. The House of Representatives supported the Senate, and Hughes and his colleagues from the Packer organizations were banned altogether from Parliament House. They were not allowed to enter King's Hall, the library or the refreshment rooms.

The then Postmaster General, Senator Ashley, was one of the lone parliamentary voices to oppose the ban. He said the penalty was too drastic. The Australian Journalists' Association also opposed the ban, saying it was wrong and unjust. Newspapers condemned the action by the parliament, seeing it as another blow against freedom of the press.

So Hughes and his colleagues retired to a nearby hotel. From there, and other places, they continued their cover of parliament. Other reporters, despite a threat by parliament to withdraw privileges if they provided information to the beleaguered *Telegraph* staff, sneaked in tips. Some ministers and, of course, members of the Opposition, also kept a tenuous contact. In the initial stages of the ban Hughes provided a bulky reminder to members of their timid parochialism by sitting at the main table of the Hotel Canberra lobby after the house rose each day. He said he did it to discomfort those among them who had done nothing to help him.

The Clerk of the House of Representatives, Frank Green, who was a friend of Hughes, added to the discomfort of members by striding in each afternoon, giving Hughes full notes of events in the House and telling him loudly not to hesitate to contact him if he needed further information.

For these actions and many other kindnesses, Hughes put Green into his subsequent list of mandarins. He defined mandarins as 'superior beings with inborn authority, realistic but generous, self disciplined and resilient. The true mandarin knows his friends and he knows his enemies and he has a talent for using both categories while rewarding the friends and coping with the enemies.'

The ban lasted four months. It ended when a carefully worded statement came from Packer's organization. The statement said Hughes' article was interpreted as a personal attack on individual members of the Senate. This was not intended by Hughes or by the *Sunday Telegraph*. Nor was the article intended to imply disparagement of parliamentary institutions. Everyone's dignity was intact. But Hughes had had enough of parliament and his feelings about the silliness of the ban, and indeed, of his own precipitation of it, were to remain with him for the rest of his life.

The ban and the repercussions that flowed from it made news on the domestic front, but inexorably the war was coming closer to Australia. American troops poured into the country, led by the charismatic General MacArthur. Darwin had been hit again by Japanese aircraft, enemy midget submarines had terrified Sydney when they sneaked into the 'impregnable' harbour and attacked shipping, and an Australian division had been lost in Malaya. Japanese forces had taken Rabaul and Port Moresby was in danger.

But, much to his disgust, Hughes remained in the thick of the domestic news. Brian Penton was editor of the *Daily Telegraph* and he drove his journalists by brilliant example but with little of the charm of Sid Deamer. With Deamer, Hughes was at home, each revelling in the impish wit of the other. With Penton there were clashes. He was a complex, wonderfully able journalist and has been rightly called one of the great editors. He and Hughes, however, clashed repeatedly. Some of the confrontations were of Hughes' making. One such involved Hughes shouting — intending Penton to hear — 'What's that stupid bastard thinking of doing today?'

But Penton knew talent and by early 1943 Hughes was on his way to help cover the North African campaign. He travelled via the United States, resplendent in his uniform as an accredited war correspondent. He renewed some of his friendships, blew into brief flame again some of his romances with the American women he had met a year earlier, then happily resumed his writing about the war.

In Washington he found confusion among U.S. officials about Australia's policy on service overseas in wartime. Under this policy, militia units were not allowed to serve outside Australia. Hughes, his memories of far off schooldays when he would march through Melbourne proudly wearing his 'No' badge opposing conscription still vivid, had difficulty explaining his country's apparent unwillingness to prosecute the war to the limit.

It was difficult, he said, for Americans to understand 'the restrictive, traditional and prejudiced emotional opposition so many Australians have to conscription'. (Subsequently, militiamen were allowed to serve in theatres of war outside Australia. Many of them helped throw back Japanese forces menacing Port Moresby.)

He found instant empathy with Americans, however, in their emotional involvement with the war against Japan. He found they understood the policy of defeating Hitler first, but their real hate was against the Japanese.

He arrived in Algiers as the Allies were pounding Berlin from the air and as the Russians were launching their offensive East of Leningrad. Nearer home, Allied air forces destroyed a Japanese convoy of ten warships and twelve transports in the Bismarck sea, effectively wiping out heavy Japanese reinforcements for the campaign in New Guinea.

Hughes' first encounter with the Mediterranean war was a chastening experience he had not expected. He arrived with the American invasion, ready to go to the front in Tunisia, but found most of the people around him embroiled in politics, with the Americans suspicious of the British, the British contemptuous of the Americans, and the French distrusting both. It was an unpleasant, unhelpful atmosphere far from Hughes' liking, and it continued in spite of the determined efforts General Dwight Eisenhower was making to bring his Allied command together.

The jealousies and resentments slipped over into the Allied press corps, which was far too big for the size of the operations. Too many correspondents had been accredited to go to the front and Hughes found no alternative, although he was the only Australian newspaperman there, but to hang about the command press headquarters waiting for the daily communique. Hughes was scornful of this treatment and lashed out at the daily 'buffoonery', as he called it, of scores of reporters waiting for scraps of often misleading speculation and news from a front hundreds of kilometres away.

He was even more disdainful of the news agency men scrambling over one another to be first to the wires with what the communiques had to say.

Initially, his time in Algiers provided a chance for a welcome reunion with his friend and colleague from Melbourne newspaper days, Alan Moorehead, by then a distinguished war correspondent of the London *Daily Express* and other newspapers. The meeting at the British press hotel was not as Hughes had hoped, however, and was in fact a lasting disappointment.

They had been good friends in their younger days on rival newspapers in Melbourne in the 1930s and had last seen one another on the Melbourne docks the day Moorehead left to try his luck in London. But by Algiers, 1943, it seemed they had not much in common, not even an accent or the same uniform. Hughes, in his Australian army outfit, felt a stranger to this typical British war correspondent in immaculately tailored battledress, talking about getting out his latest book. It was a time when Hughes could have done with some friendly help and guidance, but it was not forthcoming.

The days of frustration, enlivened by rough Algerian wine, eventually passed and almost overnight he was at the front watching Montgomery's victorious desert army face up to its last battles in Africa.

Hughes fell into the trap awaiting most war correspondents on their first assignment. He overwrote. But his writing soon developed into an

Family portrait showing Hughes with his father and mother and young sister, held by his mother, in Melbourne in 1910.

Hughes in pith helmet, with two of his Daily Telegraph colleagues, King Watson (L) and Cyril Pearl at a party in Sydney in 1938.

Hughes interviewing a Japanese underworld luminary in Tokyo in 1948 when he was researching a story about Japanese crime. The man standing is a bodyguard, a one-eyed, scarred tough who got his injuries defending his boss against six rivals. He told Hughes he killed three of the attackers and wounded the remainder. 'He seems a very mild, pleasant, peaceable sort of fellow,' Hughes said at the time.

easy blend between the bald, official style many affected, and the chatty yarn-over-the-backfence method. He had crossed to North Africa with an American convoy and his first stories were about the Americans and their easy assimilation into the life of the mysterious, polyglot North Africa that Algiers then epitomized.

The U.S. maxim of maximum occupation with minimal internal dislocation was working beautifully, he wrote in his first despatch. Courtesy and generosity were winning the local people, and these attributes, together with unrivalled transport facilities and plenty of petrol and candy, made the occupation a cinch.

He was frightened and confused when he first came under fire as General Montgomery's forces chased Rommel near the Mareth line. 'There is bewildering bedlam. There's the ceaseless thunder flashes of unseen batteries, belching apparently at random, crazy patterns of coloured lights, black smoke curtaining the sky and lazily drifting yellow flares that make evil masks of the faces of friends. From the camp bed where I'm typing this under a blazing sun, I can see thousands of trucks scattered across the sand and half hidden in the gullies and the palm and olive trees.

'There are wild flower meadows too. This is no war of marching columns, sand-bagged trenches and bayonet charges — except in the front line — and the whole scene is like a huge furniture removalists' picnic celebrating an Australian summer holiday.'

Enemy aircraft plummeting out of the sun brought the first taste of bombing. All the correspondents reacted the same way, he said. 'We were all shaken, scared and embarrassed by our need to conceal our fear by exaggerating it.' After the bombs fell he found he had broken his nails digging his fingers into the earth where he lay.

The first soldier he saw killed affected him deeply. The soldier was hit by shell fragments as he plodded along to his camp one bright, sunny morning. 'I can still see — and I will see forever — the expression of pure amazement on his face as he fell. His tall, thin body lay quite still and within seconds seemed to blend into the sand', he wrote emotionally.

His first experience of infantrymen going into battle came near Wadi Karit after Mongomery's skilful outflanking of the Mareth line: 'Earlier, we could hear snatches of ribald song, most in pure Cockney, and odd bursts of laughter from invisible camps under far off stars. Then, when the British barrage started at 4 am, the ground shook as the explosions swung into a dreadful rhythm that broke out of step and swelled again to angry, confused pandemonium. The sandy, mile-wide no man's land where the little men with bayonets had to advance became a stage as the eastern sky lightened out over the Mediterranean, and we could see the little men only occasionally through the smoke and flying sand.'

Montgomery's forces rolled on inexorably and Hughes and the other correspondents tagged along. It was an austere life for them all. A few hot beers now and then and a rare bath were the only luxuries and reminders of other, halcyon days.

In Sfax, Hughes reported on the reception given to the British troops — for whom, incidentally, he had enormous respect — through the eyes of a French family. He saw the family at an airfield. There was the father, wife and small daughter, all dressed in their Sunday best. He wore a jaunty beret that flaunted a tricolour and his small daughter clutched a bouquet of red, white and blue wildflowers. The Frenchman hoisted his daughter onto his shoulder and was hugging his plump wife. They were crying with happiness.

By early May the Allied armies were in control. Fifty thousand German and Italian troops were running hard and more than 100 000 others were scattered. Ships were trying to evacuate Axis troops from Cape Bon as Allied warplanes bombed and strafed them ceaselessly. In Tunis, he found the people 'mad with joy' as Montgomery's victorious troops came in. Flowers showered down on them and the grinning troops were mobbed as they arrived in the city.

Towards the end of May the Allies had captured 150 000 prisoners, thousands of motor vehicles and guns and some 250 tanks. The end was near and Hughes was at Cape Bon when the final, humiliating episode was played out.

'Today I saw a German army corps throw away its arms and imploringly wave the white flag. The whole of Cape Bon peninsular was a mass of waving white flags. Thousands of German soldiers, some good humoured, all resigned and many bitter, poured back along the coast road under a cover of fluttering handkerchiefs, shirts, underpants and sheets. Many rode on their own transports, others waited patiently along the roadsides to be picked up. Mostly they were docile and humble. This was the cream of Hitler's troops, some iron cross veterans from Russia, some bronzed stalwarts who once were in sight of Alexandria.'

He tried to find the reason why brave soldiers who had fought so long and so gallantly were now so dejected. He said many of them felt they had been betrayed by their leaders. This bitterness, he felt, could have been the spark that exploded their dramatic collapse and the surrender at Cape Bon was indisputable proof that when Germans cracked they cracked wide open and their swastika became a white flag overnight.

Hughes met Montgomery briefly during the North African campaign. His control over the huge machine of destruction he had fashioned, his dedication to victory and the sheer brilliance and certainty of his every move fascinated Hughes, but he could not warm to the austere General who was the antithesis of the free-wheeling, romantic and larger than life figure most of the correspondents wanted him to be. There was something too Calvinistic about the little, hawk-like man, an omnipotence that seemed to make him walk alone.

He had a happier reaction to another of the great war time leaders, Lieutenant General Sir Bernard Freyberg. Like Montgomery, Freyberg also had a high voice, but he was a character and likeable legends had grown up around him as he led his brilliant New Zealanders into the thick of some of the North African fighting. Known among his troops as 'bung 'em in Bernie', the former dentist and wine expert Freyberg had won a Victoria Cross in the First World War and, although not a military genius in Hughes' opinion, was responsible for the 'left hook' movement that kept Germany's Rommel reeling back in confusion.

Winston Churchill had a more classical nickname for the enigmatic Freyberg. He called him 'the salamander of the British Empire', obviously a reference to the mythological spirit supposed to live in fire.

When Hughes first met Freyberg the big man, built like a rugby forward, was standing gloomily on a ridge a couple of kilometres from the mountain citadel of Takrowna. Shells from New Zealand 25-pounder batteries were thumping into the wild hills on the farther side of the citadel. A handful of brave New Zealanders had scaled the steep cliff face and driven out the Italian garrison at bayonet point. But the shoulder of the mountain was still held by Germans and the guns were softening up the German defences.

'The air above the ridge where we stood was alive and menacing as the New Zealand shells swished and whistled to the target. Freyberg lumbered morosely toward us and nodded towards the citadel. "Good shooting" he said in his curious high-pitched voice. "Good shooting."

'He seemed to take for granted the amazing heroism of his men as they clambered up the wall of what was really a citadel of death.'

When Hughes first encountered the New Zealanders, he formed the opinion, shared by friend and foe, that they were the cream of Montgomery's army. The New Zealanders had been kept on after the last of the Australian divisions had gone on to the Pacific war after their decisive role at El Alamein. The New Zealanders had distinguished themselves in the 'left hook' movement that forced the Afrika Korps to abandon the Mareth Line and all hope of hanging on in Tunisia.

The tough desert veterans welcomed Hughes as a fellow Anzac, but the warmth of their welcome was overshadowed by the intellectual stimulus he found among them. Although they had lived in the desert for almost a year and were tired, he found himself engrossed in the freshness of their ideas and their idealism. The talks that went on long into the cold desert nights were as stimulating as any he had ever had.

And among them he met one of the most remarkable men he had

encountered in the North African war, Captain Paddy Costello, who had joined the New Zealanders as a private after a classical education that took in Cambridge. He was chief of Freyberg's intelligence section when Hughes met him and they formed an instant liking for one another. The tall, elegant Costello, articulate and witty, found in Hughes a fellow spirit who gloried in the exchange of views on every subject under the sun. And like Hughes, he was a renegade Catholic. 'Monsignor' and 'Bishop' became their customary greeting to one another.

Costello had a breadth of mind rare in any company. He made no effort to hide his communist sympathies but he was a free spirit of such remarkable panache and infectious warmth that this aspect of his nature was ignored. Hughes' anti-communism at the time was not as vitriolic as it became later and the disparate political views they held did nothing to affect the friendship each treasured.

Fluent in French, German, Italian, Greek and Russian, Costello's intellectual attainments never overshadowed the earthy quality of his ribald, irreverent attitude towards so many of the conventional views others held. He shared with Hughes the gift of being acceptable on all levels. Condescension in any form was equally foreign to them both.

Bruce Hewitt, then a young war correspondent with the New Zealanders and later to become a distinguished newspaperman in New Zealand and Australia, remembers what he called 'a kind of Gallagher and Sheen' conversational crossfire between Hughes and Costello in which they chastised the 'cardinals' running the war and praised 'the sheep and lambs' called on to do their bidding. Hewitt recalls being intrigued at the time by the disparate backgrounds of Hughes and Costello and amazed at the progression each had made from such modest beginnnings. Costello's talent for languages, for instance, seemed all the more remarkable considering he had grown up in a small North Auckland township where English and broken Maori were the only languages spoken.

Hughes could not match Costello on the intellectual level but he was equally articulate and witty and had a grasp of international affairs Costello admired. The New Zealander would 'fill in' Hughes with his brilliant intelligence summaries culled from his questioning of German and Italian prisoners of war. As a consequence, Hughes' despatches and predictions about the course of the war had a distinctly authentic ring to them many others lacked.

Hughes wrote often to his then teen-aged son, growing up happily in distant and peaceful Melbourne. In one letter he told his son about having dinner at the hotel in Casablanca where Churchill lived and had some whisky, which, 'through some oversight no doubt, Churchill had left behind'.

The comparative fleshpots, after the rigours of the desert campaign, were tasted in Carthage. There, with a curious feeling like breaking up for school holidays affecting all the correspondents, Hughes had a hot bath and breakfast with roses on the table of a flower-hung French villa. The war seemed over and won, but all the correspondents knew this was a dangerous illusion despite the children playing on the beach, nurses wheeling prams in the sun and church bells that wakened them that morning.

By July Hughes was in Cairo and revelling for a while in the splendour of women and soft beds and drinking wine on roof gardens under discreet lights. The war seemed far away. He saw a great similarity between war-time Cairo and Shanghai: 'There are the same dramatic contrasts of Western luxury and Eastern poverty, of marble-pillared hotel lounges and slum factories, limousines and hideously deformed beggars, pet dogs on leashes and native women festooned with babies.

'Across the noble bridges over the Nile at night truck loads of singing troops pass. Then would come a line of shining cars, half a dozen horse drawn gharrics followed by a string of soft padding camels each with a hurricane lamp on its rump.

'We can watch the searchlights wheeling over the palm trees and white-sailed feluccas drifting down the wide and silent river.

'But I find myself recalling the gambling cabarets on Bubbling Well road in Shanghai and Chinese coolies plunging into the Whangpoo river to scrabble for rubbish from liners anchored off the Bund. But there is one fundamental difference between the Shanghai I knew in 1940 and Cairo of 1943. Shanghai knew the war was moving remorselessly nearer. Cairo knows the war is moving steadily further away.'

He found it impossible at times to believe there was a war on somewhere, remote and distant from the Cairo of poverty and wealth, grandeur and squalor where he felt so strangely ill at ease. He joined with the other correspondents in singing a song called 'What's it all about?' when Cairo newsboys dodged through the streets calling 'Mussolini mafeesh'. Most of the lines of the song were unprintable but two of the mildest summed up their feelings of frustration:

'We never write a line and we never get a beat;
We only keep our weight off our big fuckin' feet.'

So Hughes went looking for his likeable New Zealanders and found them on a beach near Alexandria where they were camped before sailing for Italy. They lazed about the beach, swimming, drinking beer and arguing about one of Hughes' pet projects — the unification of Australia and New Zealand.

Hughes tried to get Freyberg to agree to take him with the New Zealanders to Italy. Paddy Costello's added his plea to Hughes impassioned appeal, but nothing either could say changed the situation. Freyberg rejected the request because of Hughes' lack of accreditation from the American command across the Mediterranean.

So he returned to Cairo and to the juvenile pranks he and other correspondents dreamed up to pass the time. He affected a monocle, which he managed to screw under his eyebrow and hold in place by keeping his mouth slightly askew. The 'in' place for army officers, many of whom had spent a comfortable war sipping cold drinks on the broad terraces, was Shephards Hotel. There, Hughes and his companions would swing into their act, calling each other 'your grace', 'rabbi' and 'monsignor' and flaunting their ability to wear monocles without the tape many of the English officers used.

It was a childish war of attrition, aimed no further most of the time than securing a comfortable chair when the English could not stand the barracking any longer and left. They over-tipped the waiters, smoked the biggest cigars they could find and womanized and moaned about the war they were missing.

Some of the correspondents had managed to get to Italy. Hughes would have been with two of them when they were killed during the campaign. He reflected on this in Cairo when a letter came from one of the dead friends: 'I owe you a bottle of plonk too. Will fix later. Meantime please try to get some silk stockings for my wife and I'll collect them later.' Hughes got the stockings and mailed them to Australia.

Frustrated at the lack of action, Hughes and his companions stepped up their baiting of the pale English officers, drank, swopped lies, played practical jokes on each other and bickered through the lazy Cairo days.

Hughes kept his stories flowing into his newspapers, however, and war stories were replaced by snippets about Egyptian life, the cost of living, the political situation, wounded soliders — many of whom he visited in hospital — and inconsequential asides about soldiers climbing the pyramids in record time.

When he visited Alexandria he usually stayed at the Cecil Hotel. After one stay, a germ that came closer to killing him than any bomb or shell struck at his huge frame and within days he was strapped to splints on his arms and legs and near death from rheumatic fever. He hovered near death for days, sometimes in a coma, and in his half-dream state he wandered again along the suburban streets of his childhood and heard the far off 'Right away' cry of his railway days as imaginary trains rushed into the nights. His physique saved him and, although he dropped weight alarmingly, he gradually began to feel some stirrings in his muscles and began the long road to recovery.

Hughes knew the war was over for him. He could use two fingers however and when he began to recuperate he had his portable typewriter brought to his chair and propped up. He tapped out a weekly diary, most of the material culled from Egyptian newspapers and from snippets brought to him by fellow correspondents who regaled him with stories of their exploits in free-wheeling Cairo. They too were frustrated as the war in Italy began to build to its climax. Gradually they wandered off and Hughes' days tapered rapidly to boredom.

Across the street from his bed where he was recuperating he often saw a strikingly handsome Egyptian girl. Occasionally in the evening she would join in a make-believe, long distance drink with the lonely big man strapped to his splints. Eventually she came to see him and the strange friendship between them bloomed. She epitomized the emerging Egypt and her dark, intense beauty fascinated him. So, in time, she ministered to him in the only way either of them could manage, and the loneliness that came always to him as the long aching days eased to dusk was assuaged. When he left his sick bed for the long haul back to Australia he raised one last imaginary glass to her and smiling, gave her his adopted episcopal blessing with gratitude and love.

4 Sydney & Hiroshima

America was in full cry, wartime blood was boiling, when Hughes passed through on his way home. His 1941 forecast that the American war effort would become the greatest industrial revolution in the world's history had come true. Ships and aircraft and tanks and guns were being turned out in vast numbers at unbelievable speed. War fever had lifted patriotism to new heights and uniforms — particularly when worn by a big handsome war correspondent complete with a limp and a walking stick — were like catnip.

Hughes was entertained royally and the reception brought back much of his old ebullience and lust for living. Cairo and the long hot days of his illness faded and he enjoyed himself immensely, rekindling old romances and making new ones and forming instant friendships with strangers eager to hear of his exploits. He met old friends too. One of them dropped to his knees and grabbed and kissed the grinning Hughes' hand as he gave his mock blessing. Two nuns passing at the time did a double take, then hurried on when the two men shouted exuberantly in a non-clerical fashion when the act ended.

Australia was a little more blasé and his home-coming relatively muted. He went to Melbourne to see his son and his family and sat long into the night to tell of his experiences. His teen-age son was too old now for the train rides of his childhood, with his father pretending to drive the train, and too old also for 'I'm Forever Blowing Bubbles' that he sang to him in infancy. Like so many Australians, Hughes had difficulty showing his affections to those dear to him including his son. He was aware that to his son he was a bluff, distant father who came home occasionally, provided money for education and clothes, yet rarely heeded the boy's need for closeness and touching. So he took comfort in the boy's closeness to his grandfather and his Uncle Walter and the enveloping, if distant, love his grandmother lavished on him.

Hughes' aunt, the nun Sister Sebastian — known to them all as 'Aunt Posey' — was also a great comfort to him because she lavished on young Richard the love and gentleness engendered by her order. She would tell the boy before she died in 1943 that when she got to Heaven — and he had no doubt about this — she would storm paradise for the three Richards ... his grandfather, father and himself. He was a religious boy, a good student and an avid reader. Sherlock Holmes, too, was among his favourites. His uncle, a generous and affectionate man, was like a surrogate father, and the boy was untroubled when his father went back to Sydney.

Hughes was aware that his son was beginning to love jazz but he put it down to a youthful whim, sure that an earlier liking for Schubert and Liszt would prevail. But a chance visit by a friend of Walter's, one Will McIntyre, who came to the Hughes home in Melbourne's Windsor, was to influence the boy's life. The house rocked to 'Boogie Woogie Stomp' as McIntyre thumped the keys of the upright piano and the eldest Richard Hughes raced to make sure all the windows were shut. 'The neighbours will think I'm drunken', he said. 'This is a mockery of music.'

Mockery or not, from that moment the boy was a jazz fan for life, destined to become one of Australia's foremost jazz pianists and an authority on jazz rather than the diplomat his father wanted him to be.

Hughes returned to Sydney, limping still and walking with the aid of a cane. He swung back into the newspaper business with a flair sharpened by his stint as a war correspondent, and back too into the buccaneering world of daily journalism, shouting matches with Packer and the make-believe world of the 'monastery'.

The war in the Pacific, that at one stage directly threatened Australia with invasion, was receding as American might pushed the Japanese back through the islands, and in Europe the end seemed close. Domestic news, particularly on the political front, was becoming more and more relevant but Hughes was beginning to hunger again for the excitement of the foreign field. Everything happening in Australia seemed so tame by comparison.

Hughes found it hard to reconcile his own liberal views, particularly about politics, with the hard-line anti-Labor attitude that Packer adhered to so rigidly with his papers. Hughes admired Curtin as one of the greatest leaders Australia had thrown up but his papers were sniping more and more openly at Curtin's Labor Government. He had a personal liking for Ben Chifley, the former railwayman now being openly tipped as a possible sucessor to the ailing Curtin. He disliked Robert Menzies, whom Packer backed.

But like his fellow journalists, Hughes was loyal to his employer while holding rigidly his right to keep his own views inviolate. He fought with Packer, but they respected each other. But with Brian

Penton there was naked animosity. Hughes knew his editor's worth as a journalist but disliked the man. Penton was not known for his humour but he was known and respected, however, for his undoubted ability as an editor and for his courage. He would stand up to Packer if he felt something was wrong and he became something of an autocrat. His ability to dictate editorials over the phone, his appeal to women and the style changes he brought about on the *Telegraph* made him a legend of his time.

So it was inevitable that Penton and the ebullient Hughes would continue to clash. One confrontation came when Hughes interceded in the case of an employee accused of having pinched a girl's bottom. 'Keep out of this. You're employed here in an editorial capacity, not as a priest', Penton said.

Hughes lumbered to his feet and glared. 'How dare you speak to me like that', he roared. He raised the stick he still needed and crashed it down on Penton's table. Both men were on their feet, trembling with anger. The rowdy newsroom behind them stilled. Then, simultaneously, each realised how ridiculous they looked. They burst into laughter and shook hands. The truce was only temporary, however, and eventually Packer moved to keep them apart as much as possible.

Cyril Pearl, calm, erudite and then editor of the *Sunday Telegraph*, encouraged Hughes with his steadfast friendship and sure journalist's flair. Early in 1944 Hughes brought out his first book, a modest little volume called *Dr Watson's Casebook*, which dealt with some of the great mysteries of the world. The pseudonym was Dr Watson Jnr and he dedicated it 'in reverent and humble tribute to the master, Sherlock Holmes "the greatest and the wisest man I have ever known".'

Among the twenty-two mystery and crime stories covered in the book he dealt again with the sad story of Reuter's Jimmy Cox who leapt to his death in Tokyo in 1940 just before Hughes' arrival. Hughes repeated his earlier contention that Cox had been driven to his death because he was convinced the police would beat a confession from him eventually. 'He was as innocent of spying as I was', wrote 'Watson'.

Another story dealt with the case of a 'teacup Borgia', one Major Herbert Armstrong. 'He was a queer little man, vain and amorous, henpecked but dogged', living with his wife in a small Welsh town. His wife suffered from heart and kidney troubles and at one stage she had delusions, 'began to roar out at night and scamper around in undignified attire'. Eventually she was dragged gibbering and twitching to an asylum. She returned home after some months so Armstrong bought some white arsenic ostensibly to kill weeds in his garden. 'For years he sublimated a very natural desire to kill his nagging wife into a ruthless slaughter of dandelions in his back garden. But eventually she died. Had the major the good sense to rest content with one murder he

58

would have been safe but he had come to the conclusion that the black sport of poisoning was simplicity itself. As long as you had weeds in your garden you could buy arsenic and as long as you had arsenic you could remove people who annoyed you.'

A 'terrified Welsh solicitor', O. N. Martin, was indeed annoying the major over the return of some money the major owed and which he could not repay. So he invited Martin for afternoon tea. 'The major was a gracious host. There was a cakestand laden with bread and butter, scones and current loaf. The major placed a buttered scone on his guest's plate. Martin went home ill and was treated by his doctor for arsenic poisoning.'

Undeterred, the major returned to the attack and pestered Martin to come again to afternoon tea. Martin, 'terrified at this teacup attack' refused time and again. When some chocolates were mysteriously delivered to Martin he tried them out on his sister in law. She became violently ill and the doctor became suspicious. The major's wife was exhumed and arsenic was found and the major was hanged.

Another story in *Dr Watson's Casebook* dealt with what Hughes called the perfect frameup, which, he contended, was as rare as the perfect murder. 'Let us ponder reverently therefore on the genius of Morten Bruns, the humble Danish peasant who framed Pastor Soren Qvist with cold-blooded vindictiveness and inspired invention.' Qvist, he said, was a remarkable man, a big broad-shouldered Dane 'with a mane of yellow hair, huge fists, a red hot temper and the biggest feet in Jutland'.

Farmer Bruns had made honourable passes at the Pastor's attractive daughter and the Pastor, disapproving, threatened to knock Bruns' teeth down his throat. 'Bruns swallowed his wrath, saved his teeth and retired, inflamed, to his farm to plot his frame-up.' He arranged for his brother, Niels, 'a bad fellow who drank too much, didn't like work and had a weakness for lying in the crisp Danish sunshine with a bottle of schnappes' to work for the Pastor. 'Niels immediately embarked on a policy of calculated provocation. He lay with his bottle of schnappes under the parsonage trees, singing ungodly songs, jeering at his fellow workers, chasing the maid around the meadow whenever he saw her and announcing that he was an atheist.'

Qvist turned the other cheek for a while but one day he had enough. 'In the presence of witnesses, Qvist did his block, slugged Niels and broke his bottle of schnappes and Niels disappeared.'

So Bruns called at the parsonage and accused the pastor of having murdered Niels. 'Running hard, Bruns managed to slam the parsonage gate behind him before the reverend Qvist could catch him'.

A long search for Niels was fruitless. Then Bruns produced a moronic native who swore he saw a figure in a long green dressing gown digging in the parsonage garden at midnight. Police were called and they dug up a battered body wearing Niels' clothes. Everybody knew the pastor wore a green dressing gown so he was arrested, tried for murder and finally hanged on the Hill of Ravens. Morten Bruns died two decades later, fat and respectable. Just after his death Niels re-appeared, quite alive but angry because his brother's remittance payments had stopped. He then confessed that Morten had dug up a month old corpse, hit it over the head, dressed it in Niels' clothes and buried it in the parsonage garden while wearing the pastor's green dressing gown which he borrowed while the pastor slept. The villagers, suitably apologetic, erected a sorrowful headstone over the pastor's grave.

The humble book, full of other such mysteries — some perhaps invented — sold well. But Sydney booksellers became more wary than ever after it appeared whenever 'Dr Watson Jnr' reviewed mystery books. They were still uneasy about the non-existent books Hughes had reviewed earlier under the 'Pakenham' byline.

This irreverent and light-hearted hoax had its counterpart, also in 1944, when two poets, James McAuley and Harold Stewart, dreamed up a meaningless concoction of words and presented it as poetry. Their aim was to debunk the then current vogue of surrealism and obscurantism in verse.

They presented their work as having been written by one 'Ern Malley', a former mechanic and insurance salesman. The sixteen poems were sent to an avant-garde magazine, *Angry Penguins* where Malley was described as 'a giant of Australian literature'. An entire edition of the magazine was devoted to his work.

When the hoax was uncovered, the two young poets responsible admitted they had produced the entire life work of Ern Malley in one afternoon. They had used a dictionary, the works of Shakespeare and a dictionary of quotations. Their object was to find out if the people who wrote or praised so lavishly some of the current poems, and particularly those published in *Angry Penguins*, could tell the real product from consciously and deliberately concocted nonsense.

The hoax became world news and the fictitious 'Ern Malley' enjoyed brief fame at a time when light-heartedness was scarce.

Hughes was in the thick of the fight in 1944 when Packer's newspapers 'took on' the Labor Government over censorship, which they claimed was too harsh. The *Daily Telegraph* and the *Sydney Morning Herald* formed a brief improbable partnership when they each reported that some American correspondents had left Australia because of restrictive censorship and as a consequence the United States was not properly informed on Australian policy. The then Minister for Information, Arthur Calwell, insisted that all reports referring to censorship had to be submitted for censorship, hence making it virtually impossible for newspapers to criticize censorship.

The next move in the bitter 'war' came when the *Daily Telegraph* published Calwell's attack on newspapers but left a blank space for the reply by the Chairman of the Australian Newspaper Proprietors' Association, Rupert Henderson, on the ground that Henderson's statement had been censored.

Calwell struck back and on Saturday, 15 April, he served an order on the *Sunday Telegraph* editor, Cyril Pearl, insisting that all matter intended for publication the following day should be submitted to the chief censor. A statement by Henderson saying his reply to Calwell had been mutilated, together with an editorial comment by Pearl were slashed. Henderson's statement was 'killed' altogether. So in the first edition of the *Sunday Telegraph* there were blank spaces where the editoral and Henderson's statement were to be printed. In the second edition, Pearl ran pictures of Calwell and Henderson, together with the comment: 'A free press . . . ? The great American democrat Thomas Jefferson said "where the press is free and every man able to read all is safe".'

Before the presses started Commonwealth police arrived and seized all copies of the *Sunday Telegraph*. Other newspapers supported the *Telegraph* stable and by Monday the *Telegraph*, the *Sydney Morning Herald*, Sydney evening newspapers the *Sun* and the *Mirror*, the *Melbourne Herald* and the *Adelaide News* were all seized. At one stage, police produced guns to prevent papers from being delivered.

The standoff was short-lived. Newspapers took their case to the High Court which granted an injunction against the Government, which eventually amended the censorship regulations. Hughes joined Pearl and others in a suitable celebration. But they agreed shortly afterwards that not all censorship was bad, and co-operated fully when details of one of the most terrible battles ever fought on Australian soil were censored.

Outside the little New South Wales town of Cowra on 5 August, 1944 more than 1000 Japanese prisoners of war tried to break out of their camp. Primarily, according to Harry Gordon's definitive and brilliantly researched *Die like the Carp*, they simply wanted to die because they believed they had lost honour by becoming prisoners.

Armed with home-made weapons — sharpened table knives, garden tools and clubs — they hurled themselves against the barbed wire. During the outbreak and in the following days 232 Japanese were killed and more than 100 wounded. Four Australian soldiers were killed and four wounded. Only the barest details of the massacre were released because the Government feared the Japanese would take violent reprisals against Australian prisoners of war, already suffering almost unbelievable privations at the hands of their captors.

As the war dragged on, Hughes took over as Acting Editor of the *Sunday Telegraph* for a period while Cyril Pearl went abroad. The country was tired of the war, tired of the restrictions and the austerity, and newspapers were beginning to reflect the mood and turning more and more to domestic affairs. As Hughes' health improved, he began to pester Packer again for an overseas posting. The staff was depleted, however, by the number of top men serving as war correspondents, so he buckled down for another year.

In the meantime, Prime Minister Curtin's health was causing concern. For three long years Curtin had carried the anxieties of a country at war for its very survival and he did superbly what he asked servicemen and citizens to do. He had a heart attack late in 1944, and died in July the following year. All Australians, irrespective of their political views, mourned the loss of the quiet, strong man who had led his country through the most dangerous years of its short existence.

Ben Chifley, who had so often helped Hughes, took over. He was said to lack Curtin's intellect and vision, but he had an unrivalled knowledge of economic affairs. He and Hughes had an easy relationship, based to some extent on their backgrounds. At times he would tip off Hughes to stories. His ever present pipe, taciturn manner and 'chicken coop' voice appealed to Hughes who was used to more roisterous company.

By the middle of August 1945 the most terrible war in history was over. Two great flares of light that subdued all other natural light as the world's first atomic bombs were dropped presaged the end. The Japanese cities of Hiroshima and Nagasaki were virtually wiped out of existence.

When Hughes saw the first eye-witness of the account of the destruction of Hiroshima, which the *Daily Telegraph* published on 6 September 1945, he began to push harder for permission to go to Japan. He argued that he knew the country, some of the language and many of the war-time leaders.

His appetite was whetted by the magnificent report on Hiroshima turned in by Wilfred (Peter) Burchett, an Australian then working for London's *Daily Express*. Burchett bluffed his way from Tokyo to Hiroshima, armed only with a 45 calibre pistol, a Japanese phrase book, an umbrella and a week's supply of rations. He travelled by troop train with Japanese officers and troops, unsmiling in case the officers thought him to be gloating over Japan's surrender.

Burchett's terrifying journey ended when he climbed out of a window of the train at Hiroshima's empty shell of a station. He was arrested and held for one night but again he talked his way out of the dilemma. He walked for several kilometres into the city and as far as he could see for kilometres around there was nothing left above the ground but rubble. For some sixty-five square kilometres there was hardly a building standing. Burchett said it was the most terrible and frightening desolation he had seen in four years of war reporting. Fires were still smouldering and there was a peculiar odour, something like sulphur.

Burchett, who was later to be described by Hughes as 'one of the best and bravest correspondents I've ever known', told of his experiences in greater detail in his autobiography *Passport*, an account of an extraordinary life that was to include raging controversy over his subsequent role in South East Asia.

When the occupation of Japan got under way Hughes was among the Australian correspondents who covered the humiliation of the beaten people. And for him it was another look at a country that had frightened him years earlier, terrified half the world in the intervening years and ultimately was to nurture a life-long infatuation.

5 MacArthur's Japan

General Douglas MacArthur wore the mantle of overlord of Japan with the charisma that surrounded him from the moment he landed in Australia to lead the long fight back against the Japanese. He relished his new role and for a while in the early days of the occupation it seemed that the Japanese had substituted his imposing presence for that of the Emperor.

Hughes knew MacArthur from his time in Australia, and from the time he, too, arrived in the humiliated country their relationship was good. Hughes jostled for space among some of the foremost correspondents in the world at MacArthur's press briefings. They were theatrical, timed-to-a-second affairs. MacArthur's progress through Tokyo's streets swept decrepit local traffic to one side when his cavalcade arrived in the morning, took him to and from lunch, and home in the afternoon. It was Hollywood stuff and Hughes relished the flamboyance and air of royalty, contrasting so starkly with the subdued and resigned Japanese surroundings. MacArthur knew Hughes by sight and as with so many other correspondents he called him by his first name. It was heady stuff in the early days and any criticism of the regime was muted.

After a while, most of the correspondents operated out of the Radio Tokyo building. It was among many of the modern buildings in the heart of Tokyo undamaged. And from this building Hughes sent off despatches, with Japanese messenger boys racing each other to the transmission point. He toured the devastated outer areas of Tokyo where Allied bombing had laid waste huge areas. Vegetable plots often occupied the site of burned out blocks and Japanese had built themselves 'humpies' — reminiscent of the Depression years desolation of Australia — to shelter from the winter.

The non-fraternization order MacArthur's command had issued did not take long to break down. As usual, children were the catalyst.

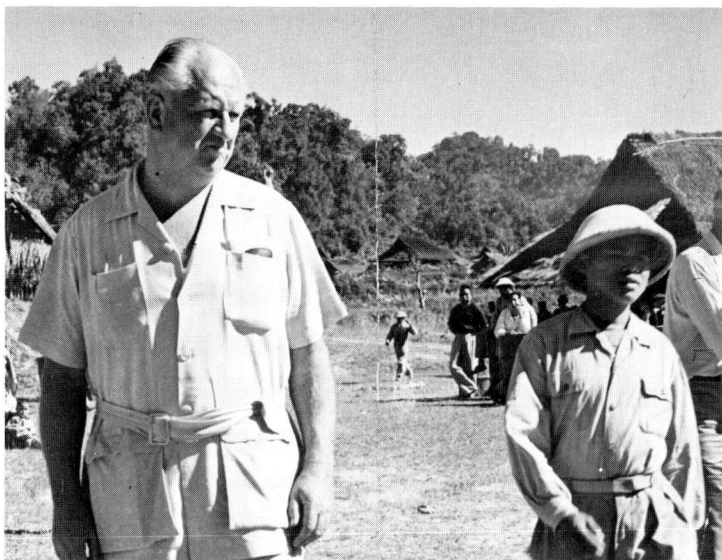

Hughes in Laos in 1959.

Author Somerset Maugham and Ian Fleming, on a tour of Tokyo with Hughes in 1959, watch a demonstration by young Japanese athletes.

Ian Fleming and Hughes at a ceremony in Kobe when cattle were being fattened 'on the hoof'. Hughes' caption for the picture attributed to Fleming a quote from Sherlock Holmes: 'I have seldom seen a better grown goose.'

Hughes and Ian Fleming in Southern Japan during their tour of the country when Fleming researched his James Bond novel You Only Live Twice.

The solemn, shaven headed little boys and doll-like girls were irresistible to the correspondents and troops of the occupation force. And through them there was a gradual mingling with the Japanese people, particularly the women.

The old Imperial Hotel, where Hughes had lived in 1940, was not available in the early days of the occupation, but many of the contacts he had made there before the war gradually emerged. The meetings were surreptitious at first, particularly with Japanese. Many Japanese bowed too low under their collective guilt and Hughes, with others, began to feel uncomfortable. The stepping-off-the-footpath routine did not appeal to his Australian sense of egalitarianism.

One of his contacts was an aide on MacArthur's staff. Among his duties was the chore of writing innocuous letters for the great man to sign. They did not require MacArthur's usual careful attention, and 'John' would pound them out by the dozen, ending them with 'Yours sincerely' or 'Yours faithfully'. He was pretty sure that MacArthur did not even read them, so he slipped 'Go and get stuffed' into a couple of them that annoyed him. Back came the offending letters, together with a pencilled note from the great man: 'I agree the "get stuffed" is deserved but in these cases let's drop the "sincerely" and just make it "yours" '.

Hughes also had contacts among the Russians, some of whom he had known before the war. He was always amused by the Russians' habit of invariably choosing a restaurant table that faced the entrance. At that stage he was developing a feeling for all nationalities which recognized few national boundaries and he regarded loyalty and generosity of spirit as top priorities.

One of his dearest friends among the Australian contingent of correspondents had a row with the committee then running the Correspondent's Club. He took up billets in a heavily bombed area of the city and relied on his friends to sneak in supplies of food and grog. This particular night, with too much of the club whisky on board, he became convinced that military police were tailing his jeep. So he took to the rubble, deserting his beloved jeep. By the time he found the vehicle two days later, the engine, wheels and everything that could be unscrewed had gone. Hughes and his friends used bribery and some pressure to have the jeep rebuilt by the U.S. Army.

Number 1 Shimbun (newspaper) Alley, where the Correspondents' Club was situated, was a five-storied building which had once been a restaurant. Here the world's press lived and congregated, drank and fought and argued and sneaked in their Japanese girl friends. It was an amiable brothel of a place where near-boiling water would occasionally swirl angrily into the cisterns to send screaming users swearing into the night. It was occasionally a one-night pad for soldiers, invited there in moments of euphoria by correspondents and for girl friends sneaked upstairs in the ancient lifts to be dined and wined and bedded. The food from the roaring kitchens down below often found its way upstairs to the guests, some of whom came from the line of hopeful girls huddled through the night in the alley. Gun-fire, and on one memorable night the roar of an exploding grenade, would scatter the members and guests occasionally and then be forgotten in what Hughes called 'the roar of disputation'.

But it was also a haven for serious, highly principled journalists. Diplomats, spies, businessmen and the more austere of the correspondents found the club an exciting venue, a thumping pulse of the noisy occupation days. It was virtually impossible to remain in touch with all the strands of Japanese and Allied life without being there.

Hughes revelled in the free-wheeling life. He wrote about it all and about the desolation of the Japanese scene and the extremes of the Allied occupation. His recall to Australia and the comparably humdrum life of a newspaper executive in Sydney remained unanswered for a few days. Then the recall tone of the cables became urgent. In one of them Packer admonished him with a 'I'll deal with you on return' line.

So he returned to Sydney and resigned, tired of the poor salary he had been getting and tired too of the interminable arguments. He could not get on with Brian Penton and his love-hate relationship with Packer had gone on too long.

When he returned to Japan, without a regular job, he found that the Japanese had begun to convert the Allied occupation into a liberation, while the Americans had converted the occupation into an annexation. He saw MacArthur, literally, as an impressive godfather to what he called 'the shabby but still hopeful son of heaven, now grazing humbly on the weeds in his once holy back yard'. The Japanese had obeyed the occupation authorities so dutifully and to such an extreme that MacArthur and the occupation people had reacted with a sort of shame and subconsciously had eased the rules.

When one of the most unlikely, ill-paid and adventurous jobs in Hughes' life was offered he accepted it gratefully. A clamorous meeting of members of the Foreign Correspondents' Club in Shimbun Alley decided to appoint a newspaperman as manager. They seemed to think that a newspaperman, a fellow journeyman, would have 'a typewriter in the pot and two jeeps in the garage' as Hughes put it. He would be able to soothe professional jealousies, be a chucker outer when necessary, would not fiddle the books and would be a father confessor to all the troubles that beset them.

Hughes was appointed to the impossible job of managing the run-down establishment and for nearly two years he presided over one of the greatest collections of talent, rogues and scoundrels ever assembled in the Far East. Occupation leaders, indigent Japanese idealists,

66

black marketeers, communists and fascists, foreign diplomats and fixers frequented the club at various times. They mixed with American, British, French, Russian, Chinese, Australian and New Zealand pressmen. There was an unofficial rule that all visitors and guests, when being entertained by residential members, must vacate bedrooms by 4 am. The rule was introduced originally to prevent the club being registered as a house of assignation. So each morning during the rule's tenuous life, there would be a muster of women guests in the club lounge. The rule was quietly rescinded eventually; it wasn't working.

The club was next door to the Soviet Embassy residential annex and Room 7 on the fourth floor — where Hughes lived — overlooked the large windows of the women's showers and bedrooms of the Russian billet. Hughes noticed that the Soviet women were randy, uninhibited brunettes rather than blondes and not as mammarian as popularly believed. He could have made a fortune double letting the room to curious resident and transient correspondents.

Below Room 7 there was a tin-roofed shed-like structure. Hughes had a habit of chewing pieces of copy paper when writing his stories, then disposing the cud by blowing it out of the window on the tin roof below. It was soon covered in great blobs.

There were innumerable brawls. One he stopped was between two temporarily violent but basically amiable members. Later one of them told him apologetically: 'Remember, Dick, he who quarrels with a drunken friend quarrels with a man who is absent'. Then he added 'I didn't make that up. A dead man did. I think it was Plato, or it might have been Confuscius.'

Hughes managed the club astutely, with a mixture of humour and toughness. He sought and got General MacArthur's backing for an attempt to have repairs and renovations made to the club premises. His diary on the incident had the following entry: 'MacArthur was sympathetic but pointed out the owners of the premises could insist that the work was a charge against tenants. He paced his office, smoking reflectively, then said: "It would be improper, of course, for me to intervene as Supreme Commander. But I don't see why I can't cover your flanks. Set up a dinner for the owners and invite them to inspect the premises. I shall send along a colonel as an observer. Observers, I have found, can be very useful."

'Later I escorted three representatives of the Japanese owners on an intensive inspection after a cordial but spartan dinner, craftily and austerely prepared. MacArthur's colonel casually stressed from time to time the Supreme Commander's special interest in the Press Club. By pre-arrangement, he questioned me closely about last week's explosion in the basement lavatory, which was not due to bomb sabotage but to some abnormality in the Club's boiler and sanitation system — also manifest in the irregular diversion of scalding water and steam geysers to the lavatory toilets. The colonel repeatedly drew attention to property disrepair and made copious notes, groaning, whistling and shaking his head. He alarmed the visitors by an apparent heavy stumble on a defective step. Later the owners agreed to pay 285 000 yen for immediate renovations. When I telephoned MacArthur with the news he said: "A good standover job by a good observer".'

The job was impossible, but it was a job and he had excellent local staff to help him. But he made enemies, inevitably. He could not be all things to all men, as the job demanded. There was a limit to his patience and at times his scathing wit hurt and his vehemence about outrageous behaviour by some of the silliest habitues of the club added to the list of those discontented with his stewardship.

He took a short trip to Australia early in 1947, remarried, and returned to Japan. When he got back he found that the club committee had fired him during his absence. He had not measured up to the demands made of him. At first Hughes was hurt. Then he became angry and vowed he would never set foot inside the Shimbun Alley club again. And he never did.

His friends were incensed. They believed he had been shabbily treated and they too withdrew from the club. One close friend heard of Hughes' sacking from a member of the committee. 'You're Hughes best friend and I think you ought to know that the committee has just decided to fire him,' the committeeman said.

Hughes' friend, a former commando, rarely swore. 'Get out of my office, you treacherous, dull dog', he roared and advanced on his luckless informant. He could not believe fellow correspondents would act in such a manner. With others, he tried to have the committee's decision over-ruled and, when this proved unsuccessful, they set up a rival organization and for a time the exiles met for lunches and long disputations about Japan, the state of the world, Sherlock Holmes, cigars, food and drink. But they had no permanent premises and after a while the secession move died away.

Years later Hughes wrote nostalgically and with great affection about the old Shimbun Alley Club. 'I went back to the site of the liveliest, lustiest, East-meets-West drinking centre in all Asia. I swear I heard the astral roar of intellectual disputation, breaking glass, knuckle play and folk singing in the packed bar and smelled the burned hamburgers, spaghetti and meat balls rising greasingly from the kitchen.'

Hughes' second wife was Adele, a beautiful, intelligent Jew. She was unhappily married when they first met, so subsequently they lived together, defying the strong conventions of the period, until her divorce came through. His friends, Cyril Pearl leading them, were completely supportive, but there was some opposition. It came from friends of Adele's husband, and at one stage an argument developed to the stage that one of them swung a punch at Hughes. It hit him in one eye. Hughes, the former light heavyweight who had been taught to box superbly by his father, did not retaliate but smoothed down the heated discussion.

He took Adele to Melbourne to meet his parents and his son. Her reception was cool but their obvious great love for each other and his parents' knowledge of the loneliness that followed his first wife's death eased the initial hostility. Hughes' father again understood and his earlier, gentle, 'It's all right if you love' remark was repeated.

In Tokyo, the brawling, ugly exciting city he was beginning to love, they settled down to a life of domestic bliss he had tasted so briefly years earlier.

Professionally, he kept his head above water by freelance writing. Australian news services, the *Wall Street Journal* and London's *Financial Times* were among his 'strings'. He tore into his reporting of emerging Japan, covered some of the war crime trials and gradually built up an amazing list of contacts. They ranged from Allied diplomats to Russian, Chinese and Japanese newspapermen and Japanese leaders. There were spies among them of course; Japan was one of the crossroads of the espionage world where virtually all the combatants in the twilight world mixed openly. Hughes rarely took notes when he saw people. He avoided raising the big question to which he desperately wanted the answer. He seemed to be interested in everything told to him. He appeared to be ingenuous, laid back, a pleasant companion rather than a keen-eyed foreign correspondent probing for secrets. He won the trust of his contacts because he respected confidences. He tipped off other correspondents to stories and they in turn tipped him off to their stories. One contemporary summed up his style: 'He gave and he got'.

His insatiable curiosity about everything and the priceless gift of being interested, together with his wit and charm — 'Australian bullshit' he was to call it later — opened doors normally closed to newspapermen. But there was a ruthless side to him. He reserved this for the few people who were mean-spirited, who did not keep their word or were disloyal to friends. One such person was a well-known Allied diplomat, famous for his illicit romances. He made Hughes a target for his wrath for some barbed comments about one aspect of the war crimes trials. Among other things, Hughes had referred to one Australian official's accent. 'It rang through the courtroom like the cracks of a bush stockwhip', he wrote for his paper. The diplomat objected. He accused Hughes of ridicule and of denigrating his own countrymen.

Shortly afterwards a story went the rounds of cocktail and

newspaper haunts saying that someone passing the diplomat's office heard a plaintive female cry: 'Sir, sir, please remove your spectacles. They're hurting my thighs.' Hughes indignantly denied authorship.

One of his most bizarre stories of the occupation dealt with a plan by a Japanese businessman to import Australian greyhounds to Japan in return for cultured pearl necklaces. Hughes met the businessman, Mr Goto, in the roaring precincts of the Shimbun Alley press club. He had plenty of capital to float a company to be known as Honourable and Democratic Dog Racing Association. He was prepared to offer seventy-five flawless pearl necklaces, valued at some $30 000 at ruling black market prices in return for twenty Australian pedigree racing greyhounds.He was hoping that General MacArthur would repeal current Japanese laws against betting.

Mr Goto had very little English but an insatiable thirst for Scotch, which Hughes kept coming as they worked out details of the scheme.When Hughes' story hit Australia the mail poured in. Some of it went to Hughes. There were photographs of lean and ferocious looking greyhounds, together with detailed descriptions of the animals' speed, ferocity and potency.

The next move came when Hughes had a visit from a tough looking, bullet-headed Japanese flanked by two bodyguards, who drank huge quantities of sake while he explained that his company was the only one authorized to race greyhounds in Japan. He denounced Mr Goto as a swindler and a rogue. There was some discussion about a 'rabbit car' which Hughes eventually worked out was the tin hare.

Goto was untroubled about the charges when he saw Hughes the next day and renewed his onslaught on the Scotch bottle. He assured Hughes he would not have any more visits from the sake drinker.But the plan, which Hughes was cheerfully keeping on the boil with his stories, faltered when Australian authorities warned that clearance for greyhounds to come to Japan would be difficult to get. The Japanese Government was sluggish and MacArthur had other things on his mind. The plan died with time and Mr Goto turned his attention, and presumably his pearl necklaces, to bicycle racing.

Hughes' lifelong love of Sherlock Holmes reached some sort of fulfillment in 1948 when he and other afficionados formed a Tokyo chapter of the Baker Street Irregulars. They called it the Baritsu Chapter. They reasoned, over a long, scholarly lunch, that because the solitary Japanese word Holmes used — 'baritsu' — did not appear in any Japanese dictionary, the master meant 'bujitsu'. Perhaps it had been garbled by Watson, they agreed solemnly. Bujitsu is the generic Japanese word for the martial arts, which, in addition to jujitsu, embraces the study of archery, fencing, swordsmanship and the use of arms.

Hughes was elected Chief Banto of the chapter. Among the

apologies received for non-attendance at the first meeting was one from Prime Minister Yoshida who had a prior commitment to meet General MacArthur. He promised however to attend the next meeting — even at the expense of any possible government or occupation crisis — and he kept his word. The elder statesman, Count Makino, was ill and could not attend one lunch, but he prepared a well-reasoned statement clearing up the mystery of Holmes' use of baritsu. 'For us Japanese,' Makino's statement continued, 'there is intense satisfaction in the foundation of this first Tokyo chapter of the Baker Street Irregulars.'

Walter Simmons, the Far Eastern representative of the *Chicago Tribune*, and one of Hughes' greatest friends, hosted the first historic lunch. Subsequently Hughes was authorized to arrange for the erection of a plaque in London as a tribute to Holmes. The plaque, of heavy oak and the best Sheffield steel, read: 'This plaque commemorates the historic meeting early in 1881 at the original Criterion Long Bar of Dr Stamford and Dr John H. Watson, which led to the introduction of Dr Watson to Mr Sherlock Holmes.'

Hughes had attempted to have a differently worded plaque erected in the laboratory in St Bartholomew's Hospital but the project was considered frivolous and permission was refused. So he chose a location outside the main entrance of the Criterion Hotel in Piccadilly Circus. For years the plaque was a landmark. Holmes lovers and the merely curious gathered around it, sometimes to the anger of police concerned about congestion.

When the plaque was 'ravished' — in Hughes' word — from the wall of the hotel he was incensed. He told a friend about the theft: 'There is nothing sacred. The blasphemer and the profaner, the thief and the robber run unmolested and unrebuked. A person, or persons, has or have, removed from the wall of the Criterion Hotel in Piccadilly the plaque erected by the Tokyo branch of the Baker Street Irregulars in honour of the meeting of Dr Watson and young Stamford which led to the meeting of Watson and the master.

'I am advised that the police suspect irresponsible tourist souvenir hunters. There is no evidence to arraign the news vendor, above whose stall the plaque was erected, for complicity in the rape. Former Inspector Fabian of Scotland Yard has made fruitless inquiries. It was safe and sound when I inspected it on my most recent visit to London. The news vendor, an honest appearing cockney, told me that many visitors tarried to worship before the emblem. Rest assured that I shall make a replacement on my next visit. This I pledge. You will excuse me if my heart is too heavy to write more.'

Seven years after the plaque disappeared it was returned by a mysterious stranger who claimed he found it in a cupboard of a house in Wimbledon which he had just bought He passed it to the Sherlock

Holmes society and it was replaced, much to Hughes' delight.

His life was full. He had a loving home atmosphere, although his wife's health was causing him concern, good friends, good stories and fun. He had a great capacity for fun and he made the most of the erudite, witty and highly intelligent people with whom he mixed. He took great delight in picking up and retailing the idiosyncrasies of some of the famous people around him. One of his stories involved the wife of a mission (embassy) leader known for her love of animals. She defended them passionately, particularly horses. At one obligatory party Hughes was standing in the reception line behind the head of the mission. The host asked why his lady wasn't with him. According to Hughes' story, the head of the mission replied, straight faced: 'I had to leave her at home. A touch of distemper you know.'

Hughes and his friends contrived to ensure that the animal-loving woman received Japanese news clippings saying the bears from Chicago would be paraded through Tokyo streets in open trucks prior to an exhibition at one of the big stadiums The titled woman rose to the bait and wrote a fierce letter to the Japanese editors condeming the barbarity of inflicting such pain and indignity on harmless beasts. The Japanese solemnly assured the furious woman that the bears concerned were baseball players.

'Off beat' stories — stories separate from hard news events — attracted Hughes, so when he heard about the Hairy Ainu tribe in Japan's northernmost island of Hokkaido he went there with alacrity. The Hairy Ainu were the original natives of Japan and they had a curious tradition — Hughes called it a women's lib tradition — in which the women tattooed their faces with Kaiser Wilhelm moustaches or neat beards. With Hughes were Lachie McDonald, an outstanding New Zealand correspondent whom Hughes had first met on the old *Star* newspaper, and Walt Simmons of the *Chicago Tribune*.

Before they found the tribe they called on a German mission on the island. The brown-cowled monks made their visitors welcome by producing a good supply of their own beer, brewed at the mission. Hughes delighted the monks with his hearty singing of German beer hall songs, remembered from his prewar days in Tokyo.

When they finally found the ancient tribe they were granted an interview with the Hairy Ainu king. Hughes put the king into the same mandarin category he had given to his old friend Frank Green in Canberra. He said the king was an impressive mandarin type in his own right; an amiable, honestly bearded mandarin wearing a tin and glass crown, an unbuttoned jacket and long woollen underpants.

The king was sitting on a wooden, toilet seat type of throne outside his thatched hut on the shore of Volcano Bay when Hughes and the others were ushered into his presence. He was flanked by two

72

ferocious, leashed dogs which tried sporadically to spring at the visitors' throats.

Hughes and his friends decided to ask the king for his reaction to the current RSPCA protests by foreigners in Tokyo against the ancient Ainu annual custom of spearing a captive bear cub to death to drive away evil spirits. The animal loving wife of the embassy head who had confused American baseballers with bears had urged strongly that the Ainu should abolish the custom. General MacArthur's wife had also condemned the practice.

Hughes described the scene: 'The king scratched his groin with his wooden sceptre and laughed with the tolerance of a mandarin in command. He said he could understand and sympathize with ignorant and superstitious foreign devils' protests. But they did not realise that the bear cubs, soothed by the music of holy drums and bugles while the penitent tribesmen were spearing them, did not really feel any pain, and in any event were assured of reincarnation. "Just like the crucifixion" he pointed out archly, striking one of the leaping dogs on its muzzle with his sceptre.'

Hughes said the king's homely, buxom queen, tattooed with striking sideburns and a moustache, was standing behind the throne as the king spoke. 'She whispered in his ear and the king nodded with mandarin dignity and gave us our news story lead.'

Their majesties courteously invited Madam MacArthur and the embassy head's wife to attend the next bear-slaying ceremony. They would be given spears and exhorted to participate in the mass dancing and stabbing. They would also strike a drum and blow a bugle. This way they would be cleansed of their sins. Hughes and his friends promised solemnly they would pass on the invitation.

The interview ended when Hughes asked what the king thought of democracy in view of the unsuccessful campaign by the Hairy Ainu crown prince to enter the Japanese parliament. The king referred the minor inquiry to the queen, who replied scornfully: 'What's the good of democracy if the people you vote for don't get in?'

Back in Tokyo, Hughes watched fascinated as the Japanese began their steady emergence from the shadow of the occupation. They had been so amenable to the strictures imposed on them as a beaten and humiliated people that the bonds were loosening daily. And their resourcefulness in rebuilding their shattered nation was earning them respect from the Occupation authorities.

London's *Sunday Times* put Hughes on staff in 1948 as Far Eastern representative and he had a new and exciting vehicle for his output. He relished the prospect of writing for such a prestigious newspaper, with its emphasis on serious matters.

He was becoming more and more convinced that the political rumblings coming out of Europe as the temporary wartime alliances began to crumble would develop and erupt in South East Asia. War-weary Europe would not be the testing ground for the confrontation that now seemed inevitable. South East Asia, as the last bastion of colonialism, would be the venue.

As colonial power waned even further a wave of nationalism would sweep the area, with China showing the way as she lumbered to her feet under Mao Tse Tung's communists. The Japanese, with their co-prosperity sphere dream so ridiculed during the war years, had sewn the seeds of nationalism more successfully than had been thought possible. Early defeats of the mighty powers by despised little yellow men had given to the teeming masses throughout Asia a vision of future freedom. He felt that China would be the catalyst. Mao reinforced this view when he told his followers in 1949: 'Very soon we shall be victorious throughout the country. This victory will breach the Eastern front on Imperialism and will have great international significance.'

Despite the growing disenchantment between the West and their Soviet wartime allies, Russians in Tokyo still kept a high profile. Hughes continued his friendship with many of them, reasoning that he would not be doing his job if he closed off any avenues for stories, irrespective of his own feelings. So he went to their occasional parties, drank with them and amused them by performing his party act of smashing a table with his huge hands. He had great respect for their drinking capacity. He was no mean performer himself, of course, despite his slow start. His Australian accent was uncorrupted, he was articulate and witty and he lived his life with an ebullience that appealed to the Russians and the others in the international community that made Tokyo at the time one of the most exciting and rewarding news beats in the world.

His wife's health remained a worry, however. From the tiny, vivacious and beautiful girl he had married she had developed into a virtual recluse, conscious of her swollen legs that she felt would make her an object of pity when they went out together. She took to staying at home more and more. Hughes was devoted to her and would hurry home at every chance to be with her and reassure her. He sought the best possible medical help. She was suffering from some type of lymphatic condition and doctors could do little for her.

The night before she died Hughes was home early. He worked until late and when he went to bed Adele was already asleep. He rose at his customary time of around 5 am, finished the story he was working on the night before and then took a cup of tea to her. She had died in her sleep.

Later that morning he wandered the streets, alone in his grief, unaware of the chattering crowds around him. Towards noon, he phoned two close friends and arranged to meet them at the American

Club where he told them his wife had died. He had no God to turn to; he had denounced his Catholic God years earlier. His friends tried to cheer him up and when their assumed light-heartedness became too much his control broke and he berated them for their apparent lack of care.

Again, work was the stimulus that soothed over the loss of his adored Adele but it was a long time before he could put out of his mind the hurt she had suffered when she defied convention to marry him. She was his second real love. He had his son in far off Melbourne as a legacy from his first marriage, and from Adele he had the memory of a few short years of great happiness. The memory was never to leave him.

The Korean war was on and Hughes fought with his boss in London, Ian Fleming, Foreign Manager of the *Sunday Times*, for permission to cover it. Fleming refused. 'This is an order', he cabled. The plan that Fleming vetoed was for Hughes, together with Ian Morrison, of *The Times*, Christopher Buckley of the London *Daily Telegraph*, and Colonel Uni Nayer, of the Indian Army, to fly to the tortured peninsular together. Morrison, Buckley and Nayer went and held a seat in their jeep for Hughes. It was still vacant when a landmine on the side of a Korean road killed the three of them. Subsequently when Hughes told Fleming about it Fleming said: 'Of course. It just shows the value of obeying orders.'

The fighting in Korea raged up and down the peninsular and Hughes covered much of the early part of the vicious campaign from Tokyo. He was primarily concerned with his London papers — he was then also a correspondent for the *Economist* — and as they were weeklies he had plenty of time to collect his stories and get them away. Korea was a land of extremes, with intense cold and blistering heat, and Hughes' legs were still weak from the fever he had contracted in North Africa. And there was Fleming's strict order to obey. Fleming felt that Hughes was of greater value in Japan, from where he could maintain a watch on the overall situation and report on the political aspects of the campaign, than in Korea itself. But he did visit the war later when Fleming gave his reluctant permission.

One of the great political stories of the Korean war — and indeed one of the great stories of the decade — that Hughes covered, was the dismissal of General MacArthur by U.S. President Harry Truman. MacArthur held the view that communist bases, north of the Yalu River and inside China, were supplying the North Koreans. Chinese and Russian arms were being used openly and 'advisers' from both countries were helping the battered North Koreans. MacArthur claimed that while the bases were immune from bombing attack his United Nations forces were penalized. 'On to the Yalu' was one of MacArthur's rallying cries.

Truman feared that the bombing MacArthur advocated would bring China openly into the conflict and that the resultant escalation would involve the Soviet Union. World War Three would burst then onto a world weary of killing. Truman ordered MacArthur not to involve China directly by bombing the bases. MacArthur was defiant. He felt China was already involved and that the confrontation Truman feared was inevitable eventually. Truman acted fast. He fired the great general.

Hughes was in his office in the Radio Tokyo building when the news broke. He had worked late that night and decided to have a short sleep before resuming. A friend from one of the big news agencies who monitored the news heard the 'flash' about Truman's lightning move. He owed Hughes many favours for news tips and other kindnesses. Within minutes of filing his own story the friend raced to Hughes' office. He found the big man slumped over his typewriter, sound asleep.

'Wake up, your grace', he said urgently. 'Big story.'

Hughes jerked erect. 'What is it my son?'

'Truman just fired MacArthur. It's official.'

There was a blank sheet of copy paper in Hughes' typewriter. He raised his hand in an episcopal blessing and within minutes had hammered out his story and handed it to a sleepy copyboy waiting outside to race it to the transmission point.

Tokyo was like a city in mourning when MacArthur's final cavalcade swept through on its way to the airport. Huge crowds lined the streets. They were subdued. Their surrogate emperor, the strong man who epitomized American might, was going home for the last time. It was the end of an era. Hughes rode in the cavalcade with other correspondents and watched the fat-bellied aircraft that carried MacArthur back to the U.S., and another hero's welcome finally lift off.

The Korean war, resulting in the death of more than 73 000 servicemen, finally ended in July 1953. It had lasted just three years. Its end brought relative peace to South East Asia, but it lined up inexorably the protagonists for the final showdown between democracy and communism, colonialism and nationalism, that was to come two decades later.

Hughes remained in the centre of it all through the turbulent years that followed.

6 Hong Kong & Mao's China

The May Day riots of 1952 shocked a complacent Japan and brought a fresh awareness that MacArthur's autocratic rule had ended. Japanese were becoming their own people again, the eruption seemed to say, and no longer the cowed millions who had accepted the penance of occupation.

Thousands poured through Tokyo's streets, plundering and fighting in an upsurge of hate. The demonstrators were only a minority but their frenzy whipped up a lot of anger hidden since the end of the war.

The combination of May Day and resurging communism was the flashpoint for the frightening demonstration. But many people, Hughes among them, saw the disturbance as a legacy of Japan's defeat in the war. Japan had accepted defeat too easily; had buckled down to the humiliation of the occupation too quickly. May Day gave the demonstrators a chance to vent their hate and frustration. To many who roamed the streets of Tokyo, communism had nothing to do with it. May Day was an excuse for their rage and gave it some degree of respectability.

Hughes reported the outbreak from his Radio Tokyo office. In a later letter to a friend he used his biblical tone to describe the scene: 'Our windows in Radio Tokyo were cracked by stones thrown with the same evil purpose and menacing force as those that drove holy St. Stephen, bruised and panting, to the redeemer's knees.

'With a portable altar loaded in the back of my parish jeep I was proceeding at a temperate pace towards the Plaza when the mob burst out and overturned two large army cars. There was a certain amount of plundering and violence, with the cops wielding the waddy judiciously but with some enjoyment. Undaunted, I instructed my driver to make a smart turn and drive swiftly back the way he had come.

'We executed this manoeuvre at the cost of jettisoning the portable altar, which I had hoped to erect for an outdoors revivalist meeting as the May Day boys went home.'

But the story he wrote about the riots made the point forcefully that communism could not be tucked away comfortably as belonging only to the Russians and the Chinese. It was latent too in Japan and there was no room for complacency.

The 'bare arse and the branding iron' incident, as Hughes later called it, happened when Hughes wrote a story about a visit to Japan and Korea by the then Australian Army Minister, Josiah Francis. Hughes reported that Francis was photographed exchanging toasts with the Soviet Ambassador, A. P. Kislenko, at a reception given by the Australian Ambassador, Colonel Hodgson. Francis later rebuked the photographer and destroyed the film. Kislenko confirmed the story to Hughes and commented: 'We Russians apparently have greater freedom of behaviour than your Australian ministers are permitted abroad.'

In his story of the incident Hughes recalled that in 1948 Francis, against General MacArthur's advice, had insisted on calling on the Japanese Emperor, and was restrained from shaking hands with a maid at the entrance whom he mistook for the Empress.

Hughes' story of the exchange of toasts had big impact in Australia and was widely published in other countries. In the United States, for instance, newspapers played up the angle of the Russians jesting about their comparative freedom. In Australia, where the Communist Party had been suppressed (the bill was later declared unconstitutional) and where anti-communism feelings were running high, the story was a winner.

Francis called the story a malicious falsehood. The Australian ambassador called it a 'lying story', and threatened to have Hughes' accreditation removed. Hughes rode out the storm calmly. Several days after the story appeared his phone rang. It was 2 am. 'I was just laying a book of sermons on the occasional table beside my cot when the phone rang' he said at the time. 'I thought I knew who was responsible. I got out of bed, poured myself a large drink, reopened my book of sermons and settled back into bed.' The phone continued to ring, in three minute bursts, until 3.30 am.

Explaining his handling of the exchanges of toasts story Hughes continued: 'Francis denied my earlier story about trying to shake hands with the maid at the Emperor's palace, so when this one popped up it was like having a bare arse in front of me with a sizzling branding iron handy . . . So pssst.'

Hughes rejoined the Packer organization in 1953, not long after the death of Brian Penton. He saw Penton just before he died. A wasted Penton was troubled about the visit because of the way he looked but the two former enemies shook hands emotionally.

Packer too was an emotional man beneath his tough exterior. He was pleased to have Hughes back and Hughes was equally happy to be back in the fold. Packer had a sentimental attachment to the people he had hired and he liked to remain surrounded by the brilliant men he had helped to shape. Also he liked Hughes for his wit, irreverence and his ruggedness. Both shared a dislike of regimentation of thought. At the time Packer was reported to have said that he did not think of himself as an implacable enemy or that he carried hate for a long time.

Back in Japan, Hughes was seeing the country in a new light as the memory of the occupation years faded and the people's renascent nationalism became more evident. A Japanese friend summed up the mood when he told Hughes:

'We Japanese are very proud people. We have never been humbled before and there can be no pride without some acquaintance with humility. Remember that not all Japanese have had the opportunity to travel abroad and observe Western customs and culture.

'You know, Richard, in the shock of defeat some young Japanese might have easily mistaken military victory for superior culture. But happily the occupation brought its own culture to Japan, its own living habits, and our people were able to study for themselves the behaviour of the West.' He paused reflectively and then delivered the *coup de grâce*. 'We were thus able to reassure ourselves gratefully of the enduring superiority of the Japanese way of life.'

The Japanese way of life was insidious and more and more Hughes found himself easing into the male-oriented culture. He began to fear the dreaded 'Bring the bastard back. He's gone native' recall cable that hung over the heads of correspondents grown comfortable. Japanese friends too had helped deaden the pain of Adele's death and gradually he began to pick up the threads of a social life he had partially shunned.

The *Sunday Times* and *Economist* liked the stories he was sending, so he made his second visit to London. His son, now graduated from university, was visiting Europe at the time.

They had a happy reunion though there was a sad touch to it. Hughes told his son about May's suicide. He had agonized for years about having left his son when May died. He was aware that some saw his action as abandonment of his responsibility; that his son had become a victim of his ruthless determination to succeed. But it was his loss and his alone, he reasoned. Young Richard had grown up surrounded by love, had never wanted for anything material and got the education he himself had been denied. The casualty had been closeness, and all the letters in the world and all the care he had lavished from a distance did not compensate.

So one small step towards the touching he wanted was to tell his son the painful story of how his mother died. He told it in detail and explained why he had left young Richard with his grandparents after May's death. Although he did not remember his mother, young Richard was shaken and Hughes sensed the hurt that the long deception had caused him. Unlike his father, however, he had strong faith imbued in him by his grandmother and this, together with his grandfather's conviction about after-life, comforted him and the hurt passed.

One night, soon afterwards, Hughes, his son and a friend from Japan were sitting in a car and looking down towards the lights of London from Hampstead Hill. The night was cold and still and there was a rare moon. It was a time of sentiment and the closeness that had eluded father and son was almost tangible. Hughes' friend mentioned how the moonlight spread over a quiet street leading towards shadowed Hampstead Heath and he quoted part of Alfred Noyes' poem, 'The Highwayman':

'And still on a winter's night, they say,
'When the wind is in the trees
'When the moon is a ghostly galleon tossed upon cloudy seas,
'When the road is a ribbon of moonlight over the purple moor . . .'

The reunion with his son was not the only highlight of Hughes London visit. He renewed friendship with his boss, Ian Fleming. The two had met earlier. Fleming, lean and beautifully turned out and with a youthful Oscar Wilde touch to his looks, had formed an instant liking for the huge Australian.

Despite their disparate backgrounds, their friendship flourished over the years. Hughes, who Fleming called 'my comprador', was the antithesis of the sophisticated Fleming, with his public school background and aristocratic friends. He was the man of action that Fleming always wanted to be, tough, immensely knowledgable, ebullient and sure. They would have lunch together at Fleming's favourite spot, then stroll through Green Park, Fleming with his hands clasped behind his back and Hughes' bulk towering above him.

Back in Japan, Hughes found domesticity beckoning again and he set up house with a Japanese mistress. Like so many Japanese women — particularly mistresses — she kept in the background. Hughes' friends who visited him at his home occasionally glimpsed the swish of a kimono. Otherwise, despite his efforts to bring her more into his circle of friends, she remained mysterious. She looked after him impeccably, however, and his gentle life at home was a sure contrast to the heavy days.

Fleming, who was rapidly becoming a cult figure for his James Bond books, decided to visit the Far East as part of the research necessary for a non-Bond book, *Thrilling Cities*, and he asked Hughes to accompany him on part of the trip. In the subsequent book,

80

Fleming referred to Hughes as 'my friend and philosopher . . . He is a giant Australian with a European mind and a quixotic view of the world.'

Macao, 'the pimple on the arse of China' as Hughes once delicately referred to it, was one of the cities Fleming wanted to include in his fascinating book. They limbered up for their night's sortie with dinner at the Portugese colony's Loving Buddha, then descended on the Central Hotel 'whose function and design I recommend most warmly to the attention of those concerned with English morals' as Fleming put it. It was devoted solely to the vices.

The Central's outstanding feature, as guide Hughes pointed out pontifically, was that the higher you went the more beautiful and expensive were the girls. The stakes at the gambling tables were higher, the music better, and the atmosphere more refined, according to Hughes. He had visited the hotel on an earlier occasion 'in the course of a visit to the parish to help bring the heathen to the fold' and the two men jubilantly worked their way towards the Elysian heights at the top of the building.

Fleming and Hughes reached the sixth floor and continued their 'pursuit of information which would be in accordance with the readership of *The Sunday Times*', as Fleming wrote diplomatically in his book.

Fleming lost some money at the fan tan tables, and called the game 'dainty piracy'. They also tried their luck with a strange game — something like the American game of craps — called 'hi-lo'. Again no luck, so they made their way to the dance floor. One of the beautiful 'hostesses' who joined them at their table was called Garbo — 'same like film star'. Fleming read her hand, told her she had three children and was under-sexed. The hilarity they generated brought more girls to their table and the drinks flowed with abandon.

According to Hughes, the evening 'ended decorously in a shower of twenty dollar notes'. Fleming, too, drew a decent veil over the evening. Later that night the two friends strolled back through the hot Macao streets to their hotel, contented with the results of their research.

Macao then was an exciting city, living on its collective wits, a centre of intrigue and villainy of every description. Smuggling, racketeering on a huge scale and prostitution were high on its list of priorities. Hughes had unrivalled sources for the type of information Fleming was seeking and he was able to steer the author to all the right people and satisfy his curiosity.

Towards the end of their visit, they were standing one evening on the balcony of the Bela Vista Hotel, watching the junks ghosting in on the Pearl river. It was a time of tranquil beauty. Fleming was tired of Europe and the interminable business harassment that followed in the wake of his James Bond books. He was relishing the peace of the warm, clear evening and the strange melancholy the evening engendered. 'You know Dick, I suppose a man could be happier here than anywhere else in the world', he said reflectively. He sipped his drink then added: 'For about a fortnight'.

The next day they headed back to Hong Kong on the ferry and Fleming flew off in search of other cities that excited or appalled him.

Many of the top correspondents in the world were in Hong Kong around this time, waiting for permission to enter China itself and to write about the great upheaval that Mao Tse Tung had brought about. They waited, drank and argued and got into trouble, and waited again. One of them was a dear friend of Hughes. He decided to make a fleeting visit to Macao after Hughes told him of what he called 'the nubility and skill of the local beauties'.

Hughes told another friend at the time: 'But the Chinese press in Macao immediately reported his shy arrival, member in hand, as a shrewd and secret move to enter China across the Portuguese border instead of from Hong Kong.

'They hailed his missionary zeal, called him a brave man in search of a big story. The more angrily he denied the reports from the sweated depths of cathouse pillows the more specifically were the reports repeated.

'They even stressed that, to avoid detection, he was travelling without his typewriter. He had rightly decided, of course, that this useless appendage was not essential for his real research purposes in Macao. When he got back to Hong Kong he complained bitterly that he had never before in his life indulged in such interrupted and public fornication.'

In a letter to a friend at this time Hughes regaled him with details of his and Fleming's 'revivalist mission' to Macao, and touched on some other of his travels:

'Parochial duties and the work of the Lord have caused this hiatus in my flow of pastorals to your diocese. I've been to Thailand to feed the hungry and clothe the naked following the recent revolution in that great democratic state and have been involved in spiritual distractions in my home diocese. But the Holy Ghost (to whom all submission) has inflicted me with a savage attack of gout in the left big toe and I'm pledged to severe dieting and implacable teetotalism for, alas, three months. I promised my doctor and father confessor I would persevere until I lost forty pounds in weight. Your prayers are invoked for my intentions.'

His weight at that time was about 114 kilos but his 184 centimetres carried it handsomely. 'He looked like a cross between the actor Sydney Greenstreet and Santa Claus' a critical friend said.

He had another happy visit to Macao, this time with a Fleet Street friend, Frank Owen. He called it a 'pious visit for the incidence of the Chinese new year'. For some obscure Oriental reason, the master light switch for the room was located in the hotel corridor and when Hughes climbed the stairs after an exuberant session with his friend he inadvertently switched on the light for the large room adjoining his.

There was a cry of alarm from within the suddenly lighted room. 'Who is it? What is it?' came the quavering cry from within.

Hughes, on some impish impulse, cried out gutturally, 'It is the polizza'. He then turned out the light and ducked into his own darkened room. Through the thin wall, he heard the wretched occupant of the next room fumbling in the dark and calling out: 'Yes. I am coming. What is it? I have seen the police already.' At the same time Hughes could hear the man murmuring reassurance to his female companion whimpering in the darkness.

He heard the man fling open his door and address the silent corridor. 'Where is the police?' He raised his voice and shouted this time. 'Where is the police!' His roar brought the night porter sprinting up the stairs. 'What is the matter? Is there a burglar? Why do you want the polizza?'

The enraged man, whom Hughes guessed from his accent was part Portuguese, snarled: 'I do not want the police. They want me. Why? I do not know. I do not know. I do not know. They turn on the light suddenly. They shout out menacingly. Then they turn off the light and sneak away.' He mastered his rage long enough to make soothing noises to his female companion, whose whimperings were increasing in scale.

The portly assistant manager, angry and breathing hard after mounting the stairs, arrived. What was all the excitement and shouting about, he demanded. He too began to shout. 'Why do you want the polizza?' He didn't wait for the Eurasian to reply. 'Ha, now you do not want them. Why then did you cry out for them?' There were no polizza in the hotel. Hughes could hear the woman sobbing and the Eurasian shouting at her in pure Portuguese.

Finally, unable to control his laughter and feeling the situation was rapidly getting out of control, Hughes hammered on the wall. 'Knock it off', he roared indignantly. There were murmurings of 'Scuse, scuse' from the assistant manager and the uproar subsided.

The next morning the room next to him was empty. He asked the assistant manager the reason for the commotion. The bleary-eyed man apologised profusely.

'It was the Portuguese person in the room next to yours. I dare say he had the nightmare. He was of excitable temperament. Obviously of bad conscience. He claimed the polizza came and he frightened them away. This I do not believe. Anyway he has gone. And with him the woman — his wife they say.'

In the cold light of day Hughes felt slightly embarassed about the previous night's incident. But there was something about Macao — its antiquity, its villainy, its charm — that appealed to Hughes' impish nature and he relished his visits there.

On his second visit to China he went again to his favourite Chinese city, Shanghai. 'I visited the reformatory for penitent whores there', he wrote. 'It was a sad, grey, afternoon and I found myself brooding over the lechery of my friends who had doubtless personally brought some of these poor, fallen girls to prison.'

Wherever he went in the city he was mistaken for a Russian, in favour at the time. 'Soleen' (Russian) they would call, grinning. Hughes thought this an ironic phonetic confusion in view of his bulk.

The Shanghai visit saddened him. The untamed city he visited first in 1940 was uneasy under communism, he felt. He felt nostalgia for the old, roaring days of the forties, yet he conceded that under communism it was a far better city for the Chinese people than it was in its earlier free-wheeling days. He'd had his first — and disappointing — taste of opium there, and his first — enchanting — experience with Chinese girls.

In Peking, he looked into the future — wrongly as it turned out — and predicted that Japan ultimately would be drawn into the Chinese orbit, economically and culturally, if not idealogically. The view from China, he wrote, was like looking down the wrong end of a telescope. Chinese communists regarded Japan as an instrument for their future policy and ambitions and did not attempt to conceal their supreme confidence that eventually they would be able to use Nippon for their own ends. Japanese businessmen and politicians envisaged, subconsciously perhaps, a return to the pre-1941 days when Japan ran the Sino-Japanese set-up, fixed the prices and sold the goods.

'But there are, I fear, disappointments ahead. The old, roaring, freebooting thirties in China are gone. China will have the initiative in future Sino-Japanese relations and Japan will be wise to recognize this as fact.'

He had enormous admiration for the Chinese premier, Chou En-lai. Before they met Hughes had been told by a Chinese seer that if a man's little finger extended well beyond the first joint of the third finger he would be a lucky man and could trust his friends. After he shook hands with a gracious Chou Hughes asked if he could see the Premier's hand and he pointed out the long little finger. 'I see you know our Chinese lore, Mr Hughes', Chou told him. 'I hope you too have luck and can trust your friends.'

In Canton he awoke at 6 am to catch a train to Hankow. He tried to tell a Chinese hotel servant that he would like a taxi for 7.30. Hughes had only a smattering of Chinese so after much shouting and attempted explanations he despaired of getting his message across.

Finally he scrawled '730' on the wall of his room. The servant smiled, delighted that he understood and ran off. Within a few minutes he returned to Hughes' room, dragging in his wake a dishevelled, half-asleep Chinese. 'I indicated I was pleased to meet him and inquired his interest. He glared at me and in turn inquired about my interest. I discovered later to my intense delight that he was the occupant of room 730.'

He devoted some of his reports out of China to drinking habits. 'One must open the oriental wine list naturally with shaohsing, not dry sherry. It is warm, robust and encouraging and seldom causes a hangover.'

Of mao-tai, he said the drink had a rare, fiery authority and should be sampled by 'iron-bladdered drinkers only to prove that motor fuel can be potable and exhilarating'. His first drink of mao-tai was a sip. 'Then the flames exploded and roared through my lower abdomen when I graduated from a tentative sip to a gulp'. One good slug of mao-tai was the equivalent of three double Gibsons, he declared. He also tried mare's milk. But it did not travel well outside the mares. He reserved his highest praise for sake. It was the sincere drinker's drink. You could not cellar it because the best brew died after a year in a bottle.

His session on mare's milk — he had tasted it earlier — happened at the Marching Forward commune at Urumchi in the far North West of China. He was sitting in the sun with the headman of the commune, Hasim Sasimbayu, who, although a teetotaller, kept pressing the warm, vinegary drink on an unreluctant Hughes. He found it stimulating to the extent that he, together with Hasim, began to notice the beauty of the local Kazakh women. Hasim, he said, would break off occasionally from his recital of the benefits of communist control to whistle piercingly at attractive girls and would occasionally slap a curvaceous bottom. Hasim was very contented and dismissed the need for money. He had cattle, horses and sheep and pretty women: 'He reminded me of the bloke who said he had food and drink, a place to sleep and someone to keep him warm. He lacked nothing.'

In Urumchi too he saw a street scene that made him reflect on differing reactions to violence from South East Asian people and the varying attitudes of authorities.

The scene was 'the street of grey-eyed men' — Hughes never could find out how it got its name — and involved a Chinese bus driver and a Kazakh tribesman riding a nervous white mare. The driver tooted his horn stridently and the mare reared and fell. The tribesman landed on his feet, quietened the mare, then handed the reins with quiet dignity to a bystander. He walked across to the bus, measured the driver calmly and whacked him across the nose with a huge backhander. Still without visible anger he remounted and rode off, leaving the stunned driver to pick himself out of the gutter. The driver wiped the blood from his nose, bowed to the silent spectators, bowed to his passengers, and resumed his interrupted journey.

In Peking, Hughes reflected, excited bystanders would have swarmed to the scene shouting encouragement to the brawlers. Two traffic policemen would try patiently to effect a compromise so that neither the horseman nor the bus driver would lose face. Each of the protagonists would compliment the other on some aspect of their behaviour, the horse would be left to fend for itself in the gutter and traffic would back up for miles until militiamen chanting Mao's thoughts restored order.

In Tokyo, there would be a gaggle of policemen denouncing the horseman because he was a peasant; the horseman would bow respectfully to the bus driver because he wore a uniform and then regain face by whacking the unfortunate horse.

In Singapore, a single policeman would take the number of the bus before waving it on; arrest the horseman for suspected careless riding; arrest a bystander for spitting in the street, before mounting the horse and cantering off to the nearest police station with the arrested man jogging along behind.

In Manila, a mob would assemble, pickpockets would have a field day and by the time armed police had stopped a riot, someone would have stolen the horse.

Hughes decided he liked the Urumchi way best. It was basic yet dignified and had all the appearance of justice, swiftly administered.

In all, what with the mare's milk, the happy, uncomplicated peasants and the swift and personal administration of justice, the province represented a slice of Chinese life that appealed to him greatly.

Later he visited a Chinese prison where 1200 men and forty women were serving sentences of from three to ten years. There were stone walls and armed sentries but no locks on cell doors. Prisoners did not wear uniform and corporal punishment was forbidden. Everybody worked and difficult prisoners were punished by not being allowed to work. These perverse and stubborn types could idle away the long days in their cells, stroll around the grounds or sit alone.

Officials told Hughes that these difficult prisoners suffered the silent disapproval of their comrades and sooner or later they would recognize their errors and testify to them openly. Patience, example and reason, officials said, were the only weapons they used to persuade the dissidents to come into line. There was no hurry. Hughes ended his piece on the prisons with a quote from Oscar Wilde: 'Brute reason is far more unbearable than brute force, which only hits below the belt, while brute reason hits below the intellect'.

In an aside to his prison story, he said he asked one official why there was such a difference between the sentences for adultery —

86

from five to ten years — and rape, which attracted a comparably mild two to ten years. The answer was: 'Only two are involved in rape — one sometimes unwilling — but three are involved in adultery — two willing and deceitful.'

He tried hard, and with great cunning, to get an interview with Mao Tse Tung, then at the height of his power. Always a courteous man, he laid it on thickly in his letter seeking the interview. 'May I request the honour of an interview with you on behalf of my newspaper, the *Sunday Times* of London. I sincerely believe that better under-standing between the peoples of China and Great Britain would be promoted by a personal expression of your views on world affairs to the representative of a conservative but independent and influential London newspaper.'

This failed, so he tried another approach, this time to a woman official in the information section of the Chinese Foreign Ministry. In his letter he said he felt now was the time that Chairman Mao might well be considering a direct personal statement to the world on China's plans, aspirations and principles 'especially in view of the often exaggerated and wishful thinking reports in various Western countries which often misinterpret — and continue to misinterpret — the real situation inside contemporary China.'

He put forward a most plausible argument why the *Sunday Times* would be the most suitable medium for the interview: 'If the chairman does relax his reticence at this time'. He named one great American paper, the *New York Times,* as being ideal for the interview 'but there is no possibility of this because of U.S. policy towards China'. He went on to suggest that to choose either of the two resident agencies, Reuters and Agence France Presse, would mean a slight to the other and to speak to both would, from Western capitalist standards, diminish the impact of the message. To grant the interview to friendly Eastern European or Asian correspondents would destroy, rather than diminish, its value to the West.

The first and unique interview with Mao therefore should be personalized and the choice narrowed itself to a selection from the only two available British newspapermen on the scene — Hughes himself and the correspondent of the *Daily Telegraph.*

'I do submit, with sincerity, as well as the utmost personal selfish interest, that a conservative Sunday newspaper with the influence and prestige of the *Sunday Times* would be a more useful and rewarding medium than a conservative daily newspaper even with the influence and prestige of the London *Daily Telegraph.*'

Then, in a personal aside, he wrote: 'If there is no real interest in this application, I trust you will find my arguments amusing rather than impertinent and lay it on one side with a smile rather than resentment.'

This approach also failed, so he tried again, and asked that his request should be brought to the attention of Mao himself. 'I do not doubt that, provided my application has been brought to your notice you will characteristically allow me to be informed of your response, whether favourable or not.'

But all efforts proved abortive so he set out to write whatever he could about the regime, the people and the impact China's re-emergence after its long sleep would have on the West. He wrote, sadly, that 'one of the first casualties in any Communist takeover anywhere is feminine beauty', and deplored the disappearance of the cheong sam, 'that lovely, thigh-slit gown which only the Chinese figure can sustain and adorn'.

The *Sunday Times* was delighted with the stories Hughes turned in from China. In a letter, Ian Fleming, said: 'Your tip-top stories are the best pieces you have, to my knowledge, ever written — first class, thoughtful, witty journalism. I never imagined you would be able to glean so much straw, or at least make such solid brickbats out of it, as you have managed to do. We are all delighted with the pieces.' The paper's owner, Lord Kemsley, also wrote and complimented Hughes. 'Your series had a weight and authority worthy of the best traditions of the *Sunday Times* and without any sacrifice of liveliness and readability.'

In an aside in his letter, Fleming said of his James Bond novels: 'The books go well and it looks as though we may have hit the jackpot with my diamond smuggling series' (*Diamonds are Forever*).

Tokyo, ugly and dirty and noisy but fascinating, was its usual haven when he returned. He had a cosy home life and good friends. Life was rich again. The city's night life, apart from the interminable and incestuous cocktail parties, intrigued him. There was a seemingly inexhaustible supply of beautiful women in the bars that infested the city.

One aspect of the city's night life that he remembered joyously concerned the delicate cold war between two of the city's foremost beauties — 'Dawn of Love' and 'Beautiful Crystal'. Beautiful Crystal had the inside running with her establishment until Dawn of Love, a voluptuous geisha, set up in opposition. She called her establishment 'osome' (modesty) while Beautiful Crysal's place gloried in the name of 'L'espoir' (hope). Whenever an especially distinguished man of letters visited l'espoir, Beautiful Crystal would escort him — after a decent interval — through the narrow, winding lanes to osome where she would introduce him modestly to Dawn of Love. Dawn of Love was aware of course that observant drinkers in her cabaret were witnessing a notable psychological victory by Beautiful Crystal, far transcending the sordid value of the few drinks the patron enjoyed in the rival establishment.

Hughes did most of his entertaining in the American Club and other leading places.

He kept well clear of Shimbun Alley which, he said, seemed to be infested with 'french letter and girdle salesmen, bankers and rotarians'. Occasionally he entertained at home. One night he had two friends to dinner and during the course of what he called 'a disputatious' evening one of his guests remarked on the quality of the salad dressing. 'Based on humble vinegar, my son', Hughes said, and he went to the kitchen and produced a bottle of plain white vinegar to show them.

One of his guests had a habit of swallowing his drinks by just opening his mouth and pouring it down in one gulp. He relied on the after effect as opposed to the relish of the taste. When the swallower looked away for a moment the second guest topped up his whisky glass with the vinegar. At the height of one heated argument the swallower swooped up his glass and downed the half-vinegar cocktail. Hughes, embarassed, described the scene: 'He gagged. His eyes popped and for a moment he was speechless. He glared at me, saw I wasn't capable of such duplicity and turned with a secular oath on his companion. I had to intercede to prevent fisticuffs. They went into the night, shouting obscenities at each other and didn't speak together for several days.'

He ran foul, too, of the Japanese income tax people. They sent what he called 'an amiable moron' to see him. 'He appeared to be impressed by my arguments and by the spartan conditions imposed on me by the vows of poverty of my order — at the time I was wearing only underpants with the arse out of them because of the heat — and we parted on apparently friendly and trusting terms'.

Hughes' stubborn refusal to go near the Shimbun Alley press club, his outspokenness, loyalty to friends irrespective of their faults and his rejection of implied demands to drop now dangerous friends — Russians for instance — made him enemies.

He was vitriolic in his condemnation of communists — 'commie dogs' he called them — yet he would not be brainwashed into hating individuals who had been his friends because political winds were blowing from another direction; perhaps they were bad communists. He was to say later that the only good communists were bad communists.

So he continued openly to see his friends from the Russian Embassy. Sometimes he would go swimming with them and at other times drank with them and he walked the thin line dangerously between the divided camps of the East and West. Gossip about him left him unmoved. He did not react when a visiting Australian minister called him a 'renegade' but he tucked the reference away for use at a suitable time. 'Sometimes the wounds are secret but they still ache', he told a friend. He was fond of quoting something Ian Fleming had said to him: 'A man is only as good as his friends'.

He was equally fond of quoting a list of precepts which he said provided a guide for rookie foreign correspondents. The precepts were laid down by Hotsumi Ozaki, the Japanese right-hand of master spy Richard Sorge. Like Sorge, Ozaki was hanged. Hughes knew them both slightly during his pre-war time in Japan. Ozaki, according to Hughes, milked Japanese reporters and diplomats and fed the material he gleaned to Sorge who in turn transmitted it to his Russian masters. He was a better newspaperman than Sorge, who used the cover to disguise his real job. The Japanese wrote the precepts which Hughes admired primarily as a guide for intelligence agents while claiming that they were also followed by virtually every top foreign newsman.

They were: first, 'Never give the impression you are eager to obtain news. Men who are engaged in important affairs will refuse to talk to you if they suspect your motive is to collect information.'

Second, 'If you give the impression you have more information than your prospective informant he will give with a smile'.

Third, 'Informal dinner parties are an excellent setting for news gathering'.

The precepts went on to nine, with the last two reading: 'You must cultivate trust and confidence in you on the part of those you are using as informants so you can pump them without seeming unnatural'; and 'You cannot be a good intelligence man unless you yourself are a good source of information'.

Hughes particularly commended the first, second and the final precept.

His own attitude to news gathering was to adopt the avuncular, cheerful and seemingly careless approach. He could drink copiously and eat the most exotic food, swap repartee with bar girls and madams and fellow correspondents and diplomats and businessmen, yet continue to show an absorbing interest in whatever he was told. He shunned taking notes — his long-ago training in Pelmanism honed his memory — and kept voluminous files of newspaper clippings and official records. Like many top newspapermen he had a surface knowledge of hundreds of diverse subjects, and he appeared knowledgeable in most of them by quick-wittedness in the art of diversion when he got out of his depth. He worked best in the mornings, writing his stories first in long hand, then whipping them into shape when he typed them on a tinny little portable. He wasn't very mechanically minded and when a ribbon broke he would often wrap a huge hand around the portable and carry it to a friend for fixing.

All this time Ian Fleming encouraged him, quick to pass on a tip through his unrivalled sources and ready at all times to support him. Fleming's cable address in London was 'vagabond'.

7 Burgess & Maclean in Moscow

'The big one, of course, is Burgess and Maclean', Fleming said. He was walking with Hughes through the wintery Green Park in London after lunch at his club. 'We want an interview with Bulganin and Khrushchev too — and that's the ostensible reason for your Moscow assignment.' He fitted another cigarette into the long ebony holder he affected. 'But I've got a feeling this may be the time when the Russians will produce our friends. They won't want their British visit spoiled by questions from Fleet Street about a couple of renegades.'

Earlier, over lunch, the two men planned Hughes' visit in detail. He was to go to Moscow, install himself into a leading hotel and begin a ruthless campaign to flush out the two British diplomats. Anthony Burgess and Donald Maclean had disappeared in 1951, precipitating one of the greatest spy scandals of the century. A huge dragnet flung out by Fleet Street newspapers, costing thousands of pounds, and a slightly less enthusiastic hunt by British Intelligence failed to unearth them, although it was known that they were in the Soviet Union. Their disappearance had proved a great embarassment to the British Government and Intelligence authorities and anger to those in the United States. Many people felt that security authorities, in Britain at least, would not be unhappy if the diplomats never surfaced. There were too many unanswered questions and too many other shadowy figures.

Maclean was a rising star in the Foreign Office, destined for greater office, when suspicions about him hardened. He returned to Britain from the United States, where he had been head of the American department, and was about to face his inquisitors. He had been a communist since his Cambridge University days of the thirties, and over the years had dutifully fed to Moscow enormous quantities of material available to him in his various posts.

On his thirty-eighth birthday, 25 May 1951, he worked as

diligently as ever. He knew he was under tight surveillance but when his friend Guy Burgess, also a committed communist, telephoned him at the Foreign Office and suggested an improbable dinner that Friday night he realized his exposure was imminent. Burgess, who had already been dismissed from his less exalted posts in the establishment, got his tip that Maclean must flee from sources not exposed until many years later. Burgess picked up Maclean from his home outside London in a hire car and they drove to Southampton, caught the cross-channel ferry *Falaise* to the continent and disappeared. The story broke two weeks later. It blew up into one of the greatest scandals Britain had known and its repercussions have resounded ever since.

Ian Fleming, with his own background in war-time intelligence and with impeccable sources, was in a better position than most to assess the situation He was high-principled, utterly loyal to the establishment and a patriot. Yet he was a committed newspaperman.

He and Hughes revelled in the intrigue preparatory to the onslaught on Moscow when they laid their plans over long lunches and strolls through Green Park in December 1955. Hughes had been summoned to London for leave and talks. There was a James Bond touch about the whole operation: an enigmatic cable to Hughes in Tokyo; his reply to the slightly romantic 'Vagabond' address; his installation in a luxury apartment and the briefings he had from quiet men warning him about pitfalls. All had a touch of excitement that appealed to the romantic in both men. Hughes was the man of action that Fleming saw for himself, and he was more at ease with the big man than with the intellectuals of his aristocratic background. He liked Hughes' capacity for fun, his wit, his 'European mind' — as he categorized Hughes' intelligence — and the lust he brought to everything in his life from eating and drinking to work and to women.

Fleming had a drawling, laconic style of speech that contrasted with Hughes' rapid-fire delivery. 'I think Khrushchev is ready for an exclusive interview. Try to get it and of course home-in on the Burgess-Maclean thing', he said.

'It's our prerogative, of course, isn't it?' Hughes replied drily.

'Of course.' Fleming smiled, 'I'm surprised at the implied doubt Dikko'.

He referred to the speculation that Khrushchev was about to openly criticize Stalin. 'He could use the Twentieth Congress as his forum for this. He might be carried away with euphoria and lash out rashly in other directions too. On the Burgess-Maclean thing you could go for the angle that he will be embarrassed on his upcoming British visit by questions about them. It would be better to clear the air sort of thing. He'll be harassed from the moment he sets foot in England unless he does. And the *Sunday Times* — you, Dikko — will be the right vehicle.'

Fleming tried unsuccessfully to talk Hughes into taking at least one bottle of Bourbon whiskey in the supply of good Scotch Hughes packed in his bag. 'Comparable piss', Hughes said indignantly. And he told his boss about the story attributed to Mark Twain about the relative merits of Scotch and Bourbon. Two fishermen, drinking steadily, were arguing about the relative strengths of the whiskies. The first fisherman dipped his live prawn bait into Bourbon, then hauled in a huge catch. The Scotch drinker also dipped a prawn into his Scotch. When he hauled in his catch the prawn had a stranglehold on a giant writhing trout and dumped it triumphantly before the Bourbon drinker.

London was cold and miserable when Hughes flew out, but it was mild compared to the icy blast that hit him when he stopped over at Leningrad, via an equally cold Helsinki. Soviet customs passed him through without trouble and calmed his anxiety about his treasured supply of Scotch. One official suggested, rightly as it turned out, that Hughes — who he referred to as 'Hoojis', — would develop a taste for vodka when the Scotch was depleted. He watched approvingly when Hughes threw back three sample snorts provided gratis in the dining room.

On the final leg of the flight to Moscow he was entertained by the six other passengers on the spartan aircraft. They were returning from Finland after a series of shows there. One thought Hughes was German. 'Deutsch?' he inquired.

Hughes was indignant, his memories fresh of the 1940 Tokyo days when Japanese confused his bulky figure with Germans. 'Deutsch?' he replied angrily. He tried his newly acquired basic Russsian. 'Nyet. Nyet. I am Australian.' His fellow passengers were delighted. A flautist among the entertainers tried 'God Save The Queen', another produced a flask of vodka. By the time they reached Moscow there was 'a degree of hilarity' on board, as Hughes put it.

Moscow, too, was terribly cold, but he was soon snug in Room 123 — the Persian suite — of the rambling National Hotel, with its unrivalled view of the Kremlin's daunting red walls, towers, and its five huge stars. He was greeted on his arrival by the obligatory Russian beauty. Her flashing smile and invitation, in good English, to let her know if there was anything he wanted tempted him for a moment until he remembered the dire warnings given him in London.

Within a couple of days of his arrival, his new-boy zeal had got him an interview with the chief of the press section of the Soviet Foreign Office, and with one of Khrushchev's secretaries. He gave the Khrushchev aide an outline of the type of questions he would ask the Soviet leader. He was buoyant. According to plan he sent off a cable to 'Vagabond' couched in terms he and Fleming had agreed upon in London: 'Assure my mother eyem in buoyant health' the cable read.

'Buoyant' would tell Fleming how he rated his chances.

Back in the hotel he met unexpectedly with a Russian friend of Tokyo days. They greeted each other effusively. Hughes inquired about other friends and was assured they too were in Moscow and would call on him soon in Room 123. They parted happily. But that was the last meeting and for the next three months he neither heard nor saw anything more of them.

Hughes was elated when he first met his Russian friend and he had mental visions of a renewal of their Tokyo days together. But as the days passed and nobody called he was puzzled, then hurt, and finally angry. Resident correspondents told him he was being naive to expect Moscow friendships with Russians as in the free-wheeling Tokyo times.

Many of the resident correspondents were friends of Hughes; others, like Reuter's Sidney Weiland, he met for the first time. Weiland was inclined to be a loner but he was a thoroughly professional journalist dedicated to his job of providing fast, accurate reports, devoid of sensationalism. He, with the others, helped the new boy Hughes with background on the Moscow scene. But all of them had a slightly cynical view of Hughes' professed intention to be the first 'special' to get an exclusive interview with Khrushchev. As for Burgess and Maclean, they had been trying for years to unearth them and they didn't rate Hughes' chances highly. Everyone watched everyone else, however. Some of the old hands from the Far East scene, knowing Hughes' penchant for cultivating his sources, and slightly suspicious of his arrival, kept a wary eye on him. Why did he arrive at this particular time, they asked each other. Twentieth Congress? Khrushchev's visit to England?

Opposite the cable office in Gorky street was the favourite drinking spot for correspondents. They gathered there every day. If one did not turn up there were anxious questions: 'What's that cunning old bastard up to today?' On one occasion a Russian jumped the queue and there was a slight altercation. It ended when Hughes pushed the Russian to one side. The man slipped on the icy pavement. Hughes bent to help him to his feet but two Russian policemen who had been watching stolidly grabbed the unhappy queue jumper and dragged him away. 'He was shouting something that I interpreted as "big bastard" and was frothing at the mouth. I was petrified and grinned idiotically at the policemen. But they didn't say a word to me.'

He joined with the other correspondents in visits to the civilized sanctuary of various embassies. All the time however he was bombarding officials with appeals for interviews. A subdued Christmas passed. Fleming's cables were taking on a note of urgency, along the lines of 'Thanks, good story on congress but . . .'. The Congress itself, with its rejection of Stalin and his methods, together with Khrushchev's soaring eminence, gave Hughes and the others plenty of good copy, but it was not what Hughes wanted.

And all the time there was the gossip: Khrushchev would not give an exclusive interview to anybody; Burgess and Maclean had been seen at the Bolshoi; they were in Warsaw; they were in gaol. The blasé resident correspondents even dreamed up their own cynical reply to the interminable question, particularly from the fresh-faced specials like Hughes, of 'Anything doing today?' 'Nothing much', was the yawned reply. 'Of course there are a couple of boring little men, called Burgess and Maclean or something who keep trying to wangle a lunch out of me. I just keep telling them to bugger off.'

Hughes set a record, for somebody who didn't like ballet, by going to see *Swan Lake* at the Bolshoi ten times. He listened to the same cocktail party talk night after night. He would race back to his room at the National, convinced that some small talk at one of the press conferences, embassy parties and correspondents' gatherings meant that today was the big day. There would be a message setting up the Khrushchev interview and he would finally get to ask the great man the one question that was haunting him: what of Burgess and Maclean? And night after night there was nothing. The beauty at the reception desk would smile sympathetically at him and the concierge at the head of the stairs would grin her confirmation that another wasted day had passed.

His supply of whisky had dwindled alarmingly. He took to vodka though it added to his loneliness and growing sense of failure. At times he would stand at the huge windows of his Persian suite, wondering about the strangers passing below on Gorky street. He began to feel he knew many of them. One in particular fascinated him. He was a man without legs who propelled himself along the snowy street on a little wheeled trolley. At precisely 8 each morning the legless man would inject himself into the traffic and dexterously grab the rear bumper bar of a trolley bus and be hurled along behind the bus and up the hill to his destination. He seemed to use one hand to wave to Hughes.

Another man in the thronged street did actually wave to the lonely man in the Room 123. He was a good-humoured looking traffic policeman, and they would exchange distant greetings each morning. Sometimes Hughes would pantomime pouring himself a glass of vodka; the policeman would peer ostentatiously at his watch and shake his head disapprovingly. Too early for that, he was saying.

Hughes would enter into the spirt of the little game and lift a teapot instead of a vodka bottle. The policeman would grin his approval. He was often at the same spot when the day's traffic was building to a crescendo late in the afternoon, and they would grin and wave to each other and continue the charade.

Ian Fleming's cable on 24 January was the dreaded recall

summons. It said the primary object of the assignment appeared unattainable and Hughes should return to London by 12 February.

The final humiliating blow fell for Hughes the following day. A colleague of the war in the Western Desert, Graham Stanford, roared back from Leningrad with one of the prizes Hughes had lusted for: an exclusive interview with Khrushchev. He ran to the Persian room to tell Hughes. 'I've got it, your grace', he said grinning hugely.

Hughes was pleased for his old friend. Inwardly he raged, reminding himself of the broken promises of Tokyo and Moscow and the high hopes he and Fleming had nurtured. He had failed. His prestigious *Sunday Times* had been beaten by the *News of the World*, a comparable urchin in the newspaper world. He consoled himself, first with vodka, then with a smug justification that the *News of the World*'s huge circulation had swung the issue against him.

At the end of January he cabled Fleming: 'As directed eyell retreat exmoscow February 12. Despondent regards.' He began to wind up his affairs, snarling at the concierge's greetings and ignoring the flashing smiles of the Russian beauty at the desk.

On Thursday he plodded through the snow to his bank to collect a last remittance. When he got back to the hotel the beauty called him over excitedly. There was a message for him from the Soviet Foreign Office. He should call them immediately When he got through, a suave voice on the other end of the line told him, without any explanation: 'Mr Hoojis, Foreign Minister Molotov will be happy to grant your application for an interview and will see you at noon on Saturday'.

He was puzzled. He had made no application to see Molotov, who was then a fading figure on the Soviet scene, but he accepted with alacrity. He poured a slug of vodka and settled down to draft a series of questions to put to the Foreign Minister. He began in his usual charming way, drafting his submissions carefully. He read them over. What the hell, he thought. Why not stop this diplomatic nonesense and hit out with a bullwhip? So he tore up his list of submissions, poured another slug, and wound fresh paper into his portable. He would get to Khrushchev through Molotov.

He headed his memorandum: 'For President Bulganin and Prime Minister Khrushchev. This memorandum is intended for your eyes because the points it raises will affect the success of your impending visit to England.'

He began to warm up: 'I would strongly urge you to abandon at once your protracted, futile and absurd policy of silence about the two British defectors, Donald Maclean and Guy Burgess.

'In your meetings with the British press, you will be subjected constantly to questions about these two men.

'Reports are now circulating in Fleet Street that they are dead or in

96

a Russian prison. You must recognize that the monstrous nonsense of this "We do not know" formula will utterly discredit your mission, and raise doubts of the sincerity of all friendly overtures and speeches which you may make in the United Kingdom. You will not be amused by the way in which London newspaper cartoonists will ridicule you.

'Mr Khrushchev's continued line of foolish denial makes it clear that your so-called advisers are completely ignorant of the deep and abiding British public interest in the Maclean-Burgess mystery, into which the British Government is now conducting yet another select committee inquiry.'

He read what he had written. Use the bludgeon, Hughes. He tapped away again: 'You would be wise to produce Burgess and Maclean with some sort of agreed explanation of their actions before you leave Moscow'.

He decided to slip in a small escape route: 'I do not see that there is any real problem in the fact that until now the Soviet Government has chosen to deny that it knows anything of the two men. It could be expected that a friendly government which gave sanctuary to aliens in difficulty would also respect their expressed wish at the outset that no statement be made of their presence and activities until and unless they so desired. In view of changed circumstances — apart from your own immediate and vital self-interest — that original attitude by Maclean and Burgess, which the Soviet has so scrupulously respected, might well have changed also.

'I confess cheerfully that I myself have the most selfish interest as a working British newspaperman in recommending release of this story while I am in Moscow.

'If you decide to accept my advice I naturally expect you to give me the benefit of the story. This bargain is implicit in my recommendation. I leave Moscow on Sunday week, February 12. If you agree, Maclean and Burgess should make their appearance on Saturday, February 11, and the deadline that day for my newspaper, the *Sunday Times*, should be, say 5 pm.'

He signed it with a flourish and read it back to himself, grinning at his lordly tone in the 'If you decide to accept my advice . . . ' segment. That should stir the buggers up, he thought.

He drafted some questions he planned to ask Molotov and set off for his noon interview. Molotov, normally severe, was cheerful and relaxed when Hughes was ushered in for the ninety-minute talk, the last he was to give to a Western newspaperman. He was a Stalinist and he knew that the new broom Khrushchev was beginning to wield so forcefully would sweep him into oblivion but he gave no hint to Hughes that he was on the way out.

Although there was an interpreter present, Hughes had the feeling that Molotov undertood everything said to him. He told Hughes he led a normal life. 'I get up at a normal hour and do a normal days work. I go to bed at a normal hour', he said. Then dryly: 'We Soviet communists are really quite normal people, Mr Hughes'.

Among the points he made once the interview got away from the sparring opening remarks were that there should be more face-to-face conferences between heads of state; there should be treaties of friendship between the Soviet Union and Britain and France. He called for the peaceful reunification of East and West Germany and reaffirmed his belief that the Soviet Union, China and Eastern bloc countries made the most trusting and dependable allies.

At the end of the interview Hughes reached into his pocket for his letter to Khrushchev and Bulganin. He handed it to Molotov.

'You know my background, sir.'

'Yes, Mr Hughes. Of course.'

'Well sir I would like you to read this memorandum for the President and the Prime Minister. It is urgent and important.'

Molotov bowed, shook hands and as Hughes left he handed the memorandum to his interpreter, who began to read it aloud.

The *Sunday Times* featured Hughes' interview on their front page and Fleming cabled his congratulations.

The next week went slowly and Hughes' hopes died a little more each day. He did not really expect a reply, he told himself. The memo was too tough, too opinionated, and lacked every diplomatic touch. By Saturday he was feeling sorry for himself. An abscess on a tooth was throbbing and the more he thought about Fleming's disappointment, the more it throbbed.

He began to drink again as the dusk closed in and by 5 pm — his deadline — he was half drunk and had given up. Earlier in the day he had stood at the window and raised his glass to the policeman on Gorky street, but he did not substitute the teapot for a vodka bottle when the policeman shook his head.

At 7.30 the phone rang. He answered it surlily.

For a moment he could not understand the loud, urgent voice on the other end. He switched the earpiece from the swollen side of his face to his other ear. 'What are you talking about for God sake?'

The caller slowed down. 'Mr Hoojis', he said, articulating carefully, 'can you please come round to Room 101.'

'All right. All right mug.'

He threw some more clothes into the bag. No hurry, he thought. Just the hotel manager, a civil fellow, wanting to give me a farewell drink. He finished the last of his vodka. The phone rang again. This time the caller spoke slowly but forcefully. 'Mr Hoojis, please come now.'

He lurched a bit walking down the corridor, then straightened up. Musn't show the commie dogs the decadent side of the West. Dignity,

Hoojis, dignity. He knocked on the door of Room 101 and without waiting, entered.

Five men, silent, were ranged around a small, round table, white-clothed and bare. Two of the men stood up. The others watched, still silent. The taller of the two who stood smiled tentatively and extended his hand. 'I am Donald Maclean.' The second man, sure, grinned engagingly. 'And I am Guy Burgess.'

Hughes sobered instantly. Without thought, his words came straight from Sherlock Holmes, 'Gentlemen', he said, 'this is the end of a long trail.'

His heart was hammering. He was aware suddenly of the pain in his face. He mumbled. 'This is an extrordinary shock.'

Burgess still grinning, nodded at Hughes' swollen face. 'Who hit you?'

Reuter correspondent Sidney Weiland was the only other man at the table Hughes recognized. The other two sat stolidly, watching. Burgess and Maclean each produced a packet of Russian Prima cigarettes. Weiland took out a packet of British Players and offered them around.

'Thanks but we prefer these. They're better for us because we smoke about sixty a day', Burgess said.

He reached for a brown despatch case at his feet, opened it and produced four copies of a typed document. 'One for Tass, one for *Pravda*, one for Reuters. And this one,' he winked at Hughes, 'is for the *Sunday Times*.'

The statement was headed: 'Statement by G. Burgess and D. Maclean' and covered three pages. Weiland said: 'Can we read this statement through first, or are you proposing to read it?'

Maclean looked at Burgess, obviously the leader. 'This is a strange position to be in', Burgess said. 'We don't have much to say apart from what's in the statement.'

Weiland tried another approach. 'Hardly fair, not giving us a chance to read the statement and ask questions.'

Burgess brushed aside Weiland's ploy. He stood up, and Maclean followed. 'Don't try to tell me that', he said laughing. 'I've given out too many statements to the world press in my time not to know what a story I'm giving you fellows tonight.'

Both Hughes and Weiland were still stunned. Hughes tried yet another tack. He asked where they were living. 'In Moscow', they chorused. Maclean then said his wife and children were with him. They headed for the door, Hughes and Weiland with them. The two other men in the room, correspondents for the Russian news agency Tass and the Russian newspaper *Pravda*, still sat at the table, obviously puzzled by Hughes' and Weiland's excitement.

Hughes raced for his room, scattering two portly Russian delegates to the Twentieth Congress walking sedately in the opposite direction. Weiland walked downstairs with the two diplomats, neither of whom spoke. Outside the hotel on the pavement they shook hands with Weiland, crossed the street and were swallowed in the murky night.

Upstairs in the hotel, Hughes scooped up his portable, some copy and carbon paper. There was a sudden knock on his door. Dear God, no, he thought, 'Come in.' The blonde concierge waddled in with his laundry bill. He paid it, shoving a wad of notes at her, then tore out of the Persian suite on his way to the cable office.

He had the biggest story of his life; the story the world had been waiting for. He knew that the brilliant Weiland, with his unrivalled knowlege of communications, would get his factual story into London first. So he would angle his story on the findings and the atmosphere and the way the renegades looked. Perfect timing for the *Sunday Times*, its presses already beginning to thrum in distant London.

He went flat on his back within metres of leaving his hotel, but he balanced his typewriter and the precious statement to keep them from the muck of the street. He was not wearing a top coat or overshoes. Passing Russians helped him to his feet and he started running again. Again he went down but was up again and running within seconds. At the cable office he hammered out his story — one copy for transmission, one for the censors, one to show any cuts the censors made and one for himself. Only then did he relax.

Weiland's story hit first, so when Hughes' 'I was there' came in within minutes of Reuters' first flash, the *Sunday Times* cleared their front page. 'Burgess and Maclean Appear in Moscow', the banner headline ran. 'The *Sunday Times* is the only paper represented at disclosure'.

The story was splashed in newspapers all over the Western world. In Sydney and Melbourne Hughes' old newspaper mates grinned with approval when his by-lined story appeared. 'Tonight, in room 101 of the Hotel National, overlooking Red Square and the Kremlin, I met and talked with Donald Maclean and Guy Burgess, the missing British diplomats . . .'.

The statement by the two former diplomats that followed carried no surprises. Neither admitted being secret agents. They said they were patriots, but had decided to go to the Soviet Union. 'There alone', the statement said in its strange, third person tone, 'there appeared to both to be some chance of putting into practice in some form the convictions they had always held.'

The statement ended: 'As the result of living in the U.S.S.R. we both of us are convinced that we were right in doing what we did'.

Hughes was walking elatedly through the Saturday night crowds from the cable office to the National Hotel. When he got back he

100

heard that the BBC had broadcast the Reuter story of the re-emergence of the renegades. He was in a state of euphoria, and in fancy he saw the rush by other resident correspondents to catch up on the 'beat' he and Weiland had achieved. It was the best story of his life. He decided to bask in the glory for a while, and not even the pain from his abscessed teeth detracted from his feelings of enormous achievement.

Fleming's cable of congratulations added to Hughes' happiness. But any thoughts he was harbouring about staying in Moscow to try to do follow-up stories were dissipated when Fleming instructed him to return to London. He knew Fleming was right: in London, safe from censorship, he could continue to write in detail about the renegades.

Before he left he made one last pilgrimage. He went out into the traffic of Gorky street and found the policeman who had helped him through his lonely patches. The traffic cop saw him coming, imperiously stopped the traffic and strode across to Hughes and shook hands. Drivers watched and waited as the two mimed their drinking game. 'I felt like giving him a furtive blessing', Hughes said later, 'but the drivers of the stalled cars were looking a bit hostile and puzzled as we waved our arms about and grinned.'

Hughes arrived in London to something of a celebrity's welcome. Newspapermen, radio and television commentators pumped him for every possible detail. He was guest speaker at a lunch arranged by the *Sunday Times*, was quizzed by some of the unobtrusive men who had briefed him earlier, and had long and happy lunches with Fleming. Lord Kemsley gave him a personal cheque equivalent to about $2000 and his expense account for his seventy-two days saga in Moscow, amounting to about $4000, was passed without a murmur from the watchdogs in the accounts department. He was given an extra bonus of a few days in Paris, where he celebrated a riotous fiftieth birthday, and finally climbed on board a plane for the long haul back to Tokyo.

He was still euphoric. His friendship with Fleming was strong and close, his future with the *Sunday Times* and the *Economist* was secure and, above all, he had cracked one of the great mysteries of the decade. He was going back to his beloved Tokyo. He was high on the hog.

8 Alcoholics Synonymous

The furore over Burgess and Maclean continued without let-up as Hughes flew back to Tokyo, with Fleet Street concentrating on finding the 'third man' who, it was popularly and correctly held, had tipped off the defectors. Earlier, in October 1955, Kim Philby had been named in the House of Commons as the elusive third man. Prime Minister Macmillan rejected this assumption. Nevertheless, Philby had to resign from the British Foreign service because of his former association with Burgess. Subsequently, Philby went to Beirut as correspondent of the *Observer* and the *Economist.*

Friends of Hughes who also knew Philby during his years in the Middle East from 1956 to 1963 had no inkling that the quiet man in the baggy suit and desert boots wasn't what he purported to be. He kept a low profile, did his job professionally. He was notable principally because of his penchant for drinking heavily without getting drunk and for his appeal to women. None of them had any idea that he was still a devoted Soviet agent. Perhaps a few suspected that he was still working for British intelligence. That is until he disappeared in January 1963 and the Soviet Union announced he had been granted political asylum in Moscow.

Prior to this, Hughes shared with much of Fleet Street the gut feeling that Philby wasn't entirely clean and that one day he would be produced dramatically in Moscow like Burgess and Maclean. And he resolved that, on that day, he would again be the correspondent on the spot. He would work on his contacts in the Far East and continue to ignore the gossip that he personally had some intelligence ties. He would even encourage speculation by jocularly agreeing with the innuendo: 'Of course, your grace, of course'.

Whether intentionally or not, he used terms like 'your grace' and 'monseigneur' as a subtle way of controlling and dominating many of the people with whom he mixed. He used jocular flattery or aggression to set relationships on a path suitable to himself. It often had the effect of making people play his game and was a way of gaining an advantage. Few of the people he mixed with could afford to be seen as humourless or 'square', so they felt a warmth and pride in his comradeship. He had few close personal friends, but hundreds of acquaintances. When he thought about it, he concluded that he was too wary of close ties to test them out on anyone. So, in a way, he made a mockery of many relationships and turned them into a game. It was a very successful game.

When he got back to Tokyo, another highly sensational story broke in Moscow. It was Khrushchev's secret speech denouncing Stalin. The Russian censors held the story for about a week but the resourceful Sid Weiland flew his man from Moscow to Stockholm to file from there.

Hughes and others had seen hints at the Twentieth Congress. Now it was out in the open he used his Far East datelines for erudite pieces for the *Sunday Times* and the *Economist,* forecasting the way Soviet policy was shaping under the 'new boy' Khrushchev.

But Tokyo was becoming expensive and was not the listening post to China and to other South East Asian countries, still convulsing from their colonial past. Japan was too settled; too much dominated by the vision the occupation years had brought.

So Hughes moved his headquarters to Hong Kong where the pulse of the whole area beat more strongly. He left behind his Japanese mistress and a house he had bought. Their relationship had soured. Although he regretted leaving a country he had grown to love, he had no regrets about ending this one personal relationship.

His long and mostly valued relationship with the Packer organization in Sydney ended too. There was a note of acrimony about this ending. He had accepted an offer from the Murdoch organization to join the then fledgling empire that Rupert Murdoch was fashioning so brilliantly. Murdoch offered him twice the money Packer was paying.

Murdoch made the offer when he passed through Tokyo. He also told Hughes that he planned a new newspaper. He thought of calling it the *Australian.* 'Do you think that presumptuous?', he asked. 'Not at all', Hughes said. 'First class.' He liked Murdoch. The man's restless energy and drive appealed to him. He had known Murdoch's father in Melbourne, and like most other Australian newspapermen he wanted to see if the son would match his father's brilliance. Murdoch's father had once offered him a job on the Melbourne *Herald* and Hughes often wondered how different his life might have been had he accepted.

So Hughes cabled his resignation and followed it with a letter of conciliatory explanation. He said that the money Packer was paying was not sufficient to keep him, despite his part-time work for the

Sunday Times and the *Economist*: 'I'd be forced to play a one string fiddle in Tokyo's Ginza to pay the rent'.

Packer reacted furiously. He shot off a cable to Hughes — 'On your way Judas'. Equally irate, Hughes hammered out his reply, marked it urgent and collect, and marched to the cable office to file it. It said: 'If I am to play Judas to your Jesus I don't know where Judas kissed Jesus but you know where you can kiss me'. When Packer got the cable he was still angry but he showed Hughes' reply to his dismissal notice to various executives of the *Daily Telegraph*. 'Look what the bastard sent me', he was reputed to have said, grinning at the audacity.

From Hong Kong Hughes ranged throughout his Far East diocese, visiting Laos, Burma and any other centre where news was breaking.

Of Laos, he said the Korean 'secular government stands like a pillar of rectitude in contrast to the corruption rampant in this land of a million elephants'. But the compensations included excellent food, ample supplies of French wine and crisp and sunny weather. 'The beauty of the women is, alas, equalled only by their accessibility', he wrote to a friend. 'By gracious dispensation of the Vatican I was relieved of my vows of temperance during the visit. I have, of course, far outgrown or trampled underfoot other calls of the flesh.'

In Cambodia he wrote about the rival United States and communist countries' aid pouring into the troubled and gentle country. While his material was primarily serious, he was always looking for off-beat, humourous stories. He found one such piece when he saw a rogue elephant, obviously suffering from mange, 'trying to rub its arse on a tree', near the royal court. The religious tradition of Cambodia held that elephants were sacred and must be treated with reverence and honour. They could be Buddha in the next reincarnation. This particular elephant, obviously in pain, charged a tiny red bus, a gift from Peking, in which there were six Chinese jugglers returning from an entertainment tour. 'The elephant, trumpeting, worried by his sore arse, butted the bus against a temple wall and tried furiously to overturn it and trample it.

'Inside the bus the terrified jugglers hammered in seasick frenzy against the locked door of the teetering, shuddering vehicle. A nearby imaginative court musician tried playing a sweet flute to try to pacify the elephant.' It was finally calmed down and the court chamberlain explained the situation to Hughes and offered some advice. 'Mr Hoojis, if you see the rogue elephant scrape the backside against the palm tree, toss the head and make the screeching noise do not be afraid — afraid to run.'

Hughes said the incident embarassed court officials, not because of the animal's aggression but because some might see the attack as a breach of neutralism by the sacred beast for having chosen the communist bus for attack. 'However', he reported happily, 'by chance the same elephant ran amok in the boulevard the following day and with a cunning flanking charge he trapped and tossed an unwary and elderly visitor over the wall into a temple compound. The elephant's chosen victim happened to be an American technician with the U.S. aid mission to Cambodia. Thus was restored the delicate balance between East and West.'

The relevance of the story, he wrote, was that it emphasized the essential point that the West and Asia must make a vigorous and sympathetic effort to understand the mystifying scene. There was always uncertainty about the reception and effects of foreign aid. The country giving the aid could often be perversely wrong, innocently perhaps, but the recipient was always right. It was wise to prepare for emergencies: 'And if you don't like the place and you are unwilling to be patient, flexible and realistic you'd better get out and not be afraid to run'.

Summing up his tour, he wrote that China could easily take the Far East within the following decade. He said the area was dominated by the awakening, the resurgence and the tribulations of the Chinese dragon which Napoleon hoped, many years earlier, would be allowed to sleep undisturbed. China was isolated from the rest of the world, at bitter enmity with the United States, estranged even from its ideological partner the Soviet Union, and was enduring another of its age old ordeals of hunger. 'But China is struggling forward under ruthless and able rulers who are riding the eastern winds of nationalism.'

He spoke of Mao Tse Tung as a great reformer. 'His nation, reared on agnosticism, is ripe for revenge and eager for reform. Mao took China and he could take most of Asia.' The challenge to the free world, Hughes felt, was to prevent 190 million people of South East Asia from being duped into acceptance of communism.

This could happen under the disguise of national sovereignty and 'democratic' self-determination, or by being riddled and sapped by communist infiltration or squeezed out by communist aggression. 'The legacy of colonialism — that abominated word — is a heavy one. The legacy is often unfair, undeserved and misrepresented. But this is where the need for scrupulous respect for native sensitivity is imperative.'

In his remarkably far-sighted piece, written in 1962, he said communism could not be contained in Asia by Western arms 'but only by the will and effort of the people of the non-communist states nourished as they are by high living standards'. If the West could not summon the patience, resolution and resources to undertake the long and formidable task of helping the under-developed and uncommitted nations of the Far East to stand on their own feet, it would be wise to recognize the struggle was lost. 'Then they should get out of Asia without further waste of time and money and hope.'

In a direct swipe at his own country, Hughes said geography, economics and politics must inevitably redirect Australian international policy and reshape Australian migration prejudice. Australia could not indefinitely ignore the recognition of China. This was an unpopular hypothesis at that time.

Hughes had the rare ability to be able to write an interesting story on anything because he 'always pulled out the honey' as a fellow correspondent put it. Not all his stories stood up, of course. Some were far wide of the mark. Lee Kuan Yew and the communists was one such.

He flew to Singapore in 1959 to cover the island state's elections. He was becoming more and more obsessed with a belief that communism was beginning to take over virtually the whole of South East Asia — even Japan was suspect in his view — and this obsession clouded his judgment when he met the enigmatic, brilliant Lee. He formed the opinion that Lee was collaborating with the communists and that Singapore was about to fall into the orbit of a regime he hated.

He was not alone in this view. Some of the world leaders had a similar fear. But some of Hughes' fellow correspondents saw Lee then as the strong man he was to become and they tried to ease Hughes away from his hardline approach. Hughes stayed with this line, however, and his story to the *Sunday Times* saw Lee's victory as a victory for communism. Within the week of the election Lee put the communists in gaol, abolished the party and was in complete control.

Hughes went to see Lee and apologized. He said he had written a stupid story. Lee agreed but accepted the apology graciously. He told Hughes that he had used the communists whereas they thought they were using him. He agreed he had put them in gaol, 'But they would have put me underground'.

In later years Hughes was to go back to Singapore many times, and whenever possible he would interview the man he considered one of the great statesmen of his time. He ruefully touched on his gaffe over Lee Kuan Yew in a letter to a friend. Reporting, he said, was at best a hasty, prickling and imperfect trade abounding in shallows and miseries: 'There is no ageing newspaperman whose psyche has not been scarred by ancient wounds of bad error and worse misjudgment. The wounds may be secret but they still ache.'

He ranged over his vast 'diocese', always in his light safari suit and clutching his miniscule portable in one hand and a small case in the other. Colleagues were amazed when he would produce from the small case a suit for formal occasions, a fresh safari suit, underwear, shoes, toilet articles and odd books. People he met for the first time often were puzzled — and some resentful — of his 'your grace' greeting. Some of them, too, felt strongly about his aggressive and uncompromising attitude, his 'commie dog' references. But few, if any, remained untouched by the sheer force of his personality.

His loyalty to friends and his generosity were sustaining strengths that even the rare 'knockers' recognized. He looked, and mostly acted, the part of the tough Sydney reporter, mocking polish, yet the quality of his writing refuted this image.

Hong Kong itself was rapidly usurping Tokyo in his affections. It was as free-wheeling as Tokyo was in the occupation days, although Hughes saw the colony at first as a suburb of Tokyo. It was the last of the colonies, a gourmet's paradise, a shipper's dream and Hughes revelled in the bohemian atmosphere. He saw it as 'an impudent capitalist residue of Chinese communists derriere.' The millionaire mansions, horrible slums, and teeming and hard working millions combined to bring a zest to the swollen colony and made it a dream location for a foreign correspondent.

He called the city 'ripe and throbbing and bursting' that poured slices down mountain sides and filled in waterfront shadows to make more and more room for the skycrapers and factories and the thousands pouring in from China itself. Hughes called it a 'borrowed place living on borrowed time', giving credit to novelist Han Suyin for the phrase. She was among his many acquaintances and although they argued vehemently about communism, he admired her for her strength of character and her loyalty and her great ability as a writer.

The city was full of characters. High among them, and one of Hughes' dear friends, was Jack Conder, owner of Conder's Bar and one of the best known of the Rabelaisian foreign devils in the colony. Conder was among Hughes' mandarin types. 'He is the formidable mandarin. He portrays in face and presence the popular image of the imperturbable mandarin. He has the true mandarin's pragmatism, honesty and magnetism for loyalty, with the memory of an imperial elephant.'

Conder was in the rare living legend category primarily because of his amazing escape from China. He trekked across the country for more than 2000 kilometres after escaping from the Japanese in Shanghai during the Sino-Japanese conflict. The year was 1943 and China was in turmoil, with Chinese fighting among themselves (as communism split the vast country), and against the Japanese.

A tough, tall Liverpudlian adventurer, Conder got away from his captors one darkly suitable night. He suffered incredible hardships, evaded Japanese patrols and swarming Chinese forces, foraged for food in the ravaged countryside, swam rivers, dodged Japanese spotter planes. His height and bulk made him conspicuous and at times he was mistaken for a roving missionary. Generally the Chinese people helped him, shared their meagre food with him and on one occasion even hid him in a family grave. He stayed in the grave for five hours with spiders and rustling bones for company while Japanese patrols searched vainly overhead. Seven months after he escaped he arrived safely near Hong Kong (Hughes told the full story of Conder's saga in *Foreign Devil*.)

After the war Conder established what was to become one of the world's great bars. It became a Hong Kong landmark, a bohemian meeting place for the famous and the infamous.

Conder was also among the founders of Alcoholics Synonymous, a group of dedicated talkers, drinkers and gourmets who formed their improbable organization on Guy Fawkes Day in 1955. The choice of the founding day had nothing to do with Guy Fawkes; it was simply fortuitous. The habitués of the bar decided to form the organization 'dedicated to alleviating the cares of the past week'. The reasons were a bit negative, yet strangely real in the heady postwar days. 'It was not to further the arts or to advance science and not to encourage any other lofty aspiration', the subsequent manifesto said.

The idea was born when it was realized that the shake of dice to see who would pay for drinks often caused hardship to some of the less well-off in the group. They believed the dice were not attuned to the limited resources of some of the patrons so they evolved a scheme whereby one of the group would act as chairman each Saturday. He would pay for the drinks on his day in the chair, with each member in turn becoming chairman on successive Saturdays. Membership was limited to fewer than twenty. At the first meeting there were eight British members, four American, and four others. There were to be no national boundaries or other restrictions on membership beyond keeping it male.

Each member contributed $5 and when funds built up there would be contributions to charity. Each meeting was to start at 11 am and the chairman would call for the last drink at 11.45. This was in accordance with the then British custom which gave members time for a quick trip back to their offices for a final check before going to lunch at 1 pm. The promotion of the relief of hangovers acquired during the previous twenty-four hours was one of the stated purposes. 'No meeting shall continue beyond the time when members shall have found relief and are about to contract the ailment all over again.'.

Hughes accepted with alacrity when a cherished invitation came to him to join. Newspapermen predominated but businessmen and diplomats also were among the members. Discussion on any subject under the sun was the norm; acrimony was taboo. To some, the boisterous meetings were an escape and to others an entree into a world of gossip and intrigue, but basically good fellowship was the aim.

The club flourished for some twenty-five years, moving from time to time to other premises when the much loved Jack Conder died and his bar eased into legend. On each anniversary of Conder's death, and on the death of other members, a small 'in memorium' notice would appear in Hong Kong newspapers, with the initials 'A S' the only clue to its source.

Hughes always referred to Alcoholics Synonymous as a 'cultural organization' and on his days in the chair he presided with Olympian dignity, ringing the little bell that signalled the need for more drinks with suitable gravity. Guests from all parts of the world would attend the gatherings, with each member limited to one guest.

At one meeting there was a learned discussion about the origin of the word 'dunny'. Hughes raised the subject when he told members he had used the word in the context of 'dunnies for commies' in a piece he wrote for the *Sunday Times*. Ian Fleming had cabled back 'puzzled by use of word dunnies in phrase "would like to build more dunnies for the commies" '. Hughes replied, as he recalled to A S members, saying that dunnies were privies. The bracketed word privies duly appeared after the word when the article was published.

When he raised what he called 'this sensitive semantic point' with fellow scholars at one of the A S cultural gatherings he discovered to his surprise that the word 'dunnies' was exclusively Australian. He had to reconsider this finding, however, when another learned member pointed out that John Buchan might have used the term when he referred to 'the dunnies of the Gorbals'.

He also belonged to another odd organization, the Cigar Smoker's Club. The membership number allotted to him was 007. He would recall to fellow members that he was about twenty-eight when he had his first cigar. He likened them to women. 'They need to be handled properly', he told an intrigued member watching him roll a beautiful Havana cigar between his fingers. 'Treat them gently. Regard every good cigar as potentially the most perfect. After a while they'll succumb and give you great joy. Never, ever, poke a hole in them.'

Additionally there was a thriving Foreign Correspondent's Club in Hong Kong to which he belonged. It was a favourite meeting place for local and transient newspapermen and for most notable visitors. Alcoholics Synonymous and the Cigar Smokers were strictly male only, but at the Foreign Correspondents Club wives and mistresses and girl friends added their spiced version to the rumours, lies and gossip.

The various clubs and the ubiquitous cocktail parties that made up so much of the Hong Kong scene were not time wasters, however. Membership in clubs and attendance at so many social gatherings were obligatory if a correspondent wanted to keep abreast of events.

Hughes went to them all and listened and argued. He had an old world courtliness that appealed to many women. He would kiss their hands. He was genuinely interested — in their views, their thoughts, their children. Any suggestion of chauvinism was negated by his charm and good manners. His output of letters to friends who had passed through his life was almost equalled by the letters he wrote to wives. He had several god children, and to them too he maintained a flow of letters remarkable in such a full life.

With one god child he played noughts and crosses by mail when she was very young. He was attentive to her need of a friend, albeit distant, who walked the line between parental approval and disapproval with enormous care. With each letter to the little girl he would attach a small piece of paper with his noughts and crosses contribution. She in turn would mail him her response. The love and care he poured into his letters to this particular child were, in effect, his way of showing his love for her parents.

In one of her letters the child told him — 'chairman Dikko' she called him — that she badly wanted a puppy, so he told her about two dogs that ran past the window every morning. 'They're very good friends although they look funny together because one is a huge boxer and the other is a tiny Chinese dog. You would think that the very big one would feel very superior with the little dog but he is kind and gentle. They talk to each other a lot when they rub noses and bark.'

Many people, he said, believed that dogs talked to each other. One Prince of Wales, for instance, obviously believed they could also read. He had a message engraved on the collar of his dog to introduce him to other dogs he met. The message said:

'I am His Highness' dog at Kew.
Pray tell me sir, whose dog are you?'

Over the years he pitched the tone of his letters to coincide with the girl's growth and understanding. She wrote to him once telling of her unhappiness about the behaviour of a prefect who had punished her. 'That wretched head girl', Hughes wrote in reply, 'I'll bet she's a pimply, gawky, be-spectacled girl with thick ankles who will never have a boy friend and is jealous of all other girls who enjoy themselves. We'll think of something to do about her —like getting her dentist to tell her it's time she came to see him.'

When she was having trouble with mathematics he told her she must try harder so she could go to university 'and get some sort of degree that in the long run will have nothing whatever to do with wretched maths. Keep concentrating on the sensitive and useful subjects but do try to pass in dull and tedious maths.'

When she told him he looked like Mao Tse Tung he wrote: 'If you're determined to have me look like a commie I guess Mao is the one I'd prefer to look like. Chou En-lai is more handsome but a bit of a sissy I think. Teng Shao-ping is a wretched little midget with crazy eyes who always looks as if he's recovering from a bad attack of flu. Liu Shao-chi looks like a half-witted country bumpkin. Lin Piao

110

should be training ferrets. As for that hideous, giggling, big-toothed Madame Mao — well all I can say is poor Mao.'

Hughes' output was amazing. His work came first of course and he turned in suitable pieces for his Sydney newspapers and long, scholarly stories for the *Sunday Times* and the *Economist*. But in between he wrote letters to friends all over the world. Some of the letters to friends and their wives were gossipy — who was leaving who and why, fights among correspondents, drunken escapades.

Invariably he adopted his familiar biblical tone in his letters and many of them carried, interspersed among the gossip, suitable texts from the Bible to illustrate a particular point. Some of the 'texts' he made up. Most of these letters were irreverently addressed 'very rev. mgr. in J.C.' and others simply 'your grace' or 'very rev. and dear Msgr. (in XT.J.)'

He had some other obsessions. One endearing one was to send off postcards to friends all over the world. Everyone who knew the absent friend would sign it. The finished product, usually adorned with crosses, often looked bedraggled when it arrived at its destination.

One other obsession was about the sense that unification between Australia and New Zealand would make. He believed there should be unification in an Anzac national and constitutional federation. New Zealanders, he would claim, might lack 'the musical Australian accent and their ancestors were not convicts' but they bred better racehorses and their sheep grew better wool. 'The natives happily and instinctively adjust, with a few reservations, on most personal, cultural, sporting and racial issues. Why then does the Tasman separate them into two nations?' he once wrote to an unconvinced New Zealand friend.

One other obsession — and he eased away from this in later years — was that communism could eventually engulf Japan. When he wrote about this he asked, rhetorically, whether Japan, given a world depression and the closing of essential Western markets, would turn to communism? The question, he said, should haunt the West. It was a long-range prediction, he admitted, but Peking never lost sight of it. Within two decades — he was writing in 1960 — he forecast that all of Asia, with the exception of Japan, would pass into a form of communist government, with Peking the Oriental preceptor and exemplar. In the light of the fact that the individualistic Chinese had been so susceptible to communism, would not the disciplined, obedient and mass-minded Japanese be easier prey?

In all this time Hughes never lost his interest in Sherlock Holmes. When he noticed a reference to Holmes in a Shanghai newspaper — he culled every newspaper he could find and had built up a huge personal 'library' for reference purposes — he reacted indignantly. The report from Shanghai said secret police there had attacked

111

Sherlock Holmes as 'a watchdog of the British bourgeois' and said his 'reactionary influence' was one of the factors in the deterioration of China's public security apparatus.

The article went on to say that a disgraced former police chief was a great admirer of Holmes' methods and had directed his staff to learn from the Holmesian detection technique. 'He wanted them to live like Holmes in unusual circumstances and do mysterious and secret work and to be exceptional and different from the common people . . . '

'What nonsense', Hughes thundered. 'How dare they liken Holmes' methods to mysticism and closed door doctrines.' As always, he professed, deadpan, that his readers shared his belief that Holmes not only existed but was still alive. He went on to say there was no evidence that Holmes ever visited China, 'although he did travel in Tibet for two years under the name of Sigeison'. Holmes may have visited Hong Kong, however. An obscure street in Kowloon was named Baker Street by Government decree in the nineties.

The use by the Chinese of the word 'bourgeois' raised his ire particularly. 'Commonplace, conventional, respectable, thrifty, smug, greedy? Holmes bourgeois? What rubbish.'

He recalled to friends at the time that he had once exchanged views with Arthur Conan Doyle's son, Adrian, about Conan Doyle's master detective. The exchange happened when Hughes, as Dr Watson Jnr was reviewing for his old newspaper in Sydney Hesketh Pearson's biography of Conan Doyle. Adrian Conan Doyle, writing from Lyndhurst, England on 12 October 1945, insisted: 'For the mental prototype of Sherlock Holmes we need search no further than his creator'.

In his reply Hughes, under his pseudonym, said the belief that Arthur Conan Doyle, 'who acted as literary agent for Dr John Watson in publishing the doctor's reports of Sherlock Holmes' adventures' was himself the great man was old and familiar enough. But this was the first time in his recollection that a member of the Doyle family had publicly signed a declaration to that effect. 'Therefore', Hughes wrote, 'I have forwarded photostat copies of Adrian Conan Doyle's claim to the Baker Street Irregulars, the Speckled Band, the Molly Maguires, the Moriarty Defence League and to Sherlock Holmes himself — now ninety and, except for intermittent rheumatism, well and happy among his bees on the Sussex Downs.'

The subject of Holmes often came up for cultural discussion at meetings of Alcoholics Synonymous, just as it did in the heady days of Tokyo in the occupation years. Often there were long arguments about Holmes' knowledge of the opium dens down by the old London docks, but it was conceded that the master was not known for any liking for opium. He preferred cocaine.

112

There were long discussions too about Holmes creator's belief in spiritualism. Members generally agreed, rather reluctantly, that Arthur Conan Doyle might have had a point when he declared that in the hereafter there was marriage but no sex. But spirits could drink hard liquor and smoke cigars. Hughes elaborated on this. He said he was convinced God had a great sense of humour. Perhaps He, too, might have an occasional cigar?

This acceptance of fantasy by so many of the colony's 'foreign devils' could have been their way of rationalizing their own failures or imagined failures. Subconsciously, they too were aware they were living on borrowed time in a place that in itself was an anachronism, just as Shanghai had been. The roaring days of Shanghai's glory were recalled often and with great nostalgia. Ever present, of course, was the gossip. 'It makes Tokyo seem like a Trappist monastery', Hughes told a friend.

In 1961 Hughes' mother died in Melbourne. His father wrote to him at the time, strong in his spiritualism beliefs, and said he was comforted by his certainty that they would meet again. 'She is happy and is waiting for me.'

Indo-China was boiling again as the forces of nationalism continued the inexorable dismantling of the colonialist past, so Hughes went again to Laos. There he had an experience that he was to talk about for the rest of his life, and was to make him wonder about his father's spiritualism and his own lack of belief in the conventional religion of his youth. He met 'the Blind Bonze of Luang Prabang'.

For years he had heard of the monk's amazing prophecies, so he decided to visit the holy man. He met the shrivelled, sightless, shaven-head Gandhi-like figure in a remote temple after a rough drive from the Laotian capital. The holy man was wrapped in a yellow blanket, chewing betel nut when Hughes and his interpreter entered.

The Blind Bonze (monk) turned his head as they approached, pointed one emaciated hand at Hughes and cried out, speaking rapidly and loudly.

The puzzled interpreter turned to Hughes and asked if his wife was dead. Hughes said she was. The interpreter, obviously relieved, then translated. 'The master said you had brought your wife with you. I thought at first he had made a mistake. He sees the spirit, you understand.'

Hughes was shaken. He asked the interpreter to question the holy man further. The monk turned his staring eyeballs, covered with cataracts, towards a suddenly frightened Hughes. He spoke again, still rapidly and loud. The interpreter translated — and twenty years later Hughes recalled each vivid word. 'Holy man says your wife is always with you. She came here today specially because she wishes to tell you so. Holy man says she died maybe ten years ago in some

Asian city north of here. He thinks perhaps Japan. She is a small, dark-haired woman, laughing and very gay.'

The description was quite accurate and Adele had died in Tokyo ten years earlier. Hughes swears that the Blind Bonze had not known he was coming. It was a spur-of-the-moment decision and Hughes had told no-one. No-one in the country knew anything about his private life and his interpreter, from Bangkok, thought he had just arrived from London.

He went to see the Blind Bonze again, about a year later. The holy man, walking as though he could see, came from the dark hut into the blinding sunlight. Hughes knelt in the dust, among the dogs and the filth of the compound, and asked the holy man's blessing. He wrote at the time:

'Later he raised a tatooed arm and in a surprisingly aggressive voice demanded in effect a month's truce between the opposing forces then emaciating the country. "If only for one month brother will refrain from killing brother peace will return to our beloved land. If we do not respect this period the mountain people and the forests and farms will be destroyed by war" '.

Hughes, who had brought a gift of fruit and flowers, asked through his interpeter how best the United States and Russia could help Laos. The old man rattled his wooden beads and chewed reflectively on a betel nut for a moment. He said Russia and the U.S. should give no guns and should not compete as rivals in supplying food.

The bonze was about eighty years old then. For more than twenty years he had been the oracle of South East Asia, his word sought by kings and generals. He had amazed all with his uncanny prediction in 1954 that communist invaders would march triumphantly across the plain after Ho Chi Minh's victory against the French at Dien Ben Phu.

The last time Hughes saw him, he said the old man appeared to remember him. His frail voice rose as Hughes backed away. The interpreter translated: 'Holy man said be sure to tell your friend goodbye. He did not say which friend.'

Later that day Hughes was driven to the airport by a friend of Korean war days, Frank Corrigan. In the confusion of the airport Hughes missed Corrigan to say goodbye. He merely waved from a window of the plane as his friend looked for him. Corrigan was killed in a plane crash a week later.

Subsequently Hughes told the story to Somerset Maugham when the distinguished author was having lunch with Fleming and Hughes in Tokyo. Maugham had just visited the ruins of Angkor Wat and he appeared fascinated when Hughes told him about the Blind Bonze. He was old and frail but he listened intently, one hand cupped to his ear.

'It's a pity you did not visit the Blind Bonze', Hughes said.

Maugham shook his head and there was a long silence while he grappled for the elusive words his stuttering made difficult to muster. 'I have no explanation', he stammered finally. There was another long silence, then haltingly he said: 'There are many things that have happened to me that I cannot explain. There are some things it is best we should not know. It's bad enough to know the past. It would be intolerable to know the future.'

9 *James Bond's Japan*

'Dear Dikko', the letter said, 'I have in mind that James Bond's next adventure shall be in Japan . . . . therefore I plan to come back and take another look . . .' The letter was from Ian Fleming in London and Hughes was delighted at the prospect of seeing his friend once again, this time in Hughes' own 'parish'.

Fleming's letter suggested that Hughes and Torao 'Tiger' Saito should accompany him. Saito was a distinguished Japanese author, photographer and architect. He was one of Hughes' close friends, a warm and erudite man who shared Hughes' aptitude for high living. Fleming had met Saito on his previous visit to Japan and had formed a liking for him.

Fleming's letter went on: 'After perhaps a couple of days in Tokyo I would like us to take the most luxurious and modern train down South to the Inland Sea and beyond to whatever bizarre corners of Japan you and Tiger can think up. I would like to see pearl girls diving. My heroine will be a beautiful Japanese girl . . . I would like to see hot baths, a live volcano for suicides and any terrifying manifestations of the horrific in Japan. There will be a mad foreigner in the old Japanese castle and it will be James Bond's task to bring him to book, with the help of Tiger as the head of the Japanese secret service. You, Dikko, will be Australia's secret service chief in Tokyo.'

Hughes started immediately and with enormous enthusiasm on organizing what he was to refer to later as 'the most instructive, enjoyable, crowded, leisurely, lively and hilarious trip I ever made in thirteen long and happy years residence in Japan'.

Out of it was to come one of Fleming's major Bondian adventures. The 'evangelic group', as Hughes referred to it, found the colour, 'spiritual inspiration and carnal folklore' that Fleming sought to bring alive yet another adventure in the fabulously successful James Bond series.

116

Hughes flew to Tokyo to plan with Tiger the itinerary for the trip. They both went to the airport to meet Fleming. He was by then a cult figure, and he added to the legend by appearing out of the aircraft complete with an expensive looking shooting stick, which he was to carry throughout the odyssey. His elegance was further enhanced by his usual polka dot bow tie, a light-weight dark blue suit and the ebony cigarette holder. His fame had preceded him to Japan and customs passed him through quickly, ignoring his supply of bourbon and his special cigarettes.

Although he was not in robust health at the time and was tired of the wrangling over some of his Bond books, Fleming felt at ease immediately with his two friends. Hughes was his 'orientalist guide, philosopher and friend', he was to say later, and there was a quality of extremism about the big man's enthusiasm that seemed to lift his spirits. He listened, fascinated, as Hughes and Tiger went over in detail the plans for the next two weeks.

Before dinner that first evening the three of them relaxed in a huge bath, mellow from the excellent sake that Tiger had recommended. Later at dinner Fleming indulged himself with two dozen fat Japanese oysters as an appetiser to the exquisite dinner Tiger chose. 'Ian was one of the best tooth men I've ever known', Hughes recalled with awe. 'I'm no slouch, mind you, but Ian made me look like a piker.'

Fleming's curiosity was insatiable. He accepted very little at face value and questioned and questioned until every minute detail was clear. He met businessmen, journalists, statesmen, shadowy figures from Tokyo's underworld, sumo wrestlers and bar girls and geishas.

To all of them he was a courteous listener. He recorded the information he wanted each night before dinner and before they left Tokyo he had filled a couple of notebooks with his neat writing. He told Hughes and Saito that he would insist on taking care of all expenses on the trip. All hotels were to be the best and all travel first class.

Hughes reminded Fleming about tipping. It was not customary, he said, and there was no question that the lack of a tip would bring the sort of reaction it did in the United States, for instance. But a reasonable tip for good service often meant the difference to the recipient of one or two meals.

They all had slight hangovers when they caught the early morning express out of Tokyo to Gamagore. But the attentive service on the train as it whistled out of Tokyo helped. Fleming filled them in on his outline for the book. To Hughes he said: 'Who do you dislike most. Dikko?'

'A bloke called Henderson.'

'Right, you'll be Dikko Henderson in the book. Head of the Australian intelligence outfit in Japan. And you, Tiger, will be Tiger Tanaka, head of the Japanese Secret Service.'

'I'll sue you if you lampoon me', Hughes warned, grinning.

'You do that and I'll tell the truth about you.'

Fleming questioned Tiger closely about the Japanese ON system — an obligation to pay a favour. It was almost as important as 'face' Tiger explained, and the person with the ON wasn't happy until it was discharged. The favour had to be discharged with a favour of equal importance. If larger the position of ON was reversed. The concept appeared to fascinate Fleming. He encouraged Tiger to use the vernacular, and if the word escaped him Hughes would help out. He had some Japanese but as Tiger pointed out it was very basic. He had picked up most of his knowledge of the language from women, Tiger explained, and women used a certain intonation at times that men normally did not. Hughes confirmed the truth of this.

Hughes claimed that sake, and other suitable drinks, had something to do with the fact that the three men did not quarrel for the two weeks of their living together. There was more to it of course. Each complemented the other. Tiger Saito had a gentle quality despite his nickname. He had enormous patience too and he had genuine liking for Hughes and Fleming. Hughes, on the other hand, gave the impression of being tough and cynical, yet underneath he was sentimental and enormously loyal. And Fleming could be himself as he seldom could be in his more familiar role in London, and he seemed to expand in the closeness of their relationship. Each was a good listener, blessed with great charm and high intelligence.

Fleming kept rather rigidly to his working schedule during the day. He was curious about everything, and with Tiger interpreting, he found out details of Japanese life and history that continually amazed Hughes. Each evening he would spend some time in his room alone jotting down his impressions of the day before joining Hughes and Tiger in whatever joyous entertainment had been slotted into their schedule. Fleming carried a supply of his beloved Bourbon with him and would occasionally have a nip but generally they stayed with sake, which Hughes credited for the absence of a hangover on the entire trip.

In many ways Fleming was an extrovert, aware of his poised, aristocratic behaviour and the effect it had on the people around him. The shooting stick, the long ebony cigarette holder, conservative dark blue suits and his near-pedantic attention to detail all were attention getters. But to Hughes, the dichotomy lay in the fact that underneath the suave, sure exterior the author was an extremely complicated, reserved individual. He drank and smoked far too much, yet when Hughes, of all people, chided him gently, he reacted with a tart reply tantamount to a don't-get-too-close rebuke.

Hughes, of course, knew that Fleming had been living for a long

118

time beyond the limits of his natural resources, and the Japanese discovery voyage should have been more leisurely than the flamboyant exercise it became. But any 'take it easy' approach was not in Hughes' nature any more than it was with Saito. Fleming knew this and encouraged every initiative by his full-blooded and enthusiastic participation. He was to say of Hughes — through the mouth of one of his characters in a Bond book — 'He is a man who lives as if he were going to die tomorrow'. He knew at the time, according to Hughes, that his next heart attack could be his last, yet the knowlege appeared not to affect his appetites for everything that Japan served up so pleasurably.

It was said of Fleming later that his Bond books were a fantasy autobiography. And his genuine liking for Hughes, too, was perhaps based partly on what he represented.

Hughes, for his part, acted the part of Dikko Henderson that Fleming saw for him. Subconciously he was probably flattered by Fleming's attention because it helped to confound those who saw a contradiction between the tough, knock-em-down Australian foreign correspondent and the erudite pieces he produced from time to time for his sophisticated London readers.

Nothing seemed to escape Fleming's attention. He went over minutely a provincial police station that he envisaged as the scene for one of Bond's adventures, talked to the full-breasted girl divers and appeared fascinated with a tour of an ancient brothel in Kyoto. The answers to his interminable questions were duly recorded in his notebooks. None of the frivolity, the sumptuous meals and the drinking ever interfered with his practice of spending an hour or so at the end of each day writing his impressions of what had happened, who he had seen.

Fleming's subsequent book, *You Only Live Twice*, showed how well he had absorbed detail. Also, he drew Hughes with great affection, yet captured the essential quality of what he saw as the best and most loyal attributes of an Australian. Dikko Henderson 'had a craggy, sympathetic face, rather stony blue eyes, and a badly broken nose'. It was Hughes to a 'T'.

One of Hughes most vivid memories of the trip is of an incident in the dining car of the train taking them back to Tokyo, when, in Hughes' words, 'we narrowly escaped fisticuffs with some dull Hun traders'.

Fleming was completely relaxed, Hughes recalled. His research was as complete as the three of them could make it and he was happy with the plot of the book and the characters he had planned for it. A few more questions in Tokyo — particularly about the ON system, which fascinated him for some reason — and then back to Jamaica. After a good dinner in the dining car and a flask or two of excellent sake, Tiger Saito went to bed, leaving Hughes and Fleming to a drowsing assessment of the two weeks saga. Perhaps Fleming's mind was clear of Bond's Japanese adventure and was ready for another swashbuckling sortie into the shadowy world of fictionalized espionage.

Three men of Teutonic appearance were at a table near them in the dining car. One was very bulky and he had long, dank hair that overlapped his collar. And Fleming had a dislike of long, greasy-looking hair.

The mission was near its end and Fleming was mischievous. He spoke just loudly enough for the hairy fellow traveller to hear. He disparaged the man, his bulk, his clothes and particularly his hair. The man under attack had his back to Hughes and Fleming but his two companions were aware that Fleming was discussing him and they avoided Fleming's mock hostile eyes while obviously filling in their companion about the nature of the attack from the rear.

Fleming finally got up, strolled past the three puzzled looking and now furtive men. He turned, openly contemptuous, glared at them and strolled on. He waited while Hughes did the same, then joined Hughes' grinning at the success of their childish prank.

When the train reached Tokyo, the hairy man alighted near Hughes and Fleming. Fleming immediately returned to the attack and stared at the long hairy man. 'Look at him. He's obviously guilty', he said to Hughes as the hairy one looked around him fearfully. Fleming approached a nearby policeman and Tiger, who had been filled in on the charade, interpreted as Fleming pointed his absurd shooting stick at the German and asked some innocuous question. The policeman pointed and that was enough for the hairy man. He grabbed his bag and broke into a run, scattering fellow passengers, and disappeared. Hughes still wonders what the German thought, what he had in his bag, what crime he had committed.

In a letter to a friend at the time Hughes summed up the trip. 'It was an hilarious experience. Tiger was in the party to give an appearance of indigenous realism to the mission. We travelled by hydrofoil, steam packet, the railroad, the new invention of the flying machine, palanquin and mule train (on the rough approaches to Mt. Aso.) We witnessed the fattening of prime Kobe beef on the hoof by a regular deluge of bottled beer into the animals' grateful gullets. We purified ourselves at the shrines of Ise. We drank turtle blood with members of Japan's secret police. It was spiritually and culturally uplifting.'

Before he left Tokyo on his way to his Jamaican home, Fleming discussed with Hughes and Saito the Japanese aphorism for the title *You Only Live Twice*. Despite their arguments that he should attribute it directly to the seventeenth century Japanese poet Basho, he insisted the attribution should be 'after Basho'. His first choice was:

'You only live twice,

Once when you are born
And once when you are about to die'
In the book he altered the last line to read; 'And once when you look death in the face'.

He also dedicated the book to Hughes and Saito.

Hughes had a strange feeling at Haneda airport, where he and Tiger Saito went to say goodbye, that he would never see Fleming again. He had a sense of melancholy, normally foreign to his cheerful nature. Fleming presented his ridiculous shooting stick to Tiger, which the Japanese had secretly lusted after, and would not listen when Tiger tried feebly to refuse it. He said something that Hughes has quoted ever since: 'We are only as good as our friends'.

Back in Hong Kong, Hughes had a postcard from Fleming from Jamaica where he was putting the finishing touches to *You Only Live Twice*. It said: 'I'm grinding away at Bond's latest but the going gets harder and harder and duller and duller, and I don't really know what I'm going to do with him. He's become a personal — if not a public — nuisance.

'Anyway he's had a good run, which is more than most of us can say. Everything seems a lot of trouble these days — too much trouble. Keep alive. Ian.' Hughes replied immediately. 'I won't answer such letters in future. What do you mean by this ridiculous "keep alive" business?'

Fleming's reply said: 'Dikko, I promise. Don't worry. I'm not worrying any more. Down with death.'

Fleming died in 1964, but the cult of James Bond that he had established brought him too into the legendary category. In an obituary to Fleming Hughes wrote, 'I realize now how much I owe him and how much I miss him'. And in a rare public display of sentiment he added: 'Happy Vagabond. God Bless Him.'

He recalled to friends that Fleming had saved his life when he forbade him to travel to Korea. On another occasion Fleming had refused permission when Hughes wanted to go the Pescadore Islands, where Chinese nationalists were shelling the Chinese mainland. There was no particular reason that Hughes could fathom at the time. On the way back from the Pescadores the plane he would have been on crashed, killing all on board.

He paid a final, touching tribute to Fleming in his book, *Foreign Devil*. At the end of the chapter devoted to their Japanese odyssey he also quoted from Basho:
'Morning cold;
The voice of travellers
Leaving the inn.'
The simple quote said more about his feelings for his friend than so many of the fulsome tributes others paid.

Hughes went to see Fleming's grave on a subsequent visit to London. With him was a mutual friend, Charles Wacker. They travelled by train to the semi-rural village where the author was interred, about half an hour's run from London. They searched the small cemetery with its modest grave stones but could not locate the grave. Finally they went to the curator, an elderly farmer type, who lived near the cemetery gate.

The curator led them to the grave and told them he clipped the weeds and grass off it. 'No one visits it', he told them. The grave then, Hughes said, was a bare, six inch high sheath of dirt, covered with grass and weeds. There was no stone or identification on it they could see. They had brought a bottle of whisky with them, so they drank their silent toast to Fleming and sprinkled some of the Scotch on the grave before returning to London.

Hughes was incensed. He contacted a fellow journalist on one of the big London dailies and told him of the lack of care the grave received. Next day the newspaper he had tipped off ran a big article, together with pictures, of the lonely grave and cemetery. Fleming's family told the newspaper they had authorized a handsome monument to be built over the grave, but it had not yet been finished.

During this London visit he went to see a specialist in Harley Street since he was worried about his increased weight, then some 120 kilograms. The doctor told him to cut down on drink and food and get plenty of exercise, 'not necessarily the type you get in bed'.

Back in Hong Kong, he began to cultivate even more assiduously the contacts he had built up who fed him with rare and delicious snippets from inside China. He was beginning to hit his straps as one of the great China watchers, though he tended to denigrate this role. Every Far Eastern reporter of the Chinese scene, he said, was a China watcher, whether he was a newspaperman or a diplomat. 'Even if he is a communist he is still doomed to be a China watcher because he is not Chinese.'

But he conceded that China watchers in Hong Kong who knew the Chinese scene could operate more freely, rewardingly and objectively from Hong Kong than from anywhere else, including Peking.

The information that flooded into the city was very confusing, however. There was such a mass of it. All Chinese internal radio services were monitored and translated with great speed so that government announcements were known in Hong Kong almost as quickly as in Peking. British and United States information services translated and distributed without opinion or comment relevant sections of the Chinese press. Other authorities, some of them Chinese, reasoned the motives behind some of the moves made behind the curtain and offered opinions.

Hughes' sources covered the spectrum, from the highest diplomats to the latest furtive refugee, and he showed great skill in sorting out the newsworthy and relevant from the 'shithouse rumour stuff', as he put it in a letter to a friend.

A habit of railing against what he called 'the commie dogs' resulted in Hughes being publicly associated with the strong anti-communist sentiment so dominant in the colony. Yet there is no doubt that he, and others, had discreet contacts on the other side. Some of these contacts had obviously been told to cultivate exchanges with the more influential of the foreign devil pressmen in Hong Kong. Their job was to try to use these contacts, either to further the communist cause by wrong interpretation of a particular move, or to deliberately feed in wrong information.

Hughes exploited this dangerous ploy with skill. At times he would attend friendly lunches, for just two people. Matters of mutual interest would be raised and harmless responses by the seemingly innocent Hughes were usually reciprocated so long as anonymous 'party sources' was the only attribution. He saw this role as an essential part of his job. Only the ill-informed, gullible and rivals, motivated by jealousy, saw it otherwise. Hughes rode above it all. He was secure in his faith. He was in the box seat. To one friend, he summed it up colourfully: 'Unlike the tom cat that gets it and squeals, I get it and shut up'.

His job and his full life fascinated him. But odd visits to Singapore, Bangkok, Jakarta, Tokyo and Rangoon were not enough to satisfy his restlessness and he decided on another visit to Moscow, back to the scene of his earlier triumph.

The disappearance of Kim Philby from Beirut was a big factor in his decision. What if he could turn up Philby too? One of his contacts in Bangkok actively encouraged him to make the visit. Perhaps he would have better luck this time and see Khrushchev, it was suggested. And, referring to Burgess and Maclean, the contact said enigmatically: 'There may be more to come, you know'.

Additionally he had always longed to make the still romantic trans-Siberian railway crossing. Trains were still his great love and he recalled with nostalgia the long-ago days of his stint on the Victorian Railways. That clinched it and he made arrangements for the trip.

First, he sent off an application for an interview with Khrushchev, and confident as always, he then applied for a visa. It should have been the other way around, but what the hell, he thought. Commie dogs always respected confidence whereas fawning uncertainty left them cold. This would be an attacking mission he decided. Diplomatic niceties were wasted on the Burgess-Maclean sortie whereas brutal frankness had paid dividends. He would try the same tactic this time.

From Moscow he would go to London for some leave. Tokyo was the first stop and he spent a couple of happy days with friends before boarding a ship from Yokohama to Nakhodka. But in Tokyo itself he found what he called a spiritual emptiness or mild vacuum in the lives of many of the young inheritors of modern Japan. The country, he said, seemed to have mislaid its proud discipline. But it was difficult to believe this was an irrevocable loss.

From Nakhodka he took a train to Khabarovsk. Two huge steam engines hauled the train, and in fancy he heard the 'Right away' cry before the hissing giants gathered power for the night and day run to Khabarovsk. From there to Irkutsk the journey was normally by diesel-electric train but for a reason he could not fathom all passengers were diverted to a Russian aircraft for the three-hour journey to Irkutsk. There he climbed on board another train for the four day run to Moscow.

Hughes was enchanted with Irkutsk. The gentle, centuries-old city contrasted so vividly with the full-blooded hurry of Hong Kong and smelly and ugly Tokyo that he found himself wandering contentedly through the parks and among the odd mixture of log cabins and ancient buildings. His guide there, with the improbable name of Lenin, had fought in the savage battles at Stalingrad in the Second World War.

Lenin took Hughes to a Russian Orthodox church high on a hill overlooking the city and there, kneeling on stones worn beneath the feet of millions in another age, he sought and was given a blessing by a bearded priest. The gesture was spontaneous; irreverence would have been obscene. Lenin watched stolidly and interpreted the priest's remarks: 'The holy father says he blesses you in memory of the great Pope John, who brought the people of the world of all faiths, and of no faith at all, closer together in the family of man'.

Hughes was the only English-speaking traveller on the run from Irkutsk to Moscow. But he had some French and Japanese and a Russian dictionary and the best language barrier-crosser of them all — a smile. Gregarious fellow travellers soon made him welcome, the food was excellent and the vodka plentiful at first. It was cut out however on the second day although there was plenty of beer and wine.

He had one altercation with a Russian technician who felt he had lost face when Hughes diverted his aim as he tried to shoot a glass stopper from a champagne bottle at a one-eyed Russian officer. The technician became belligerent. He tried to grab Hughes by the lapels of his jacket. Other passengers, in their night attire of identical striped pyjamas, long underpants and blue singlets joined the noisy scene as Hughes tried to reason with the drunken technician.

Finally Hughes lost his temper. He rose to his feet. 'Knock it off', he roared, brushing the technician's groping hands to one side.

The expression was taken up by the onlookers. They ran the words

124

together and began chanting in a growing swell 'knockitoff, knockitoff, knockitoff'. The one-eyed colonel got into the act too. His roar rose above the hubbub and he thundered, pointing dramatically at the door of the compartment, 'knockitoff'. The technician backed off, pursued by the refrain. For the remainder of the trip Hughes was known as 'gospodin [Mr] Knockitoff'.

Another, happier, incident involved a maudlin German engineer. He and Hughes were taking a nightcap just before midnight and the sad-eyed German, almost in tears, told Hughes that the next day was his birthday. He was far away from home, he said in a mixture of German, French and English, in a Godforsaken train in a God-forsaken land.

'Comrade', said Hughes, 'be of good cheer. I shall arrange a special salutation for you.'

He left the dining car and returned one minute before midnight just in time to order another round of drinks. He raised his glass to toast the weeping German and at that moment the train's whistle sounded forlorn across the steppes. 'It whistles for no man but you', said Hughes. 'It's your birthday greeting from comrade driver.' The German was overjoyed. Hughes of course had arranged nothing. But, as an old railwayman, he knew that drivers the world over on long and lonely journeys traditionally greeted the birth of each new day with a blast of the whistle.

Hughes regarded the trans-Siberia trip as the last romantic train journey on earth. His knowledge of the Vienna and Budapest journeys came only from books, but to him they were relics of a long-dead era of escalating European decay. He knew, too, the dreary run across his own country's Nullabor Plain. Its day after day sameness did little to complement the people who made the journey.

But this train was different. Not only the people on board, and they were diverse enough, but the vast, mysterious country it traversed. In Novosibirsk, now a thriving city and becoming one of the Soviet Union's main scientific centres, he reflected that it was only a small village just a few decades earlier. Now it was becoming one of the great power centres of the Soviet Union, although its long lines of workshops and factories and apartments did little for his ascetic soul. And the faces of the people were changing all the time. Earlier there had been Mongol influence in the faces, flat and high cheekboned. There was a brawling, wild look about so many of them. Now, as the great train got nearer to Europe, there were what Hughes called the 'technical' faces of the new Russian elite. They had a sober, journeyman look about them.

In Moscow he was given accommodation this time at the Metropole Hotel and not, as he had hoped, at the National. He walked past the National on his first day in the city and fancied he saw again the

125

flashing-eyed Russian beauty and the stout concierge. For old times sake he had a wistful look at the rooms — 123 and 101 — that had played such a part in the Burgess-Maclean saga seven years earlier. He looked, too, for the friendly traffic cop who had helped him over lonely days with his grin and 'teapot-not-vodka' routine. Nothing. Just memories now, he decided, and they wouldn't help him in his latest quest.

Red Square was unchanged, with Lenin's tomb flat and uninspiring compared with the beauty of nearby St. Basil's Cathedral. The Russian word for 'red' and 'beautiful' is the same, but to Hughes the expanse of the huge square could be considered beautiful only because of the cathedral on its outskirts. St. Basil's, he remembered from his history books, was erected by Ivan the Terrible in the sixteenth century. Legend had it that when the building was completed the builders were ordered to be blinded to prevent them producing anything else so beautiful.

It came as a shock to Hughes when the United States ambassador at the time, Foy Kohler, told him that Guy Burgess had died the previous day. Hughes had formed an instant liking for the tragic renegade when they met so theatrically and he felt a pang of sadness when he realized that, after twelve years of exile and unhappiness along the strange path he had chosen, the true end of the trail had come.

Burgess appeared to have frittered away an aimless sort of existence in Moscow, engaged in dead-end publishing activities. He had appeared occasionally at dull cocktail parties, looking bored and ageing noticeably. He lived a retired, hidden life in a typical Moscow apartment, crammed with books and English newspapers. Soviet acquaintances knew him as 'Elliott'.

Hughes went to the funeral and watched as Donald Maclean, stooped and moving slowly now, spoke a brief eulogy over his companion's red-draped casket. Neither Hughes nor the other correspondents were allowed to approach Maclean. There was no sign of Philby who was now the man they all wanted. But after his disappearance from Beirut, Philby's whereabouts were hidden behind the same heavy curtain that covered Burgess and Maclean so successfully for so many years.

Hughes made up his mind to try the same brutal, frontal, no frills approach, this time to unearth Philby. He hammered on doors, made demands by telephone and when they failed he tried every devious manoeuvre he knew. He used contacts from Tokyo and Bangkok days. Some of them were Russian, friends he had drunk and wenched with, friends who had made all sorts of promises to cancel the Japanese ON that Hughes held with some of them. Nothing worked. The closest he got was an interview with Khrushchev's son-in-law,

Alexei Adzhubei, who was editor-in-chief of *Izvestia*. After some pleasant verbal sparring with the engaging Adzhubei, Hughes sprang his big question: 'Let me see the British defector Philby', he asked bluntly.

Adzhubei turned to his foreign editor, looking genuinely puzzled. Hughes picked up the quick Russian words: 'Who is Philby?' The foreign editor explained and Adzhubei continued in Russian as Hughes' 'fixer' interpreted. 'Oh, no, not another one of them. Yes, I remember. Why can't we reach some arrangement with the Americans and British to get rid of these clowns.'

He explained to Hughes that it was none of his business and he wasn't interested in any case. But what did Hughes want him to do? Hughes said he and Philby had both worked for the same newspaper and they had that in common. Adzhubei finally agreed to raise the matter and would recommend that Hughes be given a chance to see Philby — if Philby agreed. He would also recommend that a statement be issued.

Hughes, still on his blunt 'kick', and with memory still fresh of the run around he had been given over the Burgess-Maclean incident, ended the interview. 'But please don't fool me . . .' The interpreter started to translate but Adzhubei broke in, speaking in English. 'You mean, don't bugger me around' he asked, smiling.

His hopes high, Hughes arranged for an extension of his visa. His 'fixer' brought the bad news several days later: no official party statement could be made, and Philby would not make a personal comment. This time, Hughes' descent on London was not the triumphal return it had been after his previous stay in Russia.

He wrote of his experience of the non-finding of Philby in a piece the *Sunday Times* called 'Lonely Trails'. He recalled the circumstances of the Burgess-Maclean interview and recapitulated on their lives in exile. At the same time he touched on some others in the list of those who had apparently thrown in their lot with communism. 'What of the survivors of this wandering, wasting company of the lost?' He touched on Donald Maclean having some sort of post with the Soviet Ministry of Foreign Affairs.

Then he mentioned his old colleague Wilfred Burchett — 'one of the best and bravest war correspondents I ever knew' — then drifting round Russia, Poland and East Europe. Briton Alan Winnington, then the *Daily Worker* correspondent in East Berlin, was a 'dignified, lonely figure who would sometimes talk with pathetic casualness when I knew him in Peking of "going back home sometime".'

He ended his story: 'I am no moralist. But it seems to me, still affected by the coincidence of Burgess' obscure funeral service at Moscow's crematorium, attended by scarcely a dozen people, with a few flowers from English friends, that all these exiles, drearily pursuing their long, lost and lonely trails, are paying in substantial measure for their acts, whether foolishly or deliberately committed.'

Hughes returned to Hong Kong, dejected over his failure to unearth Philby, or to interview Khrushchev. But within days he was planning another South East Asian foray, this time into the rapidly escalating war in South Vietnam, and to Indonesia, where the demagogue Sukarno was railing against the proposed Malaysian Federation and demanding more and more for his impoverished island empire. Sukarno was using threats, blackmail and bluff with astonishing success. His country's growing power was yet another manifestation of emerging nationalism and scorn of the West and the colonialist past.

Hughes with Japanese Prime Minister Yoshida in 1961.

Roy (Lord) Thomson

Hughes shares a joke with American playwright Marc Connelly at lunch in Hong Kong in 1970.

Hughes and American author Sid Perelman at lunch in Hong Kong in 1974.

10 Sukarno to Saigon

Hughes had held the view for years that China, irrespective of her communism, should be admitted to the United Nations. Chiang Kai-shek and his Nationalists, beleaguered on their off-shore stronghold of Taiwan, did not represent the Chinese people, he argued. So when the *New York Times Magazine* invited him to write a piece arguing for China's admission to the august body, he did so with alacrity.

The case against Peking's admission was argued forcefully in the magazine by Herbert Feis, noted economist, historian, author and former adviser to the U.S. State Department.

In refutation, Hughes wrote: 'United States' objections to the admission of communist China are founded, creditably enough, on the rash U.S. pledge to uphold the lost cause of Chiang Kai-shek. But the facts of international life in an imperfect world have at last caught up with Washington's dogged and sterile opposition. The inevitable can no longer be ignored and the admission of China is now merely a matter of time and timing. The fiction that the ageing Nationalists at bay under U.S. protection still represent the sovereign government of China and are crouched to recover the mainland has become a bad as well as a stale joke.'

Until communist China was admitted to international councils, Hughes' argument ran, there could be no realistic discussion of any vital Far Eastern issues such as the unification of Korea and Vietnam. Without Communist China, he said, the United Nations could not operate as a forum, negotiator and mediator in any Asian emergency.

He went on to say that of course Chinese membership would not automatically establish sweet and reasonable discourse of Far Eastern problems, but it could not be denied that U.N. membership incurred responsibilities and duties as well as rights and advantages: 'It is neither logical nor plausible to denounce someone in the abstract for breaking the code and rules of a club to which he does not belong . . . Somebody will have to get hurt in any Taiwan settlement but the over-riding responsibility of the United Nations is to ensure there are no more wars. For that reason alone Peking can no longer be ignored, nor Asia repudiated.'

His occasional pieces for the prestigious magazine got him into trouble at one stage. The *Washington Post*, which took syndicated material from the *Sunday Times*, objected when Hughes' by-line appeared in the *New York Times Magazine*. Hughes explained to both the *Sunday Times* and the *Washington Post* that his occasional pieces for the New York publication were never wanted or requested by the *Sunday Times* and consequently were never withheld from the *Washington Post*. But the *Post* was adamant. They did not want Hughes writing for an opposition publication: 'Petty as it may seem to high ecclesiastical circles', the *Post* editors wrote in reply to Hughes' biblical style entreaty, 'the *Post* looks on the *New York Times* as its earthly rival for such prestige as it may glean from monopolizing Washington's elite readership'.

Hughes accepted the rebuff. 'I can only add, with a humble genuflection, that it is a curious situation — the work I have been doing for the *New York Times Magazine* has been perpetrated in my Mr Hyde role . . . my normal staff work in my Dr Jekyll role for the *Sunday Times* continues as usual and the work I am now prevented from doing as Hyde will in no way increase my production as Jekyll. But if I must die as Hyde I can presumably survive as Jekyll — a feat which the original schizophrenic could not achieve.'

An executive of the *New York Times Magazine* to whom Hughes told the gloomy news wrote to say how sorry he was. He then added: 'Meanwhile, what do you think of the sneaky notion of writing for us under the pseudonym of Lao Tzu'? Hughes replied: 'Your unworthy and altogether admirable suggestion had already crossed my mind. I am afraid however that in our goldfish trade the story would leak very soon. My thought is to wait a month or until the heat is off and then make this suggestion to the *Sunday Times*. After all, the *Washington Post*'s objections has been only to the appearance of the by-line and if that were changed I can't see what logical objection they would have.'

Hughes however decided not to go along with the ploy, although the idea appealed to him greatly, because, he said: 'I have the honour to labour for gentlemen in Milord Thomson's London institution for gentlemen'. (Thomson by then had taken over the *Sunday Times* and other Kemsley publications.)

Vietnam was becoming more troublesome to the Western powers at this time. Mao Tse Tung had broken with Khrushchev earlier and the two communist powers were vying with each other for dominance in Vietnam and other South East Asian countries looking to communism as their hope. Although the United States was propping up successive weak, corrupt governments in South Vietnam, there were clear signs that the escalation of trouble there was only the beginning.

Few people at that stage however foresaw the holocaust to come, although Hughes felt strongly that China's goal still remained communist dominion over most of Asia.

In Indonesia too the storms were gathering. President Sukarno had already paid several visits to China and had invited Mao to visit. 'Brother Mao', Sukarno was reported to have said on one visit, 'the people of Indonesia are waiting to see you.' Mao did not make the visit, despite seven other invitations, according to Sukarno.

Hughes disliked and distrusted Sukarno. He would recall with a grin how a dear friend once called the Indonesian leader, face to face, 'the only living Quisling'. He decided to visit Jakarta to see how the confrontation issue Sukarno was whipping into a frenzy was progressing. In a story at the time, he said Sukarno had an instinct and talent for calculated risk. He wanted the Borneo territories and he wanted Timor. 'And if he gets these territories and he is still alive he will want East New Guinea.'

Mao Tse Tung was wielding the whip from a China that had become increasingly belligerent since Khrushchev had refused to honour his promise to supply China with nuclear know-how, and China watchers, Hughes among them, recalled one of Mao's chilling poems, part of which read: 'Cold-eyed I survey the world beyond the seas; a hot wind spatters raindrops on the sky-brooded waters'.

So the East wind was blowing and whipping up frenzy far to the south and Hughes set off again. The background to the confrontation issue between Sukarno's Indonesia and the proposed merger between Malaya, Singapore and the British territories of Sarawak and North Borneo stemmed from Sukarno's anti-imperialism. He called imperialism 'the demon with ten heads', an international conspiracy that must be fought by international means. He had collaborated with the Japanese during the Pacific war in the hope that Japanese victory would finally kill Western imperialism in Asia.

The state of Malaysia was proclaimed late in 1963 and Indonesia's immediate reaction was violent. The British embassy in Jakarta was razed, British factories were taken over and nationals evacuated. 'Smash Malaysia' was the cry throughout Indonesia. British troops gathered along the straits of Malacca and Indonesian troops went to Borneo. All the signs pointed to an eruption of violence that could have signalled the outbreak of the dreaded World War Three. Indonesian communists, numbered at more than three million, supported Sukarno. He referred to them as his 'blood brothers'.

Adding to Western fears, China exploded her first atom bomb and had assured Indonesia she would not stand idly by in the event of 'imperialist' attack.

Despite the tremendous tension, there were only minor clashes outside Indonesia and apart from the forecasts of doom that Hughes and others filed, there was little to report other than local riots.

So the foreign correspondents who had flocked to the area waited and waited in the terrible heat of Jakarta, visited troops, covered the massive students riots, got drunk, swopped lies and checked out rumours, and waited again. After a while they drifted away, most of them convinced that Sukarno's crusading zeal was waning and that the red tide they had forecast as sweeping so far south would recede northwards again.

One aspect of life in Jakarta that intrigued Hughes greatly was the habit of some Russians of going out into the fierce noon day heat. 'They wear, to the huge delight of old hands and Indonesians, that class-conscious symbol of colonial imperialism — the outmoded solar topee. Some of the topees have a weathered secondhand air about them and one British authority swore that the Soviet foreign aid administration bought up joblots from the moth ball cache at Moss Bros.'

Hughes, who often affected his monocle — 'good way to get service' — had one experience with a furious fellow correspondent that involved the monocle. They were arguing and Hughes was winning. Enraged, the other correspondent reached across and swept Hughes' monocle to the ground. Hughes reached into his pocket for his spare, screwed it into place. 'As I was saying when you so rudely interrupted me', he said, and went on with the argument.

The students' riots were the biggest stories coming out of Jakarta at that time. They were significant in that they presaged the end of Sukarno's reign, the emergence of the army as the controlling body and the demise of a communist threat. The students did not confine their attacks to British, American and other foreign nationals' property.

Peking's official New China Newsagency building also came under attack from the mobs. This was followed by attacks on the Chinese Consulate General building and on other Chinese official buildings. Jakarta was on the brink of anarchy. Then the army moved in and Sukarno was effectively removed from power. General Suharto was now Indonesia's man of destiny. The communist party was banned and peace was eventually restored between Indonesia and Malaysia.

The heat was off for the present, and Hughes, relieved to get away from a country he disliked, went back to the comparable order of Hong Kong. It too, was soon to be battered by China's sullen East wind. Mao's 'cold-eyed I survey the world beyond the seas' was to take on added significance.

The cultural revolution, which led China to the brink of chaos, was under way. It was precipitated when Mao decided that the Chinese Communist Party had become bureaucratic and counter-revolutionary. His allies were the army and the students.

Hughes' China-watching role, sorting out rumour from fact, was invaluable. Some of his contacts were businessmen who were allowed into China, and Japanese and diplomats passing through the colony. He also had very discreet contacts within the Chinese Communist Party in Hong Kong. From all these, and from his reading of the monitored radio news, he was able to draw a picture of a power struggle between the ailing Mao and his Politburo rivals. The cultural revolution was said to be operating on three levels. It was a 'within the palace' power struggle: it was also a crusade aimed at higher levels of democracy, socialism and collective spirit; and on yet another level it provided a chance for old scores to be settled in China's age-old fashion.

From it all, Hughes concluded that the heat the revolution generated would go far beyond the borders of the vast land, and towards the south. He reported on the growing deification of Mao and of the old man's uneasiness at the trend. Mao knew more than most how difficult it was to live up to a high reputation.

He also reported, gleefully, on Mao's swim in the Yangtze river. Mao was then seventy-two and Hughes took great delight in drawing his long-range picture — 'a magic carpet job' he called it — from reports filed by Japanese observers of the historic swim.

Based on the eye-witness reports, he wrote: 'Mao lowered himself, waving genially at the crowds on the banks, from a boat in mid-stream into the yellow, high running, white-crested water. He was wearing long white drawers which came below his knees. He was surrounded by a splashing escort of about a dozen strong-swimming members of the Young China League who accompanied him in a reverent circle. Occasionally Mao swam breaststroke vigorously, floating on his back, kicked up his legs, spat water into the air, and waggled his fingers playfully at two girls among his encircling patrol. After the swim, Mao, with his drawers clinging to his tough peasant legs, hauled himself into a waiting junk.' He added admiringly 'For a man of 72 who smokes too many cigarettes, who tries to cut back on mao-tai (Chinese dynamite liquor), who is lucky to be alive after his long march and who eats too much inflammatory red peppered food, Mao has every right to be proud of his splash in the Yangtze'.

Hong Kong continued with its frenetic pace, living to the full its role of making the most of each day. It was gearing up for America's increasingly active campaign in Vietnam. More and more of Hughes' old friends of Japan's occupation days began to converge on the colony as they scented the stand the United States was to make.

One friend who passed through on his way back to Australia

planned a first ever visit to Singapore and he asked Hughes' advice about a good hotel. Their farewell lunch was a long one. Hughes told his friend the name of a hotel. He recommended it highly. It was cheap and clean, he said. 'There'll be a few sheilas around but they won't bother you', he assured his friend earnestly.

Recalling the story later, Hughes' friend said: 'I got to the hotel the old bastard told me about and I was puzzled about the lack of other guests. There were no customers in the bar or the dining room when I checked in and when I asked for a single room the bloke at the desk seemed puzzled. But it was clean and the service was efficient. The thing that puzzled me though was that the place was deserted during the day and only came to life at night when I would hear the old lift wheezing up and down monotonously.' Finally, late one night, his curiosity strong, he overheard an argument between the hotel manager and two well dressed and beautiful girls. The girls were arguing that 30 per cent was too much for the hotel and the manager was berating them about their dress, behaviour and working hours. Then the penny dropped. Hughes had sent him to board at a Chinese brothel. 'Maybe he did it innocently, probably because he's an ingenuous bloke — or is he?'

By July 1965, the United States was pouring troops into South Vietnam. President Lyndon Johnson summed up the move: 'We did not choose to be the guardians at the gate, but there is no one else'. Johnson said the U.S. knew from the experience of Korea and two world wars that retreat did not bring safety and weakness did not bring peace. He said the conflict in South Vietnam was guided by North Vietnam and spurred by China. The goal was to conquer the South, he said, and to extend the Asiatic dominion of communism.

So now the East wind that Hughes had feared for so long was raging and Saigon became another of the South East Asian cities to which he commuted regularly. The fact that Australia quickly followed the United States in sending troops made the assignment more personal. The commitment against communism by the United States, followed by that of his own country, justified his long-held belief that communism was now nakedly on the initiative. Also, he would be joining again one of his dearest friends, Denis Warner, who flew in from Australia to report the conflict. He had known Warner since occupation days in Tokyo and he treasured the friendship of the tough, down-to-earth Warner above all others. Warner was an acknowledged expert on the South East Asian scene, and a brilliant writer, with unrivalled sources.

He had ranged through the huge area for two decades and had built up a world-wide reputation for solid, no-nonsense reporting. He and Hughes had met many times since the occupation days and Hughes always felt at ease with his comparably phlegmatic friend. Warner

134

was calm and supportive and he had one quality Hughes admired beyond all others — loyalty.

The Caravelle Hotel was their usual headquarters in Saigon. It still had some element of graciousness about it that was reminescent of the once elegant city. Many of the correspondents stayed there, converting their rooms into minature news rooms where they worked and slept and entertained. It was right in the heart of the booming city that was bursting at the seams as troops poured in and frightened peasants from the surrounding countryside streamed towards its comparative safety.

Hughes and Warner and many of the other British, Australian and New Zealand correspondents used the nearby Reuter office as their communication centre. The Reuter office was presided over by a slightly built, yet strangely authoritative Vietnamese. He was Phan Ngoc Dinh. Dinh, inevitably 'Gunga' Dinh, was enormously capable, knew everybody and was a superb 'fixer'. He was to distinguish himself later when he went alone into the dangerous Cholon area of the city to recover the bodies of correspondents killed in a communist ambush. Two young Australians were among them.

Saigon then was reminescent of Tokyo during the Korean War days. The fact that the war itself was closer and at times in the city itself added to the heady excitement. Sadly, there was no Shimbun Alley, but there were many of the same cynical faces, older and more stately of course, among the world's press. There were other notable differences. Not least was the uneasy lack of total belief in the Western cause.

In the Korean War, partly because it was an Allied effort, there was initially near unanimity among the correspondents about the rightness of the conflict. It was virtually a black-and-white situation. On the surface it was not necessarily a fight against communism; it was a team effort to stop the ruthless hammering of a near-defenceless people by great powers. It was an emotional response by virtually the whole of the Western world to what seemed naked aggression and correspondents found it easy to identify themselves with the action being taken to stop it.

In Vietnam, the issues were far more clouded. For a start, it was primarily internecine. Participation by great communist powers was less evident and the comparably lonely 'guardians at the gate' role of the United States and a few of her allies was not the stuff of total commitment that applied in the Korean conflict. As a consequence, not the same identification applied in the Vietnam conflict and very early reports were filed that cast doubt on the correctness of United States' action.

Hughes, totally committed as he was to anti-communism, also found himself harbouring some uneasiness when he saw the total devastation wrought by pattern bombing and the chemical slaughter of once lush foliage. Kilometre after kilometre of once luxuriant growth became as bare as Australia's Nullabor Plain. Looking down on it as helicopters swept low taking the correspondents to visit units outside the city, he was appalled. 'Bare as a badger's arse', he said gloomily when he returned, sweating, one day from a visit to Australian troops.

He was troubled too, as always, by the innocent victims of the violence from both sides. He visited hospitals in Saigon and saw the rows and rows of crowded cots with their tiny, maimed occupants, big-eyed with fear. He sat in on debriefing sessions when interrogators were told about the hopeless conditions of their fight by black-pyjamed Vietcong prisoners — some of them mere children, scrawny and frightened yet often defiant. And inevitably he thought often of the contrast to his own childhood — the sounds of children playing, cricket games with his brother, and the shining days as he tramped happily to school.

He dutifully wrote his pieces for his British and Australian papers, reporting on the tonnes of bombs being dropped, skirmishes, casualties, advances and retreats. He could often see the flash of artillery and hear the thumping of bombs from the top floor of the Caravelle.

Writing to one small god-daughter Hughes noted: 'There is much ugly fighting — and I've got the dreaded gout again. Once, when I was in a bombed village it was raining very hard and I was quite wet. A little girl about the same age as you ran out of her house and handed me a towel so I could dry myself. The little girl and her people were very poor but she would not take anything I offered her. And I forgot the gout and being wet and I felt good.'

Saigon had its compensations however. There were many old friends in the city and he swapped lies with them and smoked his cigars and drank. On occasions he even screwed in his monocle and took part in clamorous 'cultural disputation' about the state of the world, the war, Conan Doyle and the unrivalled beauty of the cheong sam-clad women, always in abundant numbers. He practiced his execrable French on the locals, many of them English speakers, and poured scorn on some of the younger correspondents who occasionally acted the role of the war correspondents, complete with weapons, as Hollywood had depicted it for them.

He had a great fondness for exotic foods, and somehow he found places in Saigon that still retained the art of French cooking from the city's French colonialist past. The fact that a bomb might whizz from a passing motor cyclist into some of the places he frequented did not deter him. Eggs benedictine was one of his favourite dishes but he swore off this tidbit when even his iron constitution rebelled at the main locally produced ingredient.

Kipling might have had Hughes in mind when he wrote that a good war correspondent needed 'the power of glib speech that neither man nor woman can resist when a meal or bed is in question, the eye of a horse coper, the skill of a cook, the constitution of a bullock, the digestion of an ostrich and an infinite adaptability to all circumstances'. Hughes had them all. And beyond that he had an enormous capacity for making the most of everying — a passion for talk, for his profession and for fun. Saigon gave him all that, but his uneasiness about the state of the war and his compassion for the wretched country troubled his conscience and he returned to Hong Kong with relief.

Hong Kong too was changing. The city was becoming more and more crowded, prices were escalating as troops from Vietnam charged in on leave with bulging wallets, and there were ominous signs that the wind from the East would soon batter the colony more savagely than the occasional typhoon smashing in from the China Sea.

Hughes went back into his role of China watching with relish. The Red Guards were rampaging through China as Mao encouraged them to uncover and rout his opponents. 'Have no fear of chaos', he told the rebel youths on one occasion. 'Disorder and chaos are always a good thing.' Reports of Red Guard extremes not far from Hong Kong itself were fed to Hughes and he feared for the future of the little colony perched so precariously on China's rump.

Earlier, the colony had a foretaste of China's unpredictability when there was an uprecedented mass exodus of refugees from the mainland. For about twenty-five days some 70 000 men, women and children poured across the frontier in a frightening exodus. Hong Kong, already swollen beyond belief from years of population growth and sporadic border crossings, could not handle the numbers and absorb them in what Hughes called 'one compulsive gulp'. The frontier comprised twenty seven kilometres of fast-flowing rivers, wooded areas, stony mountains and ravines that separated Hong Kong's so-called 'new territories' from China proper.

In effect, according to Hughes, the exodus was possible only because the Chinese communists threw open the frontier. The refugees trampled down the slender four-metre-high barbed wire fence that delineated but did not guard the frontier. Hughes had been warned from a contact in nearby Macao that China was preparing a 'thinning out' operation involving hundreds of thousands of people in order to relieve congestion in the cities and relieve pressure on food-scarce areas.

He went to the border areas to watch the human tide crashing into the drought-stricken colony. There was a thin line of British and Hong Kong police, augmented by soldiers, but they were incapable of holding back the mass. Chinese guards on the mainland directed the refugees to convenient points of entry and warned them away from areas where police and soldiers were massed most strongly. Thousands of the refugees were turned back but thousands scrambled through the thin lines of defenders. 'The extraordinary thing', Hughes said at the time, 'was that the Chinese authorities on the mainland accepted the return of the refugees with the same apparent indifference they had shown earlier when the mobs began crossing'.

Trucks and trains took the refugees who had been caught back to China.

Hughes spoke to many of the refugees who made the crossing. 'They told me of a grey, barren landscape of hardship and scarcity, failing food and dwindling hope, of hungry uprooted thousands conscripted to farm work or wandering in search of greener fields and happier lives'. The refugees were not all 'useless mouths' as first reports had indicated. The first were elderly but then came able-bodied young men and women. Some had walked for five days to reach the border.

Fear of tomorrow, he said, was among the reasons some of them gave him for their attempts to break out. They were hungry and tired and some of them were suffering from an eye ailment due to a vitamin deficiency, but they were not starving. The ones who reached the border were the fittest, they told Hughes. The old, the weak and undernourished had lagged along the road and many had died.

'There was a rare, fleeting surge of hope, adventure and excitement among the refugees who made it . . . Communism as an ideology had surprisingly little influence on the refugees. Hungry people cannot eat dogma but they do not necessarily blame the dogma for the hunger.'

The picture the refugees brought of conditions in China was authentic, he felt, and was better information than what he had gleaned from his contacts. 'The prevalent mood was one of hopeless-ness, disillusion and passive resistance to eternal back-breaking campaigns directed so often to futile ends.'

He could not give a reasoned explanation for the exodus or for the apparent permissiveness of the Chinese authorities. 'Perhaps the Chinese wanted to point out to Hong Kong that she could have been swamped into impotence if the flow had not eased. It could have been a reminder to Hong Kong of its vulnerability.' Obviously a similar flood could be released whenever and for whatever reason the communist regime decided to trample down the frontier. 'Borrowed place, borrowed time' had a new and frightening significance, he declared.

Hughes' respect grew for the British authorities' tolerance and restraint in the face of the frightening experience. One false move or sign of weakness could have been the spark to ignite a far uglier situation. But they had been firm, courteous and kind, and had kept a low profile. Their police had fed the hungry ones among the refugees, attended to the sick, and above all they had been cheerful. 'No wonder the buggers ran the world for so long', he told a friend admiringly.

Although he had heard reports from his contacts that the communist Chinese authorities were not enamoured of it, Hughes' second book, *The Chinese Communes* was selling well. He had written it as factually as possible, based on his own experiences in China. He had toured various communes during previous visits, always escorted by the obligatory band and thumping drum, and had listened to interminable speeches about the glories of communal life and the paradise to come.

Nationalist Chinese, under Chiang Kai-shek, were taking advantage of the turmoil within China itself by shelling the mainland from their off-shore bases. They were being shelled in return from the mainland.

Hughes' earlier efforts to cover the story had been frustrated by Ian Fleming. But now his friend was dead, so together with Denis Warner he flew to Quemoy. The shelling from the mainland had died down temporarily and there was little to report about this aspect. Similarly, there was little point in recapitulating on Chiang's fading dream that he would lead his armies on a glorious crusade back to the mainland to topple Mao's solidly entrenched regime.

So the two friends cast about to find a story and eventually they found a Belgian priest who epitomized Chiang's dream, and that of so many old China hands, of a victorious return to resume a lifestyle that had gone forever. The priest, Father Druetto, had spent many years in China prior to Mao's victory and the communist takeover. He stayed behind and saw many of his flock killed, was thrown into prison and treated shockingly before he too was able to flee and take sanctuary on the off-shore islands.

In Quemoy, Druetto rebuilt his shattered life and gradually gathered together a small congregation of faithful Roman Catholics. He began to build a church, alone at first, but later with the help of others. Then came a small presbytery which he and some members of his flock also built. When the shelling from the mainland became intense, Druetto dug a shelter in the rock face behind his tiny church's altar. He had already carved out a sizeable hole when Hughes and Warner met him. He told them he hoped eventually to make it big enough to shelter his flock.

The priest was middle-aged but he looked incredibly old and worn. He had a long white beard that seemed to complement his gentleness, and he spoke softly.

Hughes and Warner sat in the shade of the church with the priest as he told them, without bitterness, of the terrible inquisition he had faced under the early communist regime. All around him was evidence of his love and care for his Chinese congregation. 'The scene was strangely moving', Warner recalled. 'There was devastation all around us and yet here was this man so full of hope.'

Hughes' reaction was spontaneous, as with the Blind Bonze of Luang Prabang and the Russian priest in Irkutsk. He knelt in the rubble and emotionally asked the priest's blessing. Druetto made the sign that Hughes had so often mocked. Warner does not know even now whether the action was genuine or part of the act Hughes played throughout his life.

Hughes had met the newspaper magnate Lord Thomson on one of his London visits. He liked the rotund, quietly spoken Canadian and when Thomson came to Hong Kong in the sixties, Hughes laid on a fascinating list of engagements for 'milord', as he invariably called Thomson, to look over.

One of the engagements was a sumptuous banquet on one of the floating restaurants in Hong Kong harbour. The lights of the booming city climbed up the Peak and far to the East there were shadows of mountains occasionally lit by lightning as Hughes escorted Thomson back across the harbour. They were discussing the book, *The World of Susie Wong* and Hughes pointed out an hotel on Gloucester Road as being the site of the original hotel portrayed in the book. Thomson was fascinated. He asked Hughes to take him there — 'purely, I hasten needlessly to add, in a mood of curiosity and investigation', Hughes told a friend later. Hughes knew the hotel from an earlier visit with Ian Fleming when Fleming was researching *Exciting Cities*.

'I thought Lord Thomson and I looked a respectable pair of visitors, mature, responsible and substantial, although perhaps a shade too rotarian.' Two 'susie wongs' swooped down on them as they entered and ushered the two bowing men into a cubicle. Hughes explained that they were a couple of paymaster sergeants from a U.S. aircraft carrier that had just berthed.

'Milord', Hughes recalled, 'didn't flick an eyelash. He merely nodded solemnly and sipped his beer with a nautical air.' One of the girls addressed them both in excellent English. 'Thank you, dears', she said. 'We like it better when you boys come here not wearing uniform.' Hughes said he avoided his lordship's eye. During the ensuing desultory conversation, Thomson carefully studied the price of the drinks on the menu and made a few notes on an envelope. Then, to Hughes surprise, he asked the girls: 'How much to go upstairs?'

'Thirty dollars for an hour, dear', one replied, 'plus ten dollars for the room.' She looked hopeful.

Lord Thomson made another note on the envelope. 'Then how much for a single room unaccompanied', he asked.

'Twenty dollars', the girl said, and Hughes claimed he distinctly saw perplexity replace hope in her eyes.

Thomson made another note, nodding thoughtfully. Eventually the two men got up to go and tipped the girls generously as they were

140

bowed to the door where the Thomson limousine was waiting to whisk the 'paymaster sergeants' into the night. In the car Hughes asked Thomson why he was asking so many questions. 'You're not thinking of buying the place, are you?' Thomson replied reflectively: 'No. But I could do worse, don't you think?'

Some years later Hughes went into China with Thomson and was present when the magnate had a one hour talk with premier Chou En-lai. As they rose to say goodbye to a gracious Chou, Lord Thomson remarked that he was essentially a capitalist just as the premier was a communist, but he would be grateful for Chou's advice on whether he should continue to invest in Hong Kong. Chou laughed blandly, Hughes recalled. 'Do not worry, your lordship. I look forward to our next meeting', the premier said.

Later still, after both Chou and Thomson had died, Hughes told a friend when recounting the Peking meeting: 'Who knows? Perhaps they have now met again? After all, Lord Thomson, like myself, was born in the year of the horse — although in an earlier cycle — and Chou En-lai was born in the year of the wild boar. And as all Chinese traditionalists know, the horse and the wild boar always get on well together.'

After Thomson died, Hughes paid this tribute to him: 'The highest personal tribute I can pay to Lord Thomson, after having worked for him since he took over *The Times* and the *Sunday Times* in the late fifties, is that he is the only boss who ever asked me to unlace and take off his shoes. I did so eagerly and without any sense of class conscious, anti-union kow towing.'

The incident happened about 1972 when Thomson had just returned from addressing the Foreign Correspondent's Club. He was in his suite at The Mandarin hotel and was tired and anxious for a rest before another speaking engagement that night. 'Would you mind taking my shoes off for me, Richard', he asked, sinking on his bed. 'I can't bend down very well these days.'

Hughes said he felt a certain guilt because he had pressured Thomson into the second engagement. 'Yet I felt furtiveness at my happy response to his request to act as personal valet. As a life member of the Australian Journalists' Association who had twice been out on strike in Sydney I could well imagine my personal rage if my former employer Sir Frank Packer had improbably asked me to kneel and take off his shoes. But Lord Thomson's request was unique and an honour.'

His reaction was yet another indication of the dichotomy in his thinking and actions when he was dealing with people on different strata. He never played his 'your grace' or 'monseignor' games with senior figures — people he could not control. He was then the urbane dignified Richard Hughes. To others he often played the game of jocular flattery or aggression in order to set relationships on a path suitable to him. It was a way of gaining an advantage, and he played this game with enormous success.

11 Hong Kong Hilton Bombed

Hughes adored women. He doesn't know where the quote came from, but his bastardized version of his philosophy about them was succinct: 'Women prefer being amused without being loved to being loved without being amused'. Added to that philosophy was his old-world charm. He also had the ability to appear to be genuinely interested and he openly acknowledged women's intelligence. When the intelligence wasn't there he pretended it was, but the pretence applied only to women. With men he could be fast and cruel in the face of humbug. Above all, he was immensely loyal to his friends and he never transgressed, irrespective how tempted at times, with others' wives or mistresses. They were inviolate and because of it most women trusted him.

They often told him things they did not discuss with their husbands, perhaps because they sensed Hughes knew that few men could accept truth as women did. Also, he had a touch of arrogance about him that many women found attractive. Sometimes he acted the arrogance part and other times he went on his own way, often with outrageous views, and seemed not to care whether his friends liked or despised them. One tough American woman summed up his appeal: 'We feel he's an ally. He operates from the gut. He knows we're less vulnerable than men and we're not frightened to show our vulnerability. He's got a bit of that in him too.'

Occasionally Hughes would champion a lost cause, or take an opposite view to that of the majority, purely because he got bored quickly with the I-agree-with-you mentality. He relished the spotlight this outspokenness brought. There was seldom a gathering where he was not the centre of attention. He had the rare combination of being articulate, amusing, and ruthless and when he cut loose with all three the effect could be devastating. But wit was his rapier. If that articulate weapon failed he could fall back on brutal frankness. The knowledge of it's existence rarely made it's use necessary.

143

So he attracted people from all walks of life. Intellectuals, politicians, writers, businessmen, actors, taxi drivers and waitresses and bar girls came into his orbit. Yet he was a strangely private man despite the glare and he kept his affairs hidden. He used the best of weapons — apparent openness — to keep his love life under tight wraps. He was always aware, of course, of the 'sparrows', feared alike by foreign correspondents and intelligence operators.

Some of the shadowy men Ian Fleming had introduced him to in London had warned him about them before his first tilt at Moscow. They were not always beautiful, he was told. But they were dangerous and could compromise a foreign correspondent as easily as a businessman or an intelligence agent. They would feed back to their masters the most innocuous of pillow talk that could become a significant thread in an overall pattern being laboriously fashioned somewhere.

Hughes was reminded of this during one of his visits to China. He was walking by a lake one afternoon and the rare stillness that comes occasionally in the middle of so much noise was almost tangible. He was reflecting contentedly on the absence of temptation — his mind was free of the thought of women in a lustful sense — and he was turning over in his mind how Chinese communism had taken the colour out of life. In removing colour they had effectively wiped out one of the ingredients of temptation. The train of thought led him to think of a quote he had used in his column years earlier: one of the first casualties in any communist takeover is feminine beauty.

He became aware of the girl before she spoke. She stood on the edge of the lake, then walked towards him, her baggy blue uniform hiding effectively whatever shape she had. Hughes smiled and bowed. She was trembling obviously when she got near him and she looked up at the huge man towering above her. Then, in fair English, she said: 'I am so exciting. I am so exciting I could fall in the sea.'

'I don't understand madam', Hughes said, bowing again uneasily.

The girl was handsome rather than pretty. She had the delicate facial bone structure of so many beautiful Chinese women but it was a strong face and for a moment Hughes imagined the lithe beauty of a body that would complement such a face. He guessed her age at about twenty-five.

She was looking at him steadily now, not smiling, and his composure returned after the abrupt, obvious approach.

'You mean, madam, you are excited?'

She nodded and pointed to the placid lake. 'I could fall into the sea', she repeated. She told him she was a secretary. Where did he live?

For a wild moment he thought of the possibilities. Then caution returned. 'Look out Hughes', said a little voice in the back of his mind.

He turned on his avuncular air, smiled and bowed again. Out of the

The Duke of Edinburgh and Hughes in an intense discussion at a function in Hong Kong.

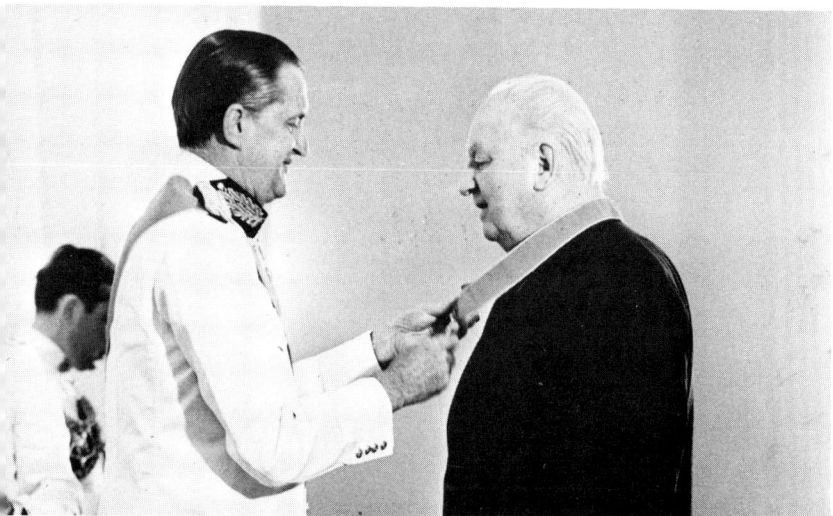

The Governor of Hong Kong, Sir Murray MacLehose, at Hughes' investiture of the C.B.E. in 1980.

Hughes with his third wife Ann and his son Richard at a 'This is Your Life' function in Hong Kong.

Hughes as guest of honour at the 35th anniversary celebrations of the Foreign Correspondents' Club of Japan in 1981 when he was given a testimonial dinner and presented with a gold membership badge. Among the guests was Australia's then Ambassador to Japan, Sir James Plimsoll (middle).

corner of his eye he could see a Chinese family, father, mother and two children, coming towards them, and they too helped break the momentary spell. He could think of nothing to say to the now forlorn looking girl, so he turned to the safety of small talk and gradually resumed his walk, alone, as the family got closer.

When he recalled the incident later in Hong Kong he told a friend that only in retrospect had the thought that the girl might have been a 'sparrow' crystallized. After all, he reflected, the Russians had introduced a lot of their tricks to the Chinese during the days of their close relationship. And the Chinese knew a few tricks of their own. But why had they picked on him, assuming the girl was a plant, and why was she so obvious? The question was to haunt him for a long time.

In Hong Kong he had an encounter with a woman that was to trouble him later too. It was an instance of his ruthlessness, rarely used, that few saw as he got older.

The woman was running for office in an organization to which Hughes belonged and she sought his support. He was polite and evasive at first, but when she became louder and more insistent and asked him repeatedly whether he would vote for her he told her bluntly he would not. Why, she asked? He said he did not think the particular office was suited for a woman. She became incensed. 'You know your trouble, don't you Richard? You're a male chauvinist pig. You're out of date.' Hughes fixed her with his cold blue eyes. He said reasonably: 'Do you think so madam? Do you think you could handle the job? You know you will come into contact with bad manners and a lot of bad language. So fuck off.'

Hughes wanted to apologize later for his rudeness, and the incident was eventually forgotten without any hard feelings.

Hughes was a prolific drinker. He put it down to his late start. Drink stimulated him and he loved nothing so much as being surrounded by friends and acquaintances talking and arguing, with drink as the common denominator. But he rarely got drunk. He often thought of himself as an escaped alcoholic and he paid deference to the influence of alcohol on his life in a piece he wrote about the relationship between drinking and reporting. 'A controversial (or scoop) story', he wrote, 'can be conceived in alcohol but in delivery it needs an unfettered mind and cool, well-considered typing fingers. In certain countries of course, another requisite is a self-protective glance over the shoulder.' He referred to Mao Tse Tung as a 'reflective and reasonable drinker' who might have said the words attributed to Ralph Waldo Emerson: 'The secret of drunkenness is that it insulates us in thought while it unites us in feelings'. Hughes went on: 'The wise correspondent should relax and invest in a snort or two with prospective sources but should never seek immediate printed advantage of alcoholic indiscretion, which preferably should be mutual indiscretion.'

He referred to master spy Richard Sorge in this drinking context. 'Sorge could drink and gamble with foreign pressmen in Tokyo's old Imperial Hotel but he never got drunk and he encouraged his running agents, who were legitimate correspondents, to pump foreign pressmen.' He also put Japan's former foreign minister Matsuoka in the top bracket with Sorge as a drinker who used alcohol properly.

At times Hughes has carried his loyalty to extremes — even to the extent that he would not write good stories if he suspected that publication would harm the innocent. One instance of this happened when a fellow correspondent from a nearby country, noted for fascist-like government, told him the story of his shameful treatment at the hands of his country's rulers.

The correspondent had written the truth as he saw it, but his reports lifted the lid on the neo-fascist rule the leaders imposed under the guise of democracy. They surrounded his terrified household one night with some forty soldiers and police and dragged him to gaol. No explanation was given, either to the man or to his wife. For months the man endured round the clock questioning. His interrogators demanded he should express regret for what he had written. He was not physically tortured but the squeeze was of the mind. He was told nothing of the fate of his wife and children.

Finally, still without explanation, he was released, but forced to leave his country and his family. He tried unsuccessfully to get a visa to another country so they could, perhaps, join him. At last he came to Hong Kong. He told the story unemotionally, but was obviously still worried about his family. He did not suggest that Hughes should not use the story.

It was the sort of story that would have been used widely but Hughes refused indignantly to write it in case harm came to the man's family. Instead, after listening for nearly an hour, he bought him, a stranger until that day, a lavish meal and encouraged him to regain his lost dignity.

Drama was attracted to Hughes like waves to a beach. If correspondents fought among themselves, divorced their wives, got into trouble with their offices, or were the victims of just plain bad luck he seemed to become involved. He was a repository of secrets and in a way he became what he mocked — a father confessor who listened and offered advice only when it was sought.

One friend whose young wife was stricken with a severe illness that crippled and sometimes killed was in despair when he told Hughes of the tragedy. Sometimes he would work throughout the night to keep his mind off his wife's suffering. Hughes would sit up with him often through the long nights, invariably cheerful, and instilling hope when

146

his friend was bereft of it. At weekends he made sure his friend was never alone. Only when the illness was partially eased and the woman began to recover did the friend realize how much he had depended on Hughes and how much the big man had given, under the seal of the confessional — Hughes style.

There were many hilarious incidents too. One involved a visiting woman correspondent, of indifferent looks, who tried to make herself 'one of the boys' to fit into what she saw as the bohemian atmosphere of the times. She was an enthusiastic member of a luncheon party where Hughes presided over some seven other correspondents. As the vodka flowed, she drew attention to herself by piling salt on the table and then setting it alight to prove it burned green. Hughes was slightly embarrassed by her antics so he reached across and took the lighter she had used and passed her a bowl of fruit. She immediately grabbed a banana and bit it in half savagely. 'I'm told bananas are regarded as prime phallic symbols', she said triumphantly.

There was a moment of stunned silence which Hughes broke. 'Christ', he said, 'that really hurt'.

Hughes made another visit to Tokyo in the mid-sixties for what he described as 'another glimpse of old days, old places, old friends (vanishing) and old memories'.

He found the city as hideous as ever but it retained its respect for the foreigner drawn back into its nostalgic embrace. During this visit he traced down the 'number one' bar boy of the old Shimbun Alley Foreign Correspondents Club. 'He was very sentimental and spoke with affection and nostalgia of you all', he wrote to a friend, also suggesting he should write to the bar boy: 'Send him a picture of yourself with your grandchildren . . . He'll show it to his friends as proof that the press gaijin (foreigners) of the forties do not forget'.

He made another visit to Singapore in the mid-sixties when it split from the Malaysian Federation after an uneasy marriage. Lee Kuan Yew did not want his island state held back by the more easy-going Malayans and his ideas about the form of guided capitalism he was implementing with such success did not appeal to the Malayans with their more conventional view. Hughes predicted, correctly, that the astute Lee would come out of the partnership intact and that tempers would soon cool.

Hughes' opposition in Singapore, at least for the *Sunday Times,* was Dennis Bloodworth of the *Observer.* An old friend, Bloodworth, like Denis Warner, was an authority on South East Asia, a brilliant reporter and author. He had two colleagues helping him with his cover. One day when the story was really on the boil, one of them disappeared but finally surfaced in the late afternoon the worse for wear. He explained his absence by saying he'd been 'dealing with the opposition'. Hughes had matched him drink for drink and so reduced *his* opposition to more satisfactory odds. He denied indignantly that he got Bloodworth's man drunk deliberately. 'Just a long cultural discussion over a civilized lunch', he explained. 'Probably the heat was too much for him'.

Singapore, like Shanghai and Hong Kong, fascinated Hughes. Its genesis was in marsh and mud, as with Shanghai, and it too owed its beginnings to a British adventurer, Stamford Raffles. Out of deference to the past, and because he had a sneaking regard for the buccaneering Raffles, Hughes always visited Singapore's Raffles Hotel when he was in the 'lion city'.

But whereas the shrewd businessmen who had founded Shanghai left it too late to learn they could not continue to rape with impunity, Hong Kong and Singapore adapted. Singapore particularly. Hughes gave most of the credit for the city's amazing progress to Lee Kuan Yew, the Cambridge-educated socialist Hughes considered to be the ablest political leader in Asia. He summed up his attitude towards Lee's critics when he wrote: 'To the earnest visitor, the twittering denigration of a political leader because of the extent of his success, founded and persisting on free voting, is like a shower of bunkum and horse manure'.

He admired Singapore's transition from iron-clad colonialism to sturdy independence. There were a few riots, admittedly, but they were primarily racial in origin and once the tough Lee had hammered the city's communists into the ground, the island rocketed ahead.

Hughes' admiration and liking for Lee Kuan Yew stemmed not only from Lee's opposition to communism. He liked the man's ruthlessness, his acceptance of things as they were and not as a starry-eyed visionary would like them to be: 'Lee would do business with the devil— irrespective of politics and race— if that business would bring investment capital to the republic'.

Over the years he developed a respectful working relationship with the charismatic Lee and he never failed to seek— and get— an interview with Lee whenever he visited Singapore. Lee, for his part, liked and respected Hughes, who never wasted his time, and knew that interviews Hughes sought were for a purpose and not just the notch-on-the-gun routine some other correspondents favoured. Perhaps each of them sensed the ruthlessness of the other.

Seeing Lee, and hearing his oratory, stirred a fervour in Hughes that could have been associated with his young days. Then a highly intelligent, tough assessor had forecast that Hughes could have become Prime Minister of Australia had he gone into politics. 'Piss on that', Hughes was to remark later when reminded of the forecast, 'I wouldn't soil my hands with politics'.

But he cultivated politicians and they in turn sought him out, sometimes to get his views on South East Asian affairs and often just

148

for the fun of his company. He could play the amiable raconteur to perfection, generous, open, ready at all times to pass on his knowledge. The buffoonery, of course, never got in the way of this primary function of gathering information for his newspapers. His discretion was, properly, taken for granted and only the gauche found it necessary to remind him at times that certain information was off the record.

Diplomats, particularly those new to the region, often sought him out too. Some were directed to him. One recalled that virtually the first quesion the Governor of Hong Kong asked him when he arrived was: 'Met Richard Hughes yet?' At their subsequent meeting and long lunch, he said he found Hughes closer to understanding the Chinese mentality than any other China watcher he had met. 'Some others are more steeped in political and economic detail, but Hughes was one of the few who knew what made the Chinese so different from the rest of us, and more importantly, why they liked to feel so different'.

This diplomat was one of the elite band Australia sent to South East Asia after the Pacific war and who were to distinguish themselves with their professionalism and do more for their country's image than many of the faded politicians who preceded them. Years later he said of Hughes: 'I have yet to hear an Australian denigrate him and yet to meet one who did not have an affection for him. It's quite remarkable that he has managed to be both successful and popular'.

Hughes would try anything, within reason, in the way of food and drink. He even tried smoking opium, but not in Hong Kong where the Chinese referred to it slightingly as 'foreign mud'. Hong Kong had been built on it, in 1843, when the first of the British businessmen saw the trade possibilities of the magnificent harbour. They harvested the wealth of China, including opium, and Hong Kong grew from its lowly beginnings as a fishing village to become one of the great ports of the world largely through the marketing of opium and other contraband.

He tried opium first in Shanghai and was disappointed. There was a heightened awareness he had been told about and the elongation of time, but none of the Elysian heights the romantics spoke about. Later, together with a medical friend, he had a few pipes in Bangkok. Hughes' response was flat again, so he decided his outlook on life and opium smoking were not bed fellows. Good food, strong liquor and cigars that yielded their fine aroma after he'd seduced them with his fingers became his opiates.

But this second opium 'bash', as he called it, gave him a more tolerant view of the habit. It was a cultivated taste, he found, and one must smoke it in agreeable company. A moderate smoker did not necessarily become a hopeless addict. The few who did become addicts probably would have been alcoholics if their taste had run to liquor. Many of the people who smoked it, Hughes found, escaped from a hopeless world under its influence. It made them gentler and kinder. It was a religion to people without hope. But its effect on him was roughly the equivalent of six whiskies — and he considered he would have had more enjoyment from the whiskies.

Hughes' medical friend, who claimed to be more interested in a medical study of opium and its effects than personal enjoyment, took him to Bangkok's Heng Lak Hung Inn for the experiment. It was the biggest opium den in the world at the time, with five thousand permanent boarders and some thousand transients daily. The boarders ate and slept at the inn, went to work each morning and returned each night to eat, smoke a few pipes and play cards and talk, then sleep on the wooden floors of their cubicles. It was eminently respectable.

Hughes and his friend tramped down a long, hot passageway to an empty cubicle, haunted by the heavy, sweet smell of the smoke. He described the scene in *Foreign Devil:*

'It was about 9 p.m. and some of the inmates were already asleep. Others, reclining on their sides, were puffing white clouds of poppy smoke from their long, gleaming pipes, held over the yellow flame of oil lamps.

'The rows and rows of prone figures-twisted and huddled, naked skeleton limbs asprawl, faces lighted by the tiny tongues of fire, silent or conversing in whispers, sleeping or smoking were not only unreal, but despite drugged movement and sibilant conversation, seemed unalive. Some smokers were being massaged by kneeling women. A few, in their cheap cotton underwear, shuffled and drifted up and down the corridors like polite sleepwalkers or dazed ghosts. Some mumbled and nodded sombre secrets to themselves. No one hurried. No one raised his voice. Over all there hung a languorous, hushed, meditative spell that became almost hypnotic.'

Hughes had six pipes. At first he puffed too hard and failed to inhale properly and the opium pill went out. His tutor was the Chinese night manager of the inn, stout and beaming. He exhorted Hughes to cultivate a relaxed, rhythmical inhalation to produce a loud hissing noise and dense smoke. Hughes said the smoke in his lungs was not quite as strong as good cigar smoke but it was strangely and delicately stimulating. His sight became keener and although his brain remained clear there were flashes of fantasy. He was aware of trivia and he noticed, fascinated, the texture of the skin of his hand.

When they went out into the night again, Hughes felt tremendous exhilaration and superiority. He felt he could have stopped the roaring traffic had he held up his hand. The street lights seemed brighter and even elegant and the hot Bangkok wind seemed cool and refreshing. He was unaware of the time, and uncaring.

His doctor friend's forecast that he would doze off with memories of a pleasant day, and sleep peacefully without dreams, was correct. But he was never to repeat the experiment. The state of euphoria the opium induced was not conducive, he decided, to the life of a foreign devil fighting dragons.

He believed fervently that in Hong Kong, as perhaps in no other place on earth with the possible exception of early post war Tokyo, the human weaknesses of eating and living, loving and dying, could be enjoyed best. One of his favourite dishes among the gastronomic treasures brought unendingly to the banquets he loved attending was beggars' chicken. It comprised tender chicken stuffed with chestnuts, herbs and shredded cabbage, wrapped in lotus leaves and baked in clay. He tried them all — bear's paw, Peking duck, stewed snake. He claimed the stewed snake should be washed down with a shot of snake's blood, which he swore was a greater aphrodisiac than Korean ginseng, Spanish fly or rhinoceros horn powder — 'according to my herbalist sources'.

Hughes also tried, but found wanting, the highly touted birds' nest soup — 'Insipid and singularly over-rated'. He referred to the soup in a piece he wrote for his Australian newspapers. 'For some reason, perhaps to do with the troubles there, the sea swallows who made the nests are leaving South Vietnam,' he wrote: 'This may seem a frivolous message with little interest to sensible Australian meat pie eaters. But it reflects profound anguish among elderly gourmets along the Chinese coast and represents a grievous body blow to the national economy of embattled South Vietnam.'

The men and boys who collect the nests climb frail bamboo ladders and swing from ropes to prize the tiny nests from the grotto roofs. One of the basic ingredients of the nests is the saliva of the swallows. Hughes suggested that a decent veil should be drawn over the other ingredients. Once the nests are harvested they are boiled and unravelled and purified prior to their final appearance before the gourmets of the world. The much touted soup, like snake's blood, also has a reputation as an aphrodisiac.

When a noted Australian humourist, Alexander Macdonald, put him in the hippopotamus category when writing a light-hearted piece on what he called 'peoples' feeding habits'. Hughes reacted with exuberance, but some asperity.

Macdonald put Hughes and author J.B. Priestley in the ranks of the hippopotami as eaters: 'I once had dinner with Hughes in Hong Kong and sat spell-bound while he disposed of a filleted Mandarin duck in two huge chomps'. Later Macdonald said he had a letter from Hughes after the original newspaper report 'was carried to Hughes in a cleft stick by a trembling coolie'.

Eventually, according to Macdonald, Hughes prowled around his mountain fastness in Hong Kong before sending a reply with the address 'Zoological Gardens, Hong Kong' which said: 'My Sydney leader has directed my attention to your classification of eaters you have known and friends who have fed you in which you have been generous enough to include me in the hippopotamus class. Always a great student of your wisdom, I am inclined to agree generally with your sensitive if empiric judgement. But with respect I suggest you should sub-divide the honest-to-God gastronomes now loosely and misleadingly clumped together under the Macdonald term "hippopotami" to provide for an important Far Eastern deviation, the rhinoceros.'

Hughes found Chinese food irresistible. He wrote of it as 'the one magnificent unifying solace for all foreign-devil expatriates in the Far East'. Anyone, he said, who had a normal Chinese dinner based on Szechwan smoked duck and steamed bread who later complained of premature hunger would be in the abominal trencherman class.

Of the myths about Chinese imperial banquets in the past he said many of them should be repudiated. Similar myths about the restorative powers and aphrodisiac qualities of some viands usually disappointed the libido but were nonetheless a delight to the palate. Rhinoceros horn, birds' nest soup, monkeys' brains, snapping turtle, eels and garlic and snake blood were reputedly delightful but he was yet to be convinced they had the powers often attributed to them.

There was evidence, he said, that some of the ancient banquets were in world class. One such, given by the Empress-Dowager in 1861 in honour of her birthday, was regarded as relatively simple. The menu was: Julienne of pork with spinach, salted vegetables, julienne of white duck meat with swallows' nest, chickens with swallows' nest, duck with swallows' nest, julienne of chicken with swallows' nest. Then followed platters of swallows' nest with julienne of pork, fresh shrimp balls, braised duck kidneys, bêche de mer. Finally there were dishes of swallows' nest with julienned roast duck, pureed chicken with mashed turnip, julienne of pork sautéed with sharks' fins, duck with bean sauce, salted vegetables, julienne of pork with egg.

Hughes' own experience of a sumptuous Chinese meal redolent of the past took place in Taipei, where his host was James Wei, a noted gourmet. Wei claimed that the art of Chinese cooking was to make the meat taste like vegetables and the vegetables taste like meat, without either losing their original texture.

Nine sat down to dinner — all 'mature and discerning diners of unbounded stomach' — as Hughes reported happily. The banquet, helped along with plenty of shaoshing wine, got off to an encouraging start with hors d'oeuvres of 'drunken' chicken, pigs' kidney, mutton and clams. Then followed Shantung fish, Szechwan chicken, Hunan curd, Hupeh meatballs, roasted Cantonese suckling pig, Lanchow steamed dumplings, Foochow fish soup and finally lotus root as the

152

sweet. At the end of the banquet, the four master cooks and the waitresses were paraded for yet another toast by the contented, gently burping, nine.

Hughes literary output was prodigious. His China-watching role alone was sufficient to keep his London and Sydney newspapers contented with his cover out of Hong Kong, yet he ranged continually over his vast region and poured in stories from Rangoon, Tokyo, Bangkok, Singapore, Saigon. He touched on everything — from polished stories for the *Economist* and *Sunday Times* about the economy and shifts in political power to more down-to-earth cover for his Australian papers about the fascinating people he met and the drama of their lives.

And then there were the letters. He wrote them by the dozen. They went to England and other parts of Europe, to the United States, to his dear friend Denis Warner in Australia, to his father and his son, to Tokyo, Singapore.

To his son he wrote letters that read like short novels. He would elaborate on the most trivial incident to make it dramatic, conjuring scenes that made magic of the most humdrum. In a way, he was trying to bridge the gap his long absences brought about.

The letters poured out in an unending flow. Many were in his familiar biblical style and he had the rare gift of talking, as opposed to writing, them. They seemed to convey his physical presence.

And letters poured back to him. A letter merely addressed 'Richard Hughes, Hong Kong' would be delivered with the same despatch as those properly addressed.

There were many women in Hughes' life, of course. Nobody could combine his charm and wit and courtliness without attracting them. But most of his affairs were transitory, smile-goodbye-the-next-morning interludes in his exuberant life; others were business-like, quickly forgotten incidents that left no scars. One day he felt there would be another Adele but in the meantime surcease of loneliness, without hurt on either side, had to suffice.

All this time Hong Kong, seemingly oblivious to its own death date — 1997 when its lease was to end — was going its rambunctious way. It was naked and unashamed, Hughes wrote, and was devoid of self-pity, regrets or fear of the future. 'It offers offence to no one, seeks help from no one and asks only to be allowed to work and live.'

He, too was optimistic about the future of the colony. The fact that Hong Kong *was* China remained the corner-stone of its survival. It was no more prone to takeover by its giant communist parent than it was under Chiang Kai-shek's Nationalists years earlier. Indeed, he reflected to a friend, the Nationalists had railed more bitterly about Hong Kong's impudent existence than Mao Tse Tung and his regime had ever done. But if the communists decided to end its existence before its allotted death date there was nothing anyone could or would do. The 'dummy run' when some 70 000 Chinese had swamped the border showed the colony's vulnerability. Also it depended on China for much of its water and its food. But Peking's tolerance of Hong Kong's existence, as with her neighbour Macao, was a mixture of pragmatism and convenience.

Macao, where Hughes often visited, was the oldest European settlement in the Far East, and it had survived since its founding in 1557 through a combination of cunning and adroit side-stepping by its Portuguese masters. Its fate when Red Guards swamped the tiny peninsular at the mouth of the Pearl River and humiliated the Portuguese — yet eventually allowed Macao to continue its comparably seedy existence — was a continual reminder to Hong Kong of its own precarious status.

But Macao was useful to the Chinese and it kept a low profile, with only decaying reminders of its freebooting past. Hughes was always saddened when he visited the city after the communists tamed it. Gaiety, like feminine beauty, was also a casualty of communism, he felt. It was one of the world's great gambling centres and gateway for gold smuggling in its heyday; now it was a constant reminder to its opulent neighbour of mortality, Chinese communist style.

When the Red Guards bellowed and rampaged through its ancient streets in 1966 and the Portuguese backed off from confrontation time after time, Hong Kong had more than a twinge of fear. It was just as vulnerable. Yet Hughes remained optimistic, and the great skyscrapers that continued to soar aloft along the waterfront and the money that continued to flow into its coffers also negated the pessimism of those who forecast its doom. His big qualification, however, dealt with a continuance of the pragmatism Peking had shown in the past. What if some new war lord took over from the Mao Tse Tung regime and with Chinese fervour removed forever the offending imperialist wart on its rump that Hong Kong represented?

Like the typhoons that irregularly screamed in from the South China Sea and battered the city, Hong Kong had its share of riots, but they were primarily industrial in origin. Gangsters and bored youths lent some semblance of a popular uprising against authority in the early eruptions.

In 1967 the pattern changed and one of the greatest and most frightening upheavals in the colony's history erupted, with full communist backing. Mao's cultural revolution that had convulsed the mainland for so long was invoked with the stated intention of overthrowing 'British fascism, imperialism and tyranny' in Hong Kong. Trained activists came in from China itself, helped exploit industrial troubles, inflamed restless youth and employed killers to bomb and maim. The Red Guards fomented the trouble initially. They were

154

young revolutionaries from universities and factories who had been trained by the army to implement the cultural revolution.

Hughes was convinced at the time the Hong Kong eruption did not have the blessing of Peking. Peking had troubles of its own, he said. But Peking's troubled leaders did nothing at first as the mobs howled through the streets in a frenzy of whipped-up hate. Pessimists recalled that similar tactics had brought about the humiliation of Macao. Why not Hong Kong then?

The difference, Hughes wrote at the time, lay in the fact that there was firm Government action in Hong Kong as opposed to Macao's abject withdrawal. But more important, he wrote, there was decisive Hong Kong Chinese reaction against the uprising. And it failed, he wrote, not because Hong Kong people loved the British more but because they loved the communists less. His views at the time were not echoed by many others; most saw the riots as the beginning of the end for the colony as they knew it, another Macao in the making.

Hughes remained convinced Peking would not give the word. Many of his sources had dried up temporarily in the confusion, but he remained firm in his belief that the end so many feared would not happen. His deep understanding of Chinese thinking was behind his optimism. There was firm government in the colony, backing from London and an efficient and brave police force. There was no backing down, as in Macao, when the ideological offensive hit Hong Kong. The anarchy that lashed the colony needed something more to feed on than ideology. It needed full-blooded support from the Chinese people in the city and Hughes was convinced this was not forthcoming.

He had been in riots in Jakarta, Tokyo, Rangoon and Singapore and they had been ugly, out-of-control eruptions of orchestrated hate. Most of them died when there was restraint and firmness — however belated — from the authorities. Yet for a while in Hong Kong even these restraints failed to quieten the howling mobs and in the absence of any real direction from Peking to halt the destruction the only hope finally lay with the Hong Kong people themselves.

There was hope, too, in Hughes' view, from frail old Mao Tse Tung in Peking when reports spoke of his growing antagonism towards the excesses of the Red Guards in China itself. They had served their purpose, Hughes' informants told him, rooting out Mao's opponents within the Communist Party and it was time for the army to take control again. But the crisis of authority provoked by the excesses of the Red Guards was not to be settled easily. They had taken literally Mao's instruction to export revolution. They were confused now, and consequently more dangerous, when Mao issued his ultimatum to anyone opposing the army. They would be committing crimes, he said, if they fought the army, destroyed means of transportation, killed people or set fires.

155

This, of course, was not known until later. Hughes, like all the other watchers, relied on some information, inspired guessing, and his instinct. Like all the foreign devils in Hong Kong, he made sporadic dashes through the rioting mobs to maintain his contacts, and continue his work, but primarily he relied on the telephone from the safety of his apartment as the echoes of Mao's thoughts rang through the streets of the city.

China watching then was at its height. Every tidbit brought from the mainland by businessmen, Japanese and the few correspondents resident in Peking was analysed and interpreted — often to conform to the views the watchers already held. In between visits to Vietnam, the watchers pored over the thousands of words picked up in Hong Kong by radio monitors. Reuters, with its unrivalled monitoring facilities, listened round the clock to every mainland broadcast and provided a translated version to correspondents.

Hughes would collect his translations from the clipboard Reuters provided, then cull the material and interpret according to the terminology the communists employed. There could be significance, for instance, when a broadcast from some remote regional station spoke of some cadres being disciplined; when a particular region was mentioned frequently; when well-known names were omitted. All provided clues and from there on it was mainly guesswork. None of the correspondents knew for sure what was going on; they merely knew the giant was convulsing.

The fear in Hong Kong became more tangible when the city's water supply from Canton was suddenly cut off. Whether the action was directed from Peking or whether Canton had acted unilaterally was the big question. Hughes plumped for Canton.

He knew Canton was a 'rogue' and that shrewd old Mao Tse Tung had not yet imposed his discipline on the area. Although he was guessing like all the others, he stayed with his belief that Peking's authority was not behind the body blow the cut water supply meant to Hong Kong. His theories were soon tested to the limit, however. Small bombs began exploding in the streets. The 'disturbances', as they were euphemistically called by an administration anxious to play down any significance, began in earnest. The bombs were of nuisance value at first. Wrapped in red paper, they were placed carefully away from areas where they could kill or maim most effectively. Many of them were dummies. Perhaps ten of 200 reported in any one day were the real thing.

The objective seemed to be to run the colony's police force ragged. The British-led force reacted superbly but they had the impossible job of trying to pick the bombs likely to be most disruptive or cause most damage. Some of the bombs would be placed carefully; others would be dropped through holes cut in the floor of cars. Targets were the exhausted police and foreign-owned buildings; seldom were the Chinese populace of Hong Kong actual targets.

One bomb was placed in one of the elevators of the Hilton Hotel. At that time the Foreign Correspondents' Club was located on the top floor, so Hughes and other correspondents had a close-up view of the terror. Two of Hughes' friends had just ridden down in the lift and were walking away from the hotel when the bomb exploded. They raced back, expecting to find mangled bodies but the lift had been empty when the explosion occurred. The ingenious plan, they discovered, involved wiring the bomb to a telephone in the lift. The terrorists then phoned the hotel switchboard and said there was a bomb in a particular lift. They waited a few minutes for the arrival of the police bomb squad, then dialled the lift telephone and triggered the device. But their timing was astray and the squad had not arrived when the bomb went off.

'Hilton Hotel bombed', screamed world and local headlines, and Hong Kong, relatively untroubled until then, began to hurt. Tourist trade eased and the thousands of troops pouring into the city from Vietnam on rest and recreation leave went elsewhere. Some Chinese began to leave and property values dropped.

The state-of-siege mentality the authorities feared began to grip when Red Guards crossed the border and killed and kidnapped some Pakistani members of the Hong Kong police force. Nobody at the time was sure the Red Guards were responsible. Could it be the Red Army itself? Were the reports true that a quarter million Chinese troops were massed on the mainland side of the bamboo border?

Yet Hong Kong, at least on the surface, functioned as before. Tourists even went to the extent of travelling to border areas to peer across at the mainland, and beaches and places of entertainment were still crowded. The rioting was controlled, the bombing was controlled and only the propaganda was loose. Communist demands for the release of imprisoned rioters in exchange for kidnapped policemen were met with firm British restraint.

In Peking itself the rioting had a sad echo when communist authorities in the capital placed Reuter correspondent Anthony Grey under house arrest and held him in shameful detention for months. There was clear implication in communist propaganda that Grey would continue to be held while Hong Kong authorities held rioters in gaol.

On the border, Hong Kong police and Ghurka troops formed a pathetically thin line facing the communist troops dispersed in the nearby countryside. One army officer told Hughes on one of his visits to the border: 'If that lot over there wanted to', and he pointed to China, 'they could line up and piss on us'.

Tension was at its highest when it was reported Chinese troops had

157

crossed the border at the village of Sha Tau Kok to capture the Pakistani policemen. The correspondent who reported the frightening escalation telephoned his boss. 'They've come across the border at Sha Tau Kok. I've put the story on the wire and now I'm going.' He did too. He had been imprisoned in Shanghai years earlier and he did not want to risk the humiliation again. He packed his bags and left the colony forever.

Primarily, the border bluffing and riots and bombings were merely splinters from the great upheaval convulsing the mainland but only hindsight made this evident. Gradually, Hong Kong's street rioting and bombings eased as Mao's Red Army began to control the frenzied Red Guards on the mainland. The guards had done the job Mao had set for them. As the tension receded on the mainland, it eased too in Hong Kong and the colony resumed its comparably frenetic but different pace.

As life began to return to normal, Hughes attended a dinner one night for a correspondent who had just come out of Peking for a rest. He was being very careful about answering the barrage of questions fired at him since he had to go back.

His wife provided one rare glimpse of the tension and fear they had known in the capital when she told Hughes and the other dinner guests her worries about her young son. She said one of the Chinese servants was teaching him to tramp around their apartment, flourishing Mao Tse Tung's Little Red Book and shouting 'Mao Tse Tung. May he live ten thousand years.' She was wary of interfering in case the servant reported her household as being opposed to the regime. She was troubled. The servant was fanatical. 'What can I do?' she asked.

Hughes advice was more succinct than helpful. 'Kick him in the balls, madam', he said.

12 Married Again

Hughes' third book, *Hong Kong: Borrowed Place, Borrowed Time* was published in 1968. He wrote it in a month, starting some days at 4 am so he could handle his normal work load during the day.

He relied on his amazing memory, his files of every story he had written, newspaper clippings and reference books as sources for what was generally acclaimed to be one of the best books about the colony ever written. The book combined a vivid survey of Hong Kong's past and its buccaneering founders with the social and economic aspects of its present and its hopes for the future. It was an instant success when it hit the bookshops and in Hong Kong alone it sold initially at the rate of 500 copies a day. The happy author spent many pleasant hours autographing copies for buyers.

There was great acclaim for the book and Hughes became a celebrity even to those who knew little of his background and other exploits. He was interviewed on radio and television and feature pieces were written about him in local newspapers. Chinese, as well as the foreign devils in the colony, continued to snap up the book as fast as it was printed.

One young television interviewer, Jack Bennett, who later became a lifelong friend, recalled the patience Hughes showed when a television feature about him and his new book went wrong. They chose an opulent house on Hong Kong's peak as the setting because the mansion's twenty-metre terrace commanded a magnificent view of the harbour and Kowloon, with the bulk of Tai mo Shan and Ma on Shan mountains rising behind the city.

Bennett was nervous as he and Hughes strolled back and forth along the terrace with the cameraman and sound technician trying to keep up and battling a rising wind. Bennett was new to Hong Kong. He had heard most of the legends about Hughes and he felt the big man would give him hell if the interview went wrong. The wind and the ancient equipment foiled all Bennett's best efforts and hardly a word of what Hughes said was recorded. Trembling, Bennett approached the sweating Hughes and told him the bad news. He recalled: 'Hughes grunted. "So we cocked it up, did we?" Then he laughed. "Ah well, let's do it again."'

Bennett, who later was to become a successful author, recalled another incident when Hughes' friendship gave him enormous face.

He was in Italy, at the Universitare per Stranieri at Perugia doing a course in Italian, and he exchanged letters with Hughes. The envelopes carrying Hughes' letters always bore his address and name: 'Hughes, Episcop. Hong Kong' followed by a cross. The woman who handled the mail was deferential when she gave Bennett his letters. She told everyone that he got regular letters from the Roman Catholic Bishop of Hong Kong.

The gestation period of *Hong Kong* presented a lot of problems. Friends, and friends of friends, vaguely troubled because Hughes was not seen so frequently at his favourite spots because of his work load, began to lay siege to him via the telephone. Finally he had to take action. It was Bond-like and could have been inspired by Bond's creator. He devised a code, given only to those with whom he wanted to keep in touch, that involved the phone being allowed to ring in different sequence. Three rings, then hang up, three more rings and hang up again. Then one ring and Hughes would answer.

The scheme worked well for a time. It stopped persistent callers in the 'I-don't-know-you but' category who passed through the colony. But it also stopped calls from many good friends, some from overseas, who did not know about the code. So when the first irate friend berated him — 'What's wrong with you, mug,' — he abandoned the idea, rather relieved. 'If I'd had a heavy night on diocesan matters of some import I'd often have trouble counting the rings the next morning', he explained.

Mornings were his good time. He loved to get up before dawn and stroll through a park, miniscule compared with those of his youth, but a sanctuary among the concrete monsters usurping every scarce few metres in the tiny, bursting-at-the-seams colony. The relative quiet of the early mornings also gave him a chance to do his eye exercises. For five minutes each morning he would roll his eyes to heaven and to the ground and to left and right, his face contorting from the effort. The few other walkers he met didn't react when the big man passed them, eyes rolling and mouth working idiotically.

He'd worn glasses some years earlier but became impatient with them. So when he read about the efficacy of exercises when there was nothing organically wrong with eyes he bought a book on the subject and took to the exercises with enthusiasm. The improvement was dramatic and within a month he stamped indignantly on his glasses,

160

which he has not needed since. He did need a walking stick however when arthritis crept into his knees and his early morning walks became painful.

During his walks he noticed that tree-sniffing was replacing street spitting as an early morning idiosyncrasy of some of the Chinese walkers he met. He claimed tree sniffing was an ancient Chinese strategem to clear the chest, throat and nostrils. 'You stand with your head thrust into the healthy leaves and inhale deeply instead of spitting noisily.'

He gave Mao Tse Tung some of the credit for the welcome change in habits. It was vindication, he said, of Chairman Mao's teachings on mass criticism and the judgement of the people. 'I can't recall any specific Mao thought on spitting of course. But he obviously had it in mind.' The fact that potential spitters who made an incautious or defiant throat clearance preparatory to an explosive delivery were fixed with an accusing stare by fellow walkers was enough. 'They must then spike the cannon or fire a guilty or embarrassed shot which loses all basic satisfaction by having aroused communal disapproval.'

Another intriguing sight on his walks were dogs and their masters. 'Most of the cunning devils resist the desperate efforts of their human attendants to lure them into public latrines. There are few more pathetic sights than a dignified foreign devil at dawn using newspaper to collect canine fallout while the pampered dogs smirk and revel over this service' he wrote in his column in the prestigious *Far Eastern Economic Review*.

He said the antics of the early walkers and their dogs, and the walkers' attempts to get their dogs to the privies did not conjure up the sophisticated atmosphere of the old hip-high Paris pissoirs. 'There a male occupant could raise his hat gallantly with the disengaged hand as a lady friend passed, smiling. There is nothing gallant about the sight of a sweating foreign devil trying to force a dog away from our precious patches of grass to perform his toilet.'

Hong Kong settled down relatively quickly after the Red Guard and Cultural Revolution riots but there was no lessening in the watch Hughes kept on the mainland Chinese scene. He maintained his regard for Mao but he feared what might happen once the old man died. What helmsman then? Hughes' contacts with informants of the China scene soon resumed after the riots and he was sure there would be more upheavals on the mainland, but peace in Hong Kong, in the days ahead.

Whenever he could, Hughes would return to Australia to see his son and father and other members of his family. The old man was eighty-six when he saw him for the last time. He was living alone in sturdy independence and enjoying an occasional brandy and a cigar. He, too, was an early riser and the pair would walk through a nearby park where his father fed birds. His father was quite contented. He was convinced, he told his son, that there was irrefutable proof death would not destroy consciousness. He had studied spiritualism for more than forty years, interviewing churchmen of all denominations, attending seances and conducting his own experiments, and had finally come to the conclusion that there was a sphere in afterlife in which laws of time were not recognized. 'Spirits there have a friendly interest in me', he said, 'and they have told me their sphere is a controlled territory, directed by an intelligent force or being. This is a constructive and creative spirit, a supreme almighty over-soul known as God.'

He told his son, quite seriously and with obvious belief, that there was indeed a rose-covered cottage awaiting him after his death and that his beloved wife Katy was there. When they discussed religion, the old man told his son that the only thing religion had demanded of him in his lifetime was to ensure a safe passage for his soul in the afterlife.

During this visit Hughes enlivened a mundane gathering of journalism cadets when he told them of some of the pitfalls of being a foreign correspondent. Among other things he gave them a graphic description of some strains of venereal disease endemic to South East Asia. He also commended the precepts of Hotsume Ozaki, the Japanese newspaperman who was the right-hand-man of master spy Richard Sorge in prewar Tokyo, as prerequisites for virgin foreign correspondents.

He visited his old mate Denis Warner and had other joyous reunions with friends before returning to Hong Kong. But he was never to see his father again. Two years later, told that the old man was dying, he caught a plane from Hong Kong to Melbourne. As soon as the aircraft landed he phoned his family from the airport. The old man had died at precisely the hour his plane landed.

The war in Vietnam was looking more and more hopeless when he next visited the country. Australia's decision to withdraw her forces, following the election of a Labor government for the first time in twenty-three years, helped precipitate the inevitable end. The United States was now virtually the only 'guardian at the gate'.

Hughes was troubled at the widening prospect of communism's downward thrust when he saw the end coming. He still believed in the United States' now lonely role, yet he despaired of the terrible damage done to the ravaged country and its people. Communism had to be stopped, but not necessarily by the means so far employed. For a start, China's isolation from the Western world was wrong. She should be admitted to the United Nations. Then the opulent Western nations should recognize the cause of the despair that had driven gentle people to rebel, pour in aid to combat the poverty, and show by example the superiority of the Western world's way of life. The excesses of the colonialist past should not be excused; rather there should be renewed determination to ensure those excesses would never be repeated.

When U.S. military involvement in Vietnam finally ended, in January 1973, Hughes was in Hong Kong. He, too, was saddened when the final casualty figures were released — more than 50 000 United States servicemen killed, thousands of others crippled mentally and physically. And more than 400 of his own countrymen died in a campaign that began in high hope and ended in humiliation for the United States and her allies.

Vague signs that China was becoming receptive to closer relations with the rest of the world began to appear in the early seventies and Hughes welcomed the initiative, tentative at first, from the West. When the almost unbelievable happened and President Richard Nixon flew into Peking early in 1972, Hughes was elated. The curtain was finally lifting and the giant he had watched so assiduously for so long was finally emerging into the light. Nixon's visit was followed by that of the Japanese Prime Minister, Kakuei Tanaka, and later by France's President Pompidou and later still by Australia's Gough Whitlam and Canada's Pierre Trudeau.

Hughes' inspired guessing game was nearly over as the visitors brought out first-hand news of the country Mao Tse Tung had led for so long. Gradually the pieces in the enigmatic jigsaw puzzle Hughes and the other China watchers had struggled to fit from a distance began to come together.

Visitors returning through Hong Kong were seized upon avidly. One returning visitor Hughes relished seeing was his old friend Francis James, a brave Australian eccentric whom Hughes had known since 1957 when they met in Peking. They shared assumed episcopal titles. Hughes called James the 'Bishop of Wahroonga' (a Sydney suburb) and Hughes was his usual 'your grace'. James, after his initial visit in 1957, returned to China in 1969. He passed through the Soviet Union on his way to London after he came out and he wrote a controversial story about an uprecedented inspection of a Chinese nuclear plant at Lop Nor. Peking angrily denounced the story and said it was a 'complete fabrication'.

Early in the seventies James inexplicably returned to China. Nobody at the time could understand why he had done so and there was no great surprise, but an enormous diplomatic furore, when he disappeared. For months there was silence. Hughes tried all his contacts and every trick he knew to try to find out something about the fate of his old, impish, mate. Every diplomatic move from Australia and other friendly countries came to nothing. Finally, a story with a Canberra dateline hinted at James' likely release. Hughes knew something was in the offing, but had not written anything about it. When the Canberra story broke he angrily denounced it as possibly jeopardizing James' chances.

Eventually James arrived in Hong Kong, emaciated and sick. He was taken immediately to hospital and allowed only a few carefully screened visitors. Hughes was one of the few. When he walked into the hospital room where James lay he was shocked at his old friend's appearance. James appeared to have shrunk, but in Hughes' words there was 'the old sparkle, irreverence, brutal humour, generosity, tolerance, independence and Aussie mateship'.

James called out feebly 'Welcome, your grace', when Hughes came into the room. 'My dear Bishop of Wahroonga', Hughes replied, 'a plenary indulgence, a plenary bloody indulgence.'

Hughes was moved when he saw James. He was moved in a different way when he became aware that a man sitting near James' bed was the real Bishop of Hong Kong. The legitimate bishop beamed at the two old friends as they gave each other their mock blessing before he withdrew gracefully.

Hughes wrote a story for his newspapers about his talk with James but he respected his friend's confidence and divulged nothing about the circumstances of the incarceration. No charge was levelled against James by the Chinese during his long detention, believedly in a Chinese hotel, and no explanation was given when he arrived weak and sick at the Hong Kong border.

Later, Hughes said he believed James had rashly given the Chinese credit for a matching Western sense of humour. An almost fatal delusion. It was his considered belief that James returned after the Chinese denunciation of his Lop Nor story in a mistaken belief he could restore good relations. Another fatal delusion.

Years later, James was flown to Hong Kong to see his old friend when Hughes was the subject of a 'This is Your Life' television programme. He told watching millions in Australia and Hong Kong the story of their gaffe in blessing each other in front of a legitimate bishop.

On the same meticulously researched programme, the organizers flew in Hughes' son, his brother Walter, Denis Warner, his old friend and mentor Cyril Pearl and Shinichi Takeda ('Shinshan') a friend of Hughes' Tokyo days. There were film tributes from London from the editor in chief of *The Times,* Sir Dennis Hamilton — 'We love Dick very much and he will never be lost to our service', he said — and from friend and author John Le Carré. 'He was introduced to me as a sort of journalist Eiffel Tower', Le Carré said. 'So good luck to you Dick and keep your arse to the sunset.'

Le Carré, whose books such as *The Spy Who Came in From The Cold* rivalled Ian Fleming's for excellence and popularity, at one time used Hughes as his model for a character in *The Honourable Schoolboy*. He called him 'Craw'. Hughes referred to it good humouredly as 'another piece of lampoonery, but if I sued he might tell the truth about me, just as Ian Fleming threatened to do if I moaned too much about Dikko Henderson'.

In a foreword to his book, Le Carré said of Hughes: 'Last there is the great Dick Hughes, whose outward character and mannerisms I have shamelessly exaggerated for the part of old Craw. Some people, once met, simply elbow their way into a novel and sit there till the writer finds them a place. Dick is one.

'I am only sorry I could not obey his urgent exhortation to libel him to the hilt. My cruellest efforts could not prevail against the affectionate nature of the original.'

Hughes acknowledged the literary likeness but shied away from Le Carré's portrayal of his counterpart's involvement in espionage. 'Craw's grossly improper undercover association with MI6 — or is it SIS? — is something of course completely beyond my ken.' He went on piously: 'Also Craw works ten times as hard and far more effectively than I do. And I must insist that he drinks ten times as much as I, and takes far more interest in ladies than I do.'

When Le Carré's bestseller appeared Hughes was standing one day at the Hong Kong Foreign Correspondent's Club urinal, with its unrivalled view over the harbour to Kowloon and the mountains sprawling over its skyline. He was joined by a newly arrived American correspondent who had just read *The Honourable Schoolboy*. He knew Hughes only slightly. He was struck, he said, by the author's portrayal of Hughes on similar lines to Ian Fleming's earlier lampooning of him in *You Only Live Twice*.

'How come', he asked, 'these two guys draw you as a spy?'

Hughes raised a free hand and gave the puzzled newcomer his episcopal blessing. 'I admit it, my son', he said, 'but I adjure you to treat this piddling admission as being under the seal of a confessional.' Back at his luncheon table he watched gleefully as the newcomer regaled his companions at their table with the tidbit.

Hughes began his association with the *Far Eastern Economic Review* in the early seventies. He contributed a weekly column, sometimes wickedly satirical, on virtually every subject under the sun. He wrote about imaginary conversations between Mao Tse Tung and various Chinese and other leaders and depicted the then U.S. Secretary of State, Dr Kissinger, disguised as a missionary, drinking rum with a secret agent in Guam.

Beneath the humour and satire of his pieces there was invariably a theme that he felt passionately about. In the Kissinger story, for instance, he depicted Kissinger, with a false beard and disguised as a Roman Catholic mission father, conferring in Guam with Agent X, a top CIA man in Manila concerned with the 'great martial law mystery in the Philippines'.

An angry Kissinger told the agent: 'The president is going nuts over some of your fill-ins on this Marcos takeover'. He told the terrified agent: 'When I left the President he felt that your last report read like a pre-reformation heresy from Martin Luther — I mean the original kraut Luther, of course.'

The agent was trying hard to calm down Kissinger and he kept sliding a glass of rum towards him. Eventually Kissinger began to sip the rum, then to gulp it down. It began to take effect, so Kissinger threw an armful of secret documents onto the table. He refilled his glass with rum, then, 'with a secular oath, he dragged off his false beard and clerical collar and threw them in a convenient Filipino thunder mug'. Finally a relaxed Kissinger called for another bottle of rum and told the agent he intended to ask for a posting to the Philippines. 'After all, this Marcos is not such a bad guy.'

Another of Hughes' columns dealt with an imaginary personal letter from Chinese Premier Chou En-lai to the Japanese Prime Minister Tanaka following Tanaka's audience with Mao Tse Tung. The letter, which Hughes said had been smuggled to him by a reliable agent, purported to have Chou upbraiding Tanaka for saying Mao referred to Nationalist leader Chiang Kai-shek as 'an excellent guy'.

Chou's letter said: 'This phraseology is absurdly goddam yankee and out of character with Mao's normal speech, which is not vulgarly Brooklynese. Please avoid this "guy" lavatory-wall-style in future.' Chou went on to suggest to Tanaka he should tell correspondents something along the lines of: 'As Chairman Mao spoke to me, his eyes softened and he grasped my arm and suggested another slug of mao-tai and said: "We Asians must stick together like shit to a blanket against the Western foreign devils and the Russian turtles". ' Chou's letter went on: 'You might perhaps add that your own eyes moistened and that you grasped Mao's hand and cried: "Did not Pearl Harbour help to atone partly for our rape of Nanking?" '

After Lord Thomson's visit to China, Hughes wrote about an imaginary discussion between Chou En-lai and a 'brooding' editor of the *People's Daily*. Chou told the editor the visit had been an amiable interlude 'in this infuriating round of diplomatic receptions'.

He went on: 'There was no pious or hypocritical talk about a Socialist drive for world peace; no reiteration of our love for the people of whatever barbarian state who sent a representative; no polite gloats or disguised threats'. But the editor was puzzled and angry about rumours that Thomson planned to take over the *People's Daily*. He asked why Thomson had shown so little interest in Chou's enquiry about the possible purchase of the newspaper. 'I wasn't told a takeover was under consideration. If I'd known I could have fabricated production costs. I could have told Lord Thomson we have no Fleet Street union problems and we're not subject to capitalist advertisers' caprice and greed. He doesn't know, for instance, that we can decree — I mean encourage — circulation according to the policy.' Chou became annoyed with the editor's petulance. 'I am reluctantly driven to the conclusion, comrade, that you accepted this urbane badinage between Lord Thomson and myself as serious negotiation. Are you out of your mind? Did you not realize we were jesting? I think you need a holiday.' Chou called for the guards and they dragged away the struggling foaming-at-the-mouth editor.

A news report that Japanese businessmen planned to build a tourist resort on Queensland's Gold Coast to attract Japanese tourists and introduce Japanese hotel and holiday habits to Australia stirred Hughes to enthusiasm in another of his columns. 'This is an evil, insidious Japanese infiltration threat which could be a deadlier challenge to Australian life, living and mores than the formidable military threat down the Kokoda trail', he wrote in mock indignation. There would be oriental appeal and carnal distraction offered to rugged sunburned Queenslanders. 'Hot springs, tatami floors, public or private mixed swimming pools, razor blades and underwear on the house, round the clock meal and massage service could represent a diabolical Trojan mare in geisha kimona. Japanese meals could pose a threat to Australian meat pies and steaks. Some of their gambling games could even pose a threat to two-up.' The threat would not be contained in Queensland. The 'pox japonica' could be carried to trusting families and neighbours even as far as remote Tasmania. 'Kokoda, in retrospect, is a shrug off. This is fair dinkum, mate. They're going to put the boot in.'

He had another light-hearted swipe at his own country when he wrote an imaginary talk between Mao Tse Tung and Chou En-lai after Gough Whitlam's historic visit. The two Chinese leaders were happy. Mao moved the mao-tai jug towards Chou. 'Have a slug of this instead of that tea you're drinking', he said. Chou refused and said he had to get rid of his latest visitors first. 'They represented an unautonomous aboriginal Australia and they were always singing some variation of "The Internationale", called, I think, "Dancing Matilda",' Chou said broodingly, according to Hughes' version. His agents were very diligent in digging up such gems, he said.

China's gradual emergence and the consequent easing on reporting restrictions made the seventies a traumatic time for Hughes. His China watching role appeared less important. Also, he had his sixty-fifth birthday. So he retired from his beloved *Sunday Times* and the *Economist,* but *The Times* snapped him up immediately. He also severed his relationship with the Murdoch organization in Australia at the obligatory retiring age. Another big Australian newspaper organization, The Herald and Weekly Times of Melbourne, took him on their payroll at once.

Hughes was not prone to introspection and he did not feel for a moment that the long trail had ended. On the contrary, he threw himself into his new duties with great vigour, expanded his local output and published his fourth book, *Foreign Devil*.

But more importantly, he married again. His wife was the daughter of General Lee kon-to who served in Chiang Kai-shek's nationalist army, and she crossed into Hong Kong in 1950 after a long journey from her home together with a sister and one brother. Oi-ying — her Anglicized name is Ann — was educated by Roman Catholics in keeping with the tradition of wealthy Chinese families and she was a practising Catholic when she met Hughes. They were married in a Hong Kong registry office.

Earlier, Hughes had written in one of his books that if foreign devils were lucky they could win enchanting lovers or proud wives. And he was one of the lucky ones. His new wife brought gentleness, love and order into his life. Years later she was to say of their relationship: 'We were lucky to find each other'.

Ann's father was educated at a leading military school in Peking and he won quick promotion in China's army before marrying one of the daughters of a tea-growing family near Hanchow. He took his large family — eventually there were six boys and seven girls — to widely scattered parts of China as the Chinese waged their impossible war with Japan. He sent one of his sons to Germany and another to England to be educated while the younger ones went to university in Shanghai.

The non-ideological revolution then convulsing the country split the family and eventually Ann, together with David, a young brother, and her sister A-cha, lived in a humble Shanghai retreat. From there the three occasionally would make the long journey to Hanchow to look nostalgically at their lost home. Her father and mother were buried there in a family tomb on a high, rocky point overlooking Hanchow's West Lake. The Japanese had wrecked the once palatial home.

When Mao Tse Tung's communists came to power Ann made one last pilgrimage to her home. It was being rebuilt and eventually became a commune-type residence for Communist Party cadres. A-cha made the break first. She went to Hong Kong by train and started work there as a clerk in a flourishing business owned by her uncle. He manufactured tooth-picks. A-cha encouraged Ann to join her. So she packed one large suitcase with clothing and other personal belongings, including some family jewellery and a few golden taels, and climbed on board a train toward exile.

The year was 1950. The Korean war was boiling and China's

communist leaders were obsessed with the possibility of invasion as MacArthur's forces scattered the North Koreans and drove towards the Korean-Chinese border. Normal surveillance of Chinese fleeing to Hong Kong lessened and the young girl boarded the train without trouble, and without a ticket. She expected to buy her ticket *en route* from railway conductors, but there were no conductors on board the slow, cheap train as it inched towards Hong Kong. As they passed through Hanchow, David boarded the train to help her. Three days and two nights later they reached the Hong Kong border.

Ann was alone now. David returned to Shanghai after escorting her to the border. A Portuguese couple from Canton had befriended her on the suffocating train and they were confident their credentials would help get her into the colony. She stayed for a day at a village bungalow 'hotel' on the Chinese side of the border, leaving her suitcase behind in case of trouble at the border, but the British guards allowed the trickle of refugees to cross without hindrance. On the Hong Kong side she met a friendly Cantonese family with Hong Kong residential status and that night the family sent their farm boy across the border to pick up her belongings. A-cha met her in Hong Kong and eventually Ann too started work in her uncle's factory.

The sisters' happiness at being reunited had a sad aftermath when they learned that David was arrested because of his father's background when he returned to Shanghai. He was released after a period of detention, married and began work as an English language teacher. Of the six boys and seven girls only the fate of Ann, A-cha and David was known. The others were swallowed up in the growing eruption as China struggled to her feet.

One of Hughes' wedding presents that he treasured beyond all others was a family walking stick that David sent him from Shanghai. It was a link to Ann's troubled but proud past.

Hughes' marriage changed his lifestyle slightly. Early mornings were still devoted to his writing and the long lunches went on as before but he always went home mid-afternoon to the gentle Ann. And in the evenings Ann went with him when possible to the banquets and dinners that were so much a part of Hong Kong. Hughes' hospitality was legendary. Guests from all over the world who tried to pick up the bill were peremptorily brushed aside. 'Conniving pom' was one of his favourite expressions when visiting Englishmen tried various strategems to try to share the financial load so many of the functions imposed.

Simple lunches with one or two people invariably developed into marathon affairs involving up to a dozen people. Hughes revelled in the talk the lunches and other functions encouraged. And every Saturday he would escort a willing guest to another much-loved function and talk-fest at a meeting of Alcoholics Synonymous.

One of his friends was Sid Perelman, the great wit and author, once rightly called 'a living national treasure' in his own United States. Perelman typified the joy a reunion with Hughes meant when he visited Hong Kong on one of his research trips for a book: 'Once more I was under the Union Jack, crossing the bay on the Star ferry to hoist a jar with my beloved friend and dean of the press corps, Richard Hughes, Australia's gift to the gaiety of nations'. Perelman described Hughes at the meeting: 'His cheeks flamed like pippins and his monocle glittered'.

Another great American among his legion of friends was the playwright Marc Connelly. He was always urging Hughes to write a thriller, based on his experiences over three decades of change in the fascinating 'parish' Hughes knew so intimately. John Le Carre, press lords, visiting editors and foreign correspondents, parliamentarians and unknown young journalists sought him out. Perhaps at first their motive was partly selfish, yet invariably they fell under his spell to become friends for life.

Periodically Hughes' doctor would put him on a strict diet and ban liquor in order to keep his weight under control. He would be restricted to white wine but he invariably got off to a good start with a couple of straight double vodkas. He excused this excess by claiming that the 'Russian water' would do no harm at all if unpolluted by ice or any other foreign mix.

Foreign Devil, which he described modestly as being made up of 'anecdotes and presumptions, excuses and reflections spread over thirty years of great events', was also a great success. He dedicated it to his son, to whom he had come closer over the years. But the father still had difficulty showing his affection. He could show it in words but not in person, and his pride showed when he wrote: 'He is a good, big generous boy with a tolerance that shames his old man and he will live a happy life, laughing'.

In his introduction to the ebullient, witty account of his life as a correspondent he wrote: 'So here comes a foreign devil's maundering anecdotes of the years of the dragon — dragons being, of course, notorious for their perverse, blundering, selfish, garrulous, snorting, incestuous and socially useless behaviour.'

Hughes devoted one chapter to what he called 'Old Hands Last Supper'. The best reporters' stories were seldom printed, he recalled, but were often told at 'spiritual gatherings' of old hands. 'Visualize an improbable grand reunion', he wrote to them, 'and give us a favourite last supper story,'

So he selected the best recollections provided by his friends. Noel Monks, John Gunther, James Cameron, Robert Shaplen, Donald Wise, Dennis Bloodworth, Sydney Brookes, Robert Miller, Denis Warner and many others were on the list. They were all brilliant foreign correspondents, Monks, particularly, had distinguished himself in the Spanish Civil War and the Second World War, in Africa and the Far East and became one of Australia's most famous correspondents and a successful author. Like Hughes, he was a big man, amiable, fearless, and with an instinct for stories few possessed. He was Hughes' oldest friend. They knew each other in their early newspaper days in Melbourne and in sentimental moments Hughes would recall how he and Monks once shared an infatuation for the same girl when they were young.

Robert Shaplen best summed up the excitement of the years covered in his recollections. He said no trip taken on psychedelic drugs could be as fascinatingly full of romantic adventure, wild discovery and sheer sensation or shock as were the years in South East Asia immediately after the war.

Donald Wise, who became a household name reporting out of Africa, was later credited with having coined the original 'Wise Law': 'In the country of the long soft, the man with the half hard is king'. In his last supper story he told how he fell in love mildly with South Vietnam's Madam Nhu. He also taught her the 'twist'.

James Cameron topped them all with his story about Hanoi and his introduction: 'I was sitting down to a glass of ale with the Prime Minister when in walked Ho Chi Minh'. He said that was as good an intro as any small story deserved.

They were funny, sentimental and serious reminescences and Hughes said of the illustrious names who contributed: 'You couldn't summon a livelier band of better friends together for a livelier dinner anywhere, anytime, anyhow.'

Hughes' earlier success, *Hong Kong: Borrowed Place, Borrowed Time* was revised completely during the mid-seventies. It was such a success that he was asked to write a film script based on it. Around that time, too, he was asked to undertake a lecture tour of the United States. When he arrived he was startled to read an obituary of Richard Hughes. But it was of the Jamaican-based novelist with the same name. He remembered a series of courteous exchanges he'd had earlier with his namesake when the other Richard Hughes suggested he should use a second name, or perhaps an initial, to avoid misunderstanding. 'It was a very civilized exchange', Hughes said. 'But I couldn't help. I don't have a second name. So I suggested he might consider altering his by-line slightly. Nothing came of it. But it wasn't a big deal. We have different styles and wrote about different things.'

The lecture tour lasted three weeks. He saw many old friends during the visit, but he was glad when the tiring tour ended and he was heading back to Hong Kong again. As he passed through San Francisco on his way home, Hughes had a slight experience that convinced him there was 'unmistakeable evidence of my advancing years and growing dissoluteness in appearance'.

'There I was', he said, 'Sitting in the Top of the Mark sipping sacramental wine. In younger and happier days I would have been approached by young women, but this time I was approached by young men. It happened on two occasions. Each time they had Sodom and Gomorrah gleams in their eyes. The first approach I tolerantly, if petulantly, rebuffed. But the second, a couple of nights later, was too much. So I handled it sternly. I lumbered to my feet and intoned: "FBI, young man. We've been waiting for you." The shocked young pederast fled in terror.' He grinned at the memory. Later, he said, an aged barman told him: 'We try to keep the cocksucking fairies out of here, sir, but I'm afraid some of our patrons defend them.'

He had a happy surprise when he got back to Hong Kong. His friends organized a surprise birthday party for him on his seventieth anniversary. They even went to the extent of flying his son Richard from Australia. Young Richard, who was kept out of sight for a couple of days before the big party to heighten the surprise, was told he would be expected to play 'Happy Birthday' on the piano. He was then one of Australia's most accomplished jazz pianists, but found himself in the embarrassing position of not knowing how to play the simple tune. So he sneaked in some practice until he mastered it and on the big night his rendition, although shaky, went over well.

The governor, Sir Murray MacLehose, headed the list of more than 100 guests. He joined in the tributes paid to a delighted but embarrassed Hughes. Presents included a Chinese army fur hat 'for covering Northern campaigns', a walking stick 'to get there' and a plentiful supply of cigars. Hughes was referred to as 'the most distinguished fur-hatted, cigar-smoking, walking stick-wielding journalist' the company had ever seen.

Hughes was deeply moved at the tribute and, in his reply to the speeches, he quoted Ian Fleming yet again: 'We are only as good as our friends'.

Another tribute that delighted him was a bust erected in the Foreign Correspondents' Club. It was executed by English sculptor David Thompson. It depicted an imperious, Roman-like Hughes. It is the only piece of sculpture in the club. It stands alongside a newsagency printer that keeps members and visitors informed of world happenings, and among the blown-up prize-winning pictures of the most dramatic news events of the last few decades. Appropriately the bust faces China.

The death of old friends always hit Hughes particularly hard. He would become sentimental about them and remember all their good qualities. Then, if others caught his mood and also became sentimental he would occasionally change the tenor of the reminescences and abruptly change the flow. Don't get too close, seemed the warning.

172

Also he appeared unable to dismiss completely some of the spiritualistic beliefs his father had held so strongly. His experience with the Blind Bonze in far off Laos and the holy man's chilling recall of the spirit of Adele left him prone to belief in omens that occasionally pierced the veil.

So he was uneasy when a vivid dream snapped him awake in 1974. He sat up in bed, sweating and trembling and told Ann the dream. 'We were in the bar of the old Tatts club just down the street from the *Daily Telegraph* office in Sydney. The old barman was there. He had a moustache. Behind him the clock said 2.45. It was the time we had our last drink before the editorial conference at 3 pm.

'We were drinking heavily. There were a lot of old faces there and I saw Sir Frank Packer coming towards me. He put his arm around my shoulder. "Come on Dick, you old bugger. We're not such bad friends after all, are we?" So we started slapping each other on the back and shouting "good on us both" and "we had those rows but what the hell".'

The next day he began to tell the story of his dream — it remained in his memory in exact detail — to some friends at the bar of the Foreign Correspondents' Club. 'Had a funny dream about Frank Packer last night' he said and started telling it. He noticed his friends looking at him strangely. 'Didn't you hear', one said, 'Frank Packer died last night.'

13 Sunset Over China

As China opened up more and more to the Western world Hughes worried that his and other China watchers' speculative functions could become obsolete. But Hughes' Hong Kong role, perversely, proved more valuable than it had been when he had to base his stories on little more than gut feeling, travellers' tales and talk from refugees.

He had the freedom in Hong Kong in which to interpret whereas correspondents resident in Peking, uneasily aware of Reuter's Tony Grey and his lonely incarceration during the cultural revolution and Red Guard excesses, had to watch their backs. There was little room in Peking for the crusading zeal that Hughes and other China watchers in Hong Kong could still muster. The perfect set-up, according to Hughes' scenario, would be to have two correspondents, each thoroughly familiar with China. They would change every six months or so: 'The Peking man could emerge regularly for fresh air in Hong Kong and thus help to quarantine his natural revulsion against an unnatural society'. There would be several pleasant advantages for unmarried correspondents in Peking returning periodically to the relative flesh pots of Hong Kong. 'It would stop them from going blind, for a start', he said mischievously, his memories of childhood myths still strong.

Hughes returned to Korea in 1975. It was one of his few visits since the Korean War. The visit was to commemorate the twenty-fifth anniversary of the war and to attend the unveiling of a memorial to the correspondents killed during the campaign. He was amazed at the changes that had taken place in the last quarter century. Seoul was a booming modern city compared with the muddied huddle of smashed buildings he left in the fifties. The reunion was an hilarious and sentimental pilgrimage and he renewed friendships with correspondents flown in from all over the world. He also paid a sad visit to the United Nations cemetery near the southern city of Pusan to see the graves of friends killed in the campaign.

174

The Koreans turned on a magnificent welcome to the correspondents, with banquets and speeches lauding the men who reported the war.

At one lavish banquet, Hughes and his fellow guests had to follow tradition and leave their shoes at the door when they went in to lunch. One of Hughes' friends had a large hole in his sock and his big toe kept popping out. 'Put that obscene toe out of sight', he remonstrated with his friend as they tried to tuck their long legs under the banquet tables and squat Korean fashion. 'It's staring insolently at the governor of the province. It's got a sneer on it — a Western sneer at that —and it's putting people off their food and it's also perving on the luscious waitresses.' He then launched into a long dissertation about the effect naked big toes could have on Korean-Australian relations. 'Think of the possible repercussions', he told a puzzled non-English speaking Korean who sat opposite him, 'of an unashamed gout-ridden member like that sneering openly at oriental customs.'

He stopped for a moment to savour a delicious tidbit that a kneeling Korean beauty chose for him from the groaning table. He leant over the table towards the uncomprehending Korean while his embarrassed friend tried to tuck away the offending toe. 'Look at him struggle' and he nodded toward his friend. 'God knows what he'll produce next. The mind boggles at the depths of depravity that diseased looking toe represents. You agree, sir, of course. Exorcism? Excellent suggestion.' He turned to his friend and ostentatiously blessed him.

His capacity for fun was enormous and throughout the trip he alternated between shouting reminescences of some of the characters who reported the war and quick, sentimental recall of some of the incidents in the fratricidal devastation the war brought to the peninsula.

Bedraggled-looking postcards were sent from all points to correspondents who were unable to make the pilgrimage and toasts to absent friends roared out from Pusan in the South to Pan Mun Jom in the North.

In China, Mao Tse Tung was on his last journey, exhorting his followers to the last on the need to carry the red banner. The frail old man who led his country for so long died in early September 1976 and China's greatest dynasty ended. Earlier that year Chou En-lai died and Mao's widow, Chiang Ching, and her radical friends now saw the way clear for their drive for power. The 'gang of four', as Mao once referred to them, was not to take over Mao's mantle however, although his reported prophesy that after he died Chiang Ching would make trouble proved true.

Hughes always had a sneaky regard for Mao. Although he never met 'the great helmsman' he admired his strength and intellect. Mao was one Chinese communist he did not object to being likened to and he knew a genuine sense of loss when he died. His stories at the time reflected this and he recalled that Mao, sensing his end was near, asked that after his death his remains should be sent to Hsiangtan, Hunan. The fact that Mao's body was embalmed and displayed in a mausoleum was the last thing the old man would have wished, he said. He predicted Mao's death would see more convulsions in China, but he was convinced there would be relative peace once Mao's wish for shared leadership came about. Mao was truly China's red sun.

Again Hughes' found that, even though China opened up to more Western correspondents, the unrivalled monitoring services available in Hong Kong, together with the stories refugees continued to bring out, still gave him a distinct edge. He was aware too that his earlier suspicions and intuitions about stories refugees had brought out when the country was virtually closed were nearer the mark than had been recognized at the time.

He outlined the role of the China watcher in *Borrowed Place, Borrowed Time:* 'He is like the sincere Sussex bird watcher who unfailingly counts all the sparrows as they pass because he knows that, on one magnificent day of revelation, they will escort, even if partly hidden, the first red-rumped tit from Iceland ever to be seen in an English autumn.'

So whenever he could he would talk to refugees still trickling into the colony and adding to its population problems. His contacts with returning businessmen and, indeed, with Chinese communists in Hong Kong, were religiously maintained. Hughes was discreet and honest and the two attributes served him well. Occasionally he would mix with the colony's marine police as they intercepted Chinese trying to cross from the mainland and glean from the frightened refugees some aspect of their homeland that helped build a picture of life behind the curtain.

The illegal immigrants — illegals in newspaper jargon — who were caught were invariably sent back to the mainland. Hong Kong already had too many mouths to feed.

But not only Chinese from the mainland tried to enter the colony. From Vietnam boatloads of scrawny, frightened people braved the run up the coast in flimsy boats to try to reach Hong Kong's shining lights. Hughes was full of admiration for the firm yet kindly way the administration handled these refugees. Marine police would intercept the boats and escort them to a holding base in Hong Kong harbour where they would be processed. Relief agencies would take over from there and if they were lucky the refugees would find another home in some distant land.

One interception he wrote about dealt with sixteen men, women and children crammed into a rotting boat with only forty-five centimetres of freeboard. It was a mere speck off Landau Island when the marine police spotted it, rocking precariously in the swell from a jetfoil ferry to Macao. When the big police vessel eased alongside, the boat people were obviously fearful at first. The police crew handed over fresh water and biscuits, inspected their tattered papers and made an inventory of the pathetic possessions on board. The boat people had only their clothes, a U.S. army compass, a few cooking pots and some fishing lines.

Some of the women on board were sick. One lay on her back under a tattered canopy, eyes big with fear staring from a face that once must have been beautiful. Her man squatted near her, brushing away flies with his hat and shielding her face from the glare. He offered her the first biscuit the police crew handed over. She turned her head away and only then did he eat it. Only the children on board showed any animation — the adults were still and patient, waiting.

Their boat was too frail to take in tow, so it stuttered along in the wake of the police vessel to the holding area, with most of the occupants standing hopefully and looking towards the lights they had come so far to find.

Hughes was always moved by the plight of the homeless flood of refugees. Some of them, he knew, were opportunists and greedy misfits but the bulk were simple peasants whose only motive was to find a better way of life. He would rail against a system that forced them to leave their own country and be equally vitriolic about the opulent Western countries that refused entry to more than a mere trickle. He felt passionately that the West should do more; that the I'm-alright-Jack philosophy so many adopted should give way to the bigness America once personified when she welcomed the tired, the poor and the 'wretched refuse' from Europe.

And he was convinced his own country could do more. It too could conceive a Statue of Liberty. He had maintained an immediate feeling for all nationalities and it seldom occurred to him to recognize national boundaries or to judge people by the colour of their skin.

In the case of China, he believed nationalism was a greater force than communism and that communism would pass eventually. He acknowledged that, under Mao, China was better, physically and economically, than in the old days, but this comparison was more a denunciation of past misery than a tribute to the present. He was an optimist and he believed that, as with China, other Far Eastern countries had opted for the expediency of communism to wipe the slate clean of colonialism. But eventually nationalism would overcome communism because it was the strongest and most aggressive force in Asia.

But he also sounded a note of warning in *Borrowed Place, Borrowed Time:* 'It is unlikely that western-style democracy will be a welcome and lasting pearl of great price anywhere in the Far East. European democracy is not for export. Ideas can be adopted and adapted but fully-fledged constitutions and foreign notions of self-government cannot be carted around and dispensed like Marshall aid or gifts of home-made jellies and preserves from the squire's lady to a south Vietnam peasant or a Kowloon dockworker.'

In the case of Hong Kong itself, he said the challenge was to disprove Karl Marx and to demonstrate, to the satisfaction of restless young Hong Kong, that the rich were not getting richer while the poor were getting poorer.

Hughes was forced to use his walking stick more and more in his seventies as arthritis continued to trouble him. He tucked it under his arm however when he went to the Foreign Correspondents' Club for his customary lunch. He was too familiar with his 'parish' not to understand the importance of 'face' and he would march to his usual table with enormous dignity and sit with his back to the wall, facing the entrance, so he could wave and nod to friends. The lunches were small ceremonial occasions, often starting with one or two people in decorous small talk and frequently ending some hours later in the uproarious 'disputation' he adored. He had other favourite spots. The Hilton Hotel was one and there too a particular table was reserved for him. As with the club, Hilton staff knew and liked him and he was given impeccable service.

He was involved, innocently, in an incident that embarrassed him greatly one day at lunch at the Hilton. The spirited discussion at Hughes' table was enlivened further by loud and outspoken contributions from two transient friends unaware of the comparably dignified behaviour required from well-known locals. Hughes cautioned them gently; they were drawing attention to his table he said tactfully. They calmed down.

But at a nearby table two middle-aged Englishmen were entertaining a beautiful Chinese girl and their schoolboy behaviour as each vied with the other to impress the girl was beginning to irritate. One of them pretended to toss a few drops of wine at his rival and the drops fell on Hughes. He fixed the embarrassed wine thrower with his sternest look and snapped, with mock severity: 'What do you mean, sir? What do you mean? That is not the sort of behaviour one expects of gentlemen.'

There was silence for a few moments at the offending table. Then the wine thrower stood up and approached Hughes' party. 'I apologize', he said lightly. 'I invite retribution of course.'

One of Hughes' overseas guests immediately stood, swooped up a full glass of water and poured it slowly and deliberately over the head of the offender. The dripping man returned to his table, gathered his friends and led them sullenly from the dining room.

'That was unpardonable', Hughes admonished his guest. 'You humiliated that poor bugger.'

178

The water tipper was unrepentant. 'I've never had the chance of tipping a glass of water with impunity over such a bloody idiot, and I wouldn't have missed it for anything.'

Hughes' daily routine varied little. He wrote in the early mornings, checked with sources before lunch, rewrote as necessary, then descended on the city from his apartment. He kept his home life inviolate on Sundays.

The British Government recognized his services to journalism in 1980 when he was awarded the CBE. Shortly afterwards he paid another visit to Australia to see his son and his family and to spend a few gentle days with his dear friend Denis Warner and wife in what Hughes called 'the wilds of Mt. Eliza' in Victoria.

During this visit he addressed the Sydney and Melbourne press clubs. There was a waiting list on a waiting list on each occasion. In Sydney he was referred to as 'the legendary doyen of Asian correspondents, raconteur, wit and self-styled old curmudgeon'. 'He has become an amiable blend of Alfred Hitchcock and Robert Morley — with the same bland, perky sense of humour' as one review of his virtuouso performances put it.

He told his audiences that he was now a 'China watcher watcher', and astonished many of his old newspaper friends when he told them he led a celibate, even monkish, life in Hong Kong.

His talks ranged over the years from the time he was a boy shunter with the Victorian Railways to his travels in China and the Soviet Union. He touched on some of the great names he had known — Sir Harold Clapp, Sir Keith Murdoch, Sir Frank Packer, Chou En-lai, Mao Tse Tung, Ian Fleming, Lee Kuan Yew among them — with affection and admiration.

One questioner at his Sydney talk asked Hughes to 'add a bit' to the Burgess-Maclean story which he referred to as 'perhaps one of the greatest beats of our time'. Hughes said he thought there was little to add beyond what he called 'the extraordinary coincidence' of his arrival in Moscow on his second visit the day after Burgess died. He said he liked Burgess the better of the two. He had a sense of humour whereas Maclean was a rather dull man. 'Burgess, you know, was not distinguished by his interest in ladies and although I liked him the better it's not because of my non-interest in ladies.'

He told another questioner that the test for wearing a monocle was to be able to wink behind it three times. 'The other test — may I put it this way — is that you should be able to have an intimate conservation with a lady who doesn't like you wearing it, and not lose it when you're kissing her hand.'

In Melbourne he had a nostalgic look at the Prahran of his childhood and talked with fellow aficianados of his great literary love nurtured there for Sherlock Holmes. One friend tested his knowledge by quoting from the first paragraph in Conan Doyle's *His Last Bow*: 'It was nine o'clock at night upon the second of August — the most terrible August in the history of the world'.

Hughes delightedly quoted the final few lines, spoken after Sherlock Holmes had revealed himself to surprised readers as the counter-spy Altamont who had outwitted the German Von Bork — 'the most astute secret service man in Europe'. It was one of Hughes' favourite Holmes stories. 'There's an East Wind coming — such a wind as never blew on England yet . . .', he quoted correctly.

His friends tried him on other Sherlock Holmes stories. Each time he showed his encyclopaedic knowledge of the character he steadfastly maintained still lived.

It was a happy visit, but tinged with some sadness because Australia's beckoning was getting stronger.

Back in Hong Kong there was an abrupt and unpleasant interlude to his routine. At three o'clock one morning three thugs burst into his apartment and dragged him and his wife from bed. Armed with an axe, they tied Hughes and his wife together with flex, bound their legs and gagged them with adhesive tape. They threatened Ann with their axe and then systematically ransacked the apartment. They tore up many of Hughes' files, scattered his papers and stole travellers cheques and goods worth about $HK16 000 before leaving the way they had entered — through some temporary scaffolding on an adjacent building site. Hughes finally loosened the flex binding him and freed his wife. The only miniscule clue the police had was that the three men spoke with a Cantonese accent. Messages of sympathy — some of them tangible — poured in from many parts of the world when the story of their robbery broke. For days afterwards Hughes had trouble walking because of the cruel wiring of his legs but he gradually recovered.

He sent off a series of postcards to concerned friends assuring them of his recovery. The cards depicted a dilapidated Chinese junk, complete with washing, several children, cooking pots, fishing gear and a scabrous dog. 'My new establishment', he wrote.

He curtailed some of his walking after the robbery and was seldom without his stick. Ann, who had started a small florists shop some time earlier, acted more and more as his 'runner' and took over many of the small chores he normally handled as she went to and from her shop.

An application for a pension from Australia was again refused. Hughes had applied earlier — on local official advice — but was rejected. Further advice indicated his second application would be favourably considered. Friends in Australia lobbied on his behalf and pointed out to members of parliament the outstanding nature of his services. He was like a touchstone to hundreds of Australians passing through Hong Kong, they said. He arranged work for many journalists through his local contacts and gave without stint his money, time and enormous encouragement to all who sought it. Additionally, they said, his services to Australian journalism for nearly four decades was unequalled.

But Canberra made no exception. The Minister for Social Security, Senator Chaney, told him he did not qualify for an age pension while he resided abroad. He could, of course, return to Australia to reside and thus become eligible. The fact that he had worked for twenty-six years in Australia before going abroad apparently did not count.

Hughes was indignant at first but he accepted the ruling philosophically. If he returned to Australia to live, he told friends, he would lose his Hong Kong income and have to start again from scratch at the age of seventy-five: it was a classic Catch-22 situation.

So he wrote a courteous reply to the Minister: 'I have brooded over your friendly response to my age pension application, which has, alas, been rejected. I note that I remain ineligible because I am not a resident in Australia: but, because of my age I could no longer get a job back in my old homeland.' He was disappointed of course, as a pension would have made life so much easier and would have enabled him to ease a work load he had maintained from the age of fourteen.

But while the Australian Government, albeit sympathetically, stuck to the letter of the law, old friends did not desert him. Rupert Murdoch, the new owner of *The Times*, was quick to reassure him he would continue to be associated with the venerable newspaper he had served for so long. Murdoch remembered his brilliant father's assessment of Hughes many years earlier and he also remembered Hughes' encouragement when he launched the *Australian*. And in London there were other friends —Sir Dennis Hamilton among them — who remembered and honoured promises.

He was depressed for a time, but soon regained his old enthusiasm for the life that had sustained him for so long. After the robbery security on his apartment block was tightened. Access to his apartment was via a steel door that was opened by a guard who scanned all visitors before alerting tenants. Hughes adopted a private method of assuring the guard he at least was friendly. He would clear his throat raspingly as he approached the door and after a time the guard recognized the peculiar sound and allowed entry, grinning at the little game they played so conspiratorially.

His writing output soon picked up again after the traumatic experience of the robbery. His sources were as good as ever and he gradually assembled into order the files and references he had so lovingly kept over three decades. He was a prodiguous reader. Newspapers from all over the world were poured over, marked and filed away; books on every conceivable subject were read avidly.

When he read that his old friend Paddy Costello had been named as a possible Soviet spy he reacted angrily. British author Chapman Pincher named Costello at a London press conference when he discussed his book, *Their Trade is Treachery*. Pincher said confessed Soviet agent Anthony Blunt had pointed the finger at Costello as a one-time communist who might have been recruited as a spy.

'Paddy a commie dog mole? Utterly absurd!' Hughes fumed. He recalled that he had visited his old friend at Manchester when Costello was Professor of Russian at the university there: 'There was nobody more loyal than Paddy.' How would a legendary figure such as Freyberg recommend Costello for the job if there were doubts about his loyalty? he asked. Freyberg was Governor of Windsor Castle when he made the recommendation.

Shortly after his seventy-fifth birthday Hughes made another nostalgic return to his beloved Tokyo. He was guest of honour at a testimonial dinner given by members of the Foreign Correspondents' Club of Japan. The club journal headed its story 'His Amazing Grace' and said the night was one of 'Hughesiana, peopled by such ghosts as Soviet master spy Richard Sorge, the immortal Sherlock Holmes, Prince Tokugawa and Prime Minister Shigeru Yoshida, punctuated by frequent toasts in red wine to the living and the dead'.

Hughes was presented with a gold membership card. Among the messages from various parts of the world was a tribute from Rupert Murdoch: 'All his friends and admirers in Britain and Australia join in saluting him and celebrating his continued strength'.

Back in Hong Kong he waded through the mass of material collected during his absence, phoned several contacts, then wound paper into his portable for yet another story on the Chinese giant beyond the mountains he had watched for so long.

He never tired of watching the sun set over China. Before it dipped into the hills he invariably turned his back on it, ceremoniously. 'Keep your arse to the sunset' has been the wish that has nurtured him, and he would cling to it to the end.

Index